FRONTERAS NO MÁS

FRONTERAS NO MÁS

TOWARD SOCIAL JUSTICE AT THE U.S.–MEXICO BORDER

KATHLEEN STAUDT
AND
IRASEMA CORONADO

First published 2002 by
PALGRAVE MACMILLAN™
175 Fifth Avenue, New York, N.Y. 10010 and
Houndmills, Basingstoke, Hampshire, England RG21 6XS
Companies and representatives throughout the world.

PALGRAVE MACMILLAN is the global academic imprint of the Palgrave Macmillan division of St. Martin's Press, LLC and of Palgrave Macmillan Ltd. Macmillan® is a registered trademark in the United States, United Kingdom and other countries. Palgrave is a registered trademark in the European Union and other countries.

ISBN 0–312–23939–4 hardback
ISBN 0–312–29547–2 paperback

Library of Congress Cataloging-in-Publication Data
Staudt, Kathleen A.
    Fronteras no más: toward social justice at the US–Mexico border/by Kathleen Staudt and Irasema Coronado.
        p. cm.
    Includes bibliographical references (p.) and index.
    ISBN 0–312–23939–4 — ISBN 0-312–29547–2 (pbk.)
        1. Social justice—Mexican–American Border Region.
2. Pan-Americanism. 3.Non-governmental organizations—Mexican–American Border Region. 4. Human rights—Mexican–American Border Region. I. Coronado, Irasema. II. Title.

HM671.S73 2002
303.3'72'09721—dc21   2002068413

A catalogue record for this book is available from the British Library.

Design by Newgen Imaging Systems (P) Ltd., Chennai, India.

First edition: October, 2002
10 9 8 7 6 5 4 3 2 1

Printed in the United States of America.

to
Maya Linda and Gabriella Marissa

to
Mosi and Asha

and to
Border People, Everywhere!

¡A Todos los Fronterizos!
¡A Todas las Fronterizas!

CONTENTS

Preface

We are blessed with the opportunity to live and work at the border. We experience an open terrain, not only in our high desert and wide vistas, but also in the ability to engage in community action. At the border, our community is binational. We have many people to thank for their help in the preparation of the book. Kathy has many good friends and engaging colleagues who share a commitment to the border region: Carla Cardoza, Sandy Deutsch, Richard Gutiérrez, Jan Harmon, Núria Homedes, Frank López, Susan Rippberger, Greg Rocha, Beatriz Vera, Bill Weaver and Irasema, among others. For this book, Kathy gives special thanks to graphic artist Joel Martínez for his help in layouts and maps and to the Center for Civic Engagement and the Center for Inter-American and Border Studies at the University of Texas at El Paso. This project began when Edmé Domínguez organized a panel at the International Studies Association on the topic of transnational organizations. Panelist Debra Liebowitz provided particularly helpful feedback. Kathy is grateful to colleagues like Edmé and others who, over the years have sustained a collective commitment to analyzing and challenging power relations, including the power of discourse: Jane Parpart, Shirin Rai, Jane Jaquette, and others.

We also thank our students who enrich our lives with ideas, experiences and insights about the border. Irasema would especially like to thank UTEP students Alejandro Sandoval Murrillo, Laura Salas, Cynthia Zuñiga, Teresa Sotelo, Ana Laura García, Sonya Saunders, Gaby Montoya and Marisa Ortiz and to Jon Amastae and the staff from the Center for Inter-American and Border Studies. Over time, colleagues and friends from the Association for Borderlands Studies have provided great ideas, support and insights into how to approach binational border research. Thanks to my family, especially my parents Gonzalo and Lupita Coronado, for raising all of us to be truly engaged binational people and may Marissa and Philip carry that legacy. To Roberto Perezdíaz and family, *mil gracias por todo*. A million thanks to

Kathy for her inspiration, support, patience and insight: You are a great role model as an academic and agent of change in the border region. Finally, a special thanks to Professor Edward J. Williams for first encouraging me to pursue the academic study of the border region and to Helen Ingram for providing me the opportunity to work on environmental issues.

Puente Libre. The international border bridge, with all its traffic and congestion.

Rio Bravo. An elevated black bridge, where some of the awful border trade allegedly occurs along these tracks.

A modern day *maquiladora.*

Casa carton. A poor home.

Casa bien. A rich home.

A cross dedicated to the women who have been abused or killed. *"Ni una más!"* All photos courtesy of the authors.

CHAPTER 1

INTRODUCTION: TOWARD SOCIAL JUSTICE
AT THE U.S.–MEXICO BORDER

Many eyes now focus on the U.S.–Mexico Border, once a frontier conceptualized as being at the margins of national political life. The U.S. Southwest, formerly a part of northern Mexico, is a place of much movement: people cross back and forth to shop, visit, and work; goods move under a new trade regime, the North American Free Trade Agreement (NAFTA), that went into effect on January 1, 1994; pollution and contamination enter air and water with no respect for national boundaries. Movies like the Academy-Award winning *Traffic* sear the imaginations of both Mexican and U.S. ("American") nationals with the greed, corruption, and sickness of post-modern societies.

We who live and work on the U.S.–Mexico border observe, experience, and analyze a fuller reality. Specifically, our vantage point is El Paso–Ciudad Juárez, a metropolitan area of two million people sitting side by side in the Chihuahuan desert with the borderline running right through the pass between a mountain range, named the Franklins on the northern side and the Juárez mountains on the southern (but all part of the larger range known as the Rockies on the northern side and the Sierra Madre on the southern side). Borders surely do complicate things, even names in common geography.

Contextualizing the Border after NAFTA

We are part of the borderlands, a zone of difference from national heartlands, yet reflecting the political and economic institutions of each national heartland. The inequalities between and within these borderlands are obscene: a wage difference of 5–10 : 1, despite cost-of-living differences far less aggravated. We have lived through time periods that range from relatively open borders to border blockades. The militarization of the border in the late 1980s accentuated the potential for conflict in this region.[1] Taking into account the war on drugs and the intense drug trafficking with its concomitant violence (both emotional and physical) on both sides of the border, the region is prone to periods of heightened conflict and tensions between both nations.

We remember the hyperbole over NAFTA when it was being negotiated in the national capitols. For some borderlanders, free trade had been occurring at a micro-level for years. Mexican nationals had been coming to the United States to buy everything from basic goods to luxury items.[2] U.S. residents have shopped in Mexico for basic foodstuffs, and have availed themselves of medical and dental services and prescription drugs. For people in the United States who do not qualify for Medicare or Medicaid and do not have employee sponsored medical and dental insurance, Mexican medical services serve as a safety valve. Without the availability of affordable doctors and medicine, many border residents would do without medical care or else inundate emergency rooms in the United States if they did not take advantage of Mexican medical services as they do at times.

NAFTA's promise was job creation and economic growth, but the delivery on that promise was spotty. In El Paso, NAFTA-displaced workers number 10–15,000 and are mostly middle-aged women. We marvel at the growth of jobs in the *maquiladoras,* export-processing factories in Mexico, numbering over 200,000 in Ciudad Juárez alone (after 2001 layoffs with the downturn in the U.S. economy) with minimum wages stuck at the equivalent of $25 weekly. Marvel extends to El Paso, with growth in telemarketing and plastic molding jobs—employment that pays a bit more than the minimum wages so common in the city's largest manufacturing sector which is garment production. Texas is a conservative "right-to-work" state; approximately five percent of the labor force is unionized in El Paso.[3]

The working-class poor of El Paso lament their loss of jobs to Mexico, and comment on the exploitive wages and working conditions that Mexican workers must endure. The working-class poor in Ciudad Juárez see the jobs in the *maquiladora* industry as an opportunity for economic advancement and job security. Hence, what may appear as exploitation to one worker is seen by another as an opportunity. NAFTA has also had its blessings for some business, accounting, and legal professionals. Among middle-class professionals on both sides of the border, optimism exists about future opportunities in El Paso–Ciudad Juárez, the gateway of the Americas. Both Hispanic and Mexican professionals bring extraordinary talents to the new age of cross-border collaboration, including bilingual capability and a deep knowledge of two countries, multiple cultures, and business or legal systems. We have hopes for a future in which both grassroots activists and professionals also bring their talents to cross-border networks, organizations, and nonprofit management. In that hoped-for future, global movements would be connected to and grounded in local action and knowledge.

Whether a blessing or curse, NAFTA put the U.S.–Mexico border back on the visible map to both U.S. and Mexican policymakers. People invest in the border and its diverse populations. On the U.S. side, politicians cultivate Hispanic constituencies, and more employers hire for diversity. According to the 2000 Census, El Paso's population is 80 percent Hispanic, or what many El Pasoans would identify as Mexican American, Mexican, *Mexicano o Mexicana*. NAFTA draws attention to the border; and its companion institutions, regulations, and rules create opportunities to grow networks, organizations, and nonprofit agencies. These opportunities are transnational, but in regional more than global terms. We focus on the opportunity structure at North American borders, within and across the United States and Mexico.

Opportunity Structures at and across Borders

Political opportunity structures refer to what Sidney Tarrow calls "consistent … dimensions of the political struggle that encourage people to engage in contentious politics."[4] To take advantage of these political openings, as Tarrow continues, groups acquire additional resources, beyond those in their group, to include not just money and power (what strong and well organized groups control), but information, networks, and new allies. In the past, the Mexican government, through its control of the media, could manipulate situations and keep them from the press. Access to the Internet has changed that drastically and now information, environmental spills, labor strikes, and human rights violations can be disseminated widely and internationally. The Internet has also allowed for closer collaboration within environmental, labor, and human rights organizations in the region.

The existence of an opportunity structure is not the same thing as democratic governance, wherein people obtain accountability through political tools, legal rights, voting and economic resources. But when spaces open up in structures that give people voice, leverage, influence, and accountability, democracies can grow, power can spread, and power relations can change.

In historical perspective, power has been concentrated among the few and democracy has been limited at the U.S.–Mexico border. On the

U.S. side, Anglo male elites have dominated economic decision-making. The majority, people of Mexican heritage, faced obstacles in the exercise of voting rights. Economic and educational opportunities have been relatively limited compared to the Anglo minority.[5] Civic capacity is relatively weak, if civic capacity is measured in terms of the proportions of people who participate in public affairs through organizations, voting, and other means. In addition to well-documented structural obstacles to participation and inclusion, many residents of Mexican heritage avoided participation for many reasons, including the lack of U.S. citizenship.

Mexican Americans have had the lowest naturalization rates of any other immigrant group in this country. California's passage of Proposition 187 and the subsequent changes in immigration laws have led to more Mexican Americans taking the U.S. citizenship oath. The fact that Mexico is finally allowing the *no perdida de ciudadanía* [no loss of citizenship], has compelled more Mexican nationals to naturalize and participate in the political process of the United States. There are, however, other reasons why people did not participate in political activity in the United States: the newly arrived compared and contrasted their circumstances in the United States with Mexico. One can look across the river to Ciudad Juárez to see that the quality of life is better in El Paso, especially if one sees a poor neighborhood, known in Mexico as a *colonia popular*. Mexican Americans rarely compared their lives with the privileged of El Paso; rather, they compared their lives with that of poor Mexicans, an assumption that precluded them from making demands on public officials and schools.[6]

On the Mexico side, the northern border, or the *frontera norte*, was distant from centralized decision-making in Mexico City in both physical and real terms. One dominant party ruled Mexico for over 70 years, although the conservative opposition party made gains in the north. While the rhetoric of economic redistribution has been strong since the close of Mexico's revolution, the reality is one of extreme disparities in wealth, with a majority of the population living in poverty and approximately a fifth below the official line of "extreme poverty."[7]

Collaboration across Borders

In this book, we examine cross-border cooperation, networks, and organizations at the U.S.–Mexico border. We focus on the largest metropolitan area that joins the so-called developing and developed economies: Ciudad Juárez and El Paso that respectively comprise 1.5 million and 700,000 residents. We examine key issue areas that transcend the border: environment and health; business and labor; human rights, including the rights of women and immigrants.

Borders: More and Less Visible

For our book, a key spatial concept is the *border*. The most significant border we examine is the territorial line that divides two nation-states: Mexico and the United States. It is a line that establishes national sovereignties, or the different authorities that make rules and regulations above and below that line. And those authorities operate in *very* different political institutions, as we address in chapter three. Yet the borderline is not so clearly defined in many other spheres of life: people live on "one side" and work on the "other side" (*el otro lado,* in local terminology, as people in the region so commonly use). International business standards are used in transnationally owned and managed factory construction, whatever the national standards and however bungling, unrealistic, or corrupt the local implementation authorities.

Conceptions of Border Places and People

The founders of border studies discussed borderlands as zones of difference in between nation-states where people, cultures, and languages are mixed.[8] Oscar Martínez differentiates between the national and the transnational borderlanders who respectively have "superficial" to "significant contacts with the opposite side of the border."[9] Martínez helped refine borderlands analysis in his four models of interaction: alienated, co-existent, interdependent, and integrated. The last two are relevant in our analysis both for the present and the future.

The U.S.–Mexico borderlands fall quite definitely into the interdependent category, according to Martínez's standards. One nation is symbiotically linked with an adjoining nation; stable international relations and economic climates permit "borderlanders on both sides of the line to stimulate growth and development that are tied to foreign capital, markets, and labour."[10] He says the usual pattern is one of asymmetrical interdependence, where one nation is dominant. This is certainly the case at the U.S.–Mexico border.

The borderlanders, known as *fronterizos y fronterizas* in Spanish, have far from equal voices in defining that vague notion development or stimulating its growth. While we address both official and nonofficial interaction, our special interest in this book is with the nongovernmental organizations (NGO), or *organizaciónes no-gubernamentales* (ONG), sectors such as civic, community-based, private, and nonprofit organizations.

Methods and Sources for Our Analysis: Our Vantage Points

Our analysis is based on a mix of methods and a variety of sources. The book first and foremost draws on social science and ethnography.[11] We work, live, and teach in the borderlands with a borderlander population. We have both pursued other border research on the environment and politics (Irasema) and on migration and the political economy, with formal interviews for those projects in the hundreds (Kathy). For this book, we have pursued formal conversations with key informants. We have engaged in even more informal conversations with leaders, activists, and residents.

As researchers, we are acutely aware of the importance of citing and documenting sources. While conducting our research, we relied on traditional sources, such as books, reports, and newspapers, as well as on participant observation. We have attended numerous meetings on both sides of the border dealing with the environment, human rights, economic development, education, immigration, and women's issues. Additionally, we have participated in various academic conferences locally, nationally, and internationally that deal with the topic of borders and cooperation. While our book is informed by traditional sources, it is important to note that members of the community provided data and information on their approaches to civic engagement and binational, cross-border organizing.

Members of the border community are by no means homogenous people. In the same family, members can be American citizens, legal residents, and undocumented. For example, one woman named Consuelo we talked with mentioned that her elderly mother has a border crossing card, but has been living with her for years illegally. Without medical insurance, the mother goes to Ciudad Juárez for medical care. Recently, immigration officials have pressed her to acquire a laser visa, a newer border crossing document, at the American Consulate in Ciudad Juárez. The family is worried that the elderly woman would not be eligible for a visa because of the strict requirements, among them documenting her financial solvency coupled with an interview with a consular official trained in detecting these kinds of irregularities. She feared that she would be "found out"and the consular official would take her old crossing document away and she would be unable to return to El Paso, her home for many years. Consuelo has just submitted her paperwork to become a U.S. citizen and is concerned that the process would be jeopardized if the INS found out that her mother has been living with her without the benefit of proper documents. One of the options is for the elderly woman to not cross into Mexico; however, she would then not be able to obtain affordable health care in the United States.

As we pursued our studies, we learned a great deal about how people experience this binational setting, with its opportunities, but also its fears and paranoia. We became concerned that information about creative binational living and working arrangements would be revealed, so we decided to treat all of our informants with anonymity except for public figures speaking in public settings.

People shared insights with us about institutions that rhetorically promoted cross-border cooperation, but that behind closed doors, contained administrators who made racist comments like how difficult it was to work with Mexicans and/or Gringos. Within inner circles of the institution, the challenges of binational collaboration were discussed in a negative light. Several institutions promoted binational cooperation only because external funding agencies were more apt to provide resources, rather than out of genuine interest or their fundamental mission.

While we learned a lot from many of the interviews, we want to ensure that people's anonymity is respected. We certainly do not want to jeopardize their work, their standing in the organization and the community, or their binational efforts. Therefore, we may be less than direct in identifying certain NGOs, though we make every attempt to be faithful to the insights that people shared regarding cross-border cooperation.

Most of our work utilizes traditional citation formats. However, in good ethnographic form, we also use pseudonyms and protect the anonymity of some sources. In most chapters, we offer what we think is a vivid, yet readable way to present organizational insights: We call them Ethnographic Moments, records of all that we have observed and experienced. But again, we usually use pseudonyms unless the events are public. Readers might use these real-life stories as ways to amplify and enrich reflection or discussion. We live here; we are not border tourists or border research tourists (although we have encountered many of these tourists over the last decades).

The book is grounded in participant observation. We are active in many organizations and partner our university courses with community organizations. We both serve on public and nonprofit boards that give us space and voices in the opportunity structures relevant to this book. Since 1998, Irasema has been a member of the U.S. Environmental Protection Agency Good Neighbor Environmental Board and served as a consultant to the U.S. Census Bureau on data collection in *colonias* (known in the United States as unplanned settlements) contributing to the sprawl around El Paso with approximately 80,000 residents. Kathy has worked with cross-border organizations for ten years, including the Federación Mexicana de Asociaciones Privadas since it began its Seeds

Across the Border/Semillas a través de la Frontera program. She has also served on nonprofit boards, such as Community Scholars and Kids Voting/El Paso, and on public boards, including the Empowerment Zone and a city zoning board. We both work in and with nonprofit organizations on both sides of the border, attending meetings and participating in training programs. We know many of these organizations from the inside out and the outside in. We are academic activists.

We also examine primary and secondary sources and studies of the border region. This book, however, is not meant to be a literature review on everything that has ever been written on the U.S.–Mexico border. Instead, this book is meant to offer comparative case analysis of three large policy areas: the environment; labor and business; and human rights, including health care for the indigent, and women's and immigrants' rights. Our geographic focus is the largest metropolitan region that spans a border dividing and joining developed and developing, or northern and southern countries.

In so doing, we draw on frameworks associated with case study research that is exploratory and descriptive.[12] It is exploratory because no one has yet addressed the central topic of our research on cross-border organizing. We ask and answer questions about cross-border collaboration: Who? What? Where? How? Our study is descriptive, and we intentionally and with pride call it "thickly descriptive."[13] We do not believe that exploratory research like this can occur without vivid and rich portrayals of a region many mainstreamers can hardly imagine or empirical researchers can grasp with superficial survey instruments and numerical metaphors.[14] Yet we believe that our research is also explanatory for the way it is set in theory-driven frameworks (in chapter two) that challenged us and will, we hope, challenge readers to thread conceptual insights throughout the text. Some of these readers, we also hope, will use the analysis to pursue studies in other borderlands.

We treasure the opportunity to teach courses on the border and on U.S.–Mexico relations. Even without those reference terms in course titles, our courses on policy, women, politics, and administration are grounded in and take border vantage points. Some of our students are borderlanders: born on one side, raised on another, and fully conversant in the language, cultural practices, and currencies of both sides. Officially, a tenth of the student body from the institution in which we teach, the University of Texas at El Paso, claims Mexican nationality, and since the late 1980s, have paid "in-state" tuition rates. Irasema is a *fronteriza* by birth; Kathy is a *fronteriza* by adoption since 1977 when she moved to the border. Irasema worked for a year at the Colegio de la Frontera Norte, a research think tank in northern Mexico; she was part of a Ford Foundation funded faculty exchange program with UTEP's Center for Inter-American and Border Studies at the Universidad Autónoma de Ciudad Juárez and worked at universities in two cities that sometimes claim a border locale: Tucson and San Antonio. Together, our years at the border represent nearly two-thirds of a century.

Toward Social Justice at the Border

We bring a normative concern to the analysis: one that seeks greater integration, not just interdependence, in Martínez's terms. Beyond that, we look toward a day in which there will be greater social justice at the border. What would a socially just border look like? Social justice would mean equality in rights, wages, and responsibilities from one to the other side of the border, rather than wage and local government budgets ten times higher comparing north to south. Some will argue that it is realistic to discuss reducing 10:1 ratios, to 5:1, or 2:1 in a specific timeframe. We do not accept this, but the reduction of inequalities would be a step in the right direction.

For interdependence and social justice to occur, greater symmetry is necessary in both economic conditions *and* civic voices. With greater social justice, economic inequalities would diminish across and within borders; respect for and enforcement of human rights would envelop both sides; and environmental stewardship would characterize life, production, and trade. Crossing would be as open to people as it is to trade.

Now, the U.S.–Mexico border is far from being socially just. Yet local organizations have moved more than global movements toward concrete problem-solving and relationship building. Many global movement activists work hard to spread awareness of inequalities, human rights abuses, and environmental damage; many borderlanders *are* already aware. They cross to work, to go to school, to shop, and to visit friends and relatives. Cross-border organizing moves awareness toward problem-solving activities and in so doing, toward opening opportunities for voices among a broader spectrum of borderlanders in governmental and nongovernmental organizations.

To move analysis to action, including policy, we go beyond the typical boundaries of case-study research in highlighting prescriptions. In the body of this book, in each of the three chapters on large policy areas, we focus on a successful case of cross-border collaboration that is tied to our framework and to a concluding chapter about future civic roadmaps for the border.

We hope in our lifetimes to experience a North American integration that parallels borderlands within the European Union. Half in jest, but half with recognition that "naming" often generates new understandings and realities, we call this the North American Union, NAU, and pronounced with sensitivity to Spanish as "now" rather than "nah" in English. We hope that ordinary people have a voice in creating and participating in an "opportunity structure" that recognizes, acts on, and offers accountability to North Americans generally, not just business and consumption through market-oriented accountability.

In the meantime, we live with borders. Where do we draw border-lines, or lines around the border zone? The following section offers some options.

Defining and Mapping the U.S.–Mexico Border

A Line?

Territorial lines are quite visible borders. At the U.S.–Mexico borderline itself, official crossing points are staffed with agents and surveillance equipment that police the passage of people and commerce in northern and southern directions. As might be expected for interdependent borders, traffic is heavy with over 40 million crossers (many of them repeated) on an annual basis (so official questioning is limited to the priority anxieties of each government).

At the official crossing points, Mexican citizens crossing southward into Mexico face queries about the value of goods they bring, undermining the "free" trade principle. Mexico worries about gun smuggling, from the United States and its own citizens, and lots of road signs near the crossings show a big black gun with a diagonal red line through it. The "real" border is nearly 20 miles to the south (measured in kilometers), with extensive customs checks on cars and vehicles.

Most people crossing northward into the United States are asked their nationality and what they are bringing (including liquor in Texas, for state government taxes). What drives officials' queries are concerns about drugs and undocumented travelers. Special lines are in place for trucks from the export-processing factories, or *maquiladoras* or *maquilas* for short. For the tidy annual fee that amounts to 14 weeks of full-time mini-mum wage work in Mexico, *maquila* managers can zip through the Dedicated Commuter Lane (DCL) instead of the usual wait of at least ten minutes, but more often thirty or more minutes. Since September 11, 2001, the waits have been far longer. The exhaust fumes themselves surely have effects on the border bureaucrats who staff the bridge traffic. Delays like these deter busy people, among them the cross-border activists.

A Zone?

Definitions of the border range from the line itself to the zone of residents who live within a radius, often drawn at 25 miles north or south of the borderline. Border maps often highlight this space, what could be called the border zone. According to the 2000 Censuses, the population of U.S. border counties is 6,296,497, while that of municipalities in Mexico totals 7,862,194. The population in this border zone is approximately 14 million people (bigger than many states in the United States), and their living and crossing circumstances vary considerably depending on the range of urban to rural ranch and desert environs.

From west to east, the major urban areas are Tijuana–San Diego (although San Diego is 17 miles from the actual border); *ambos* (both) Nogales, towns with the same name but divided by a steel wall that is two miles long and 14 feet high; the largest binational metroplex, Ciudad Juárez–El Paso, in the pass between the differently named Río Bravo/Rio Grande river and the Sierra Madre/Franklins at the end of the Rocky Mountain range; Nuevo Laredo–Laredo, a huge truck-traffic stop from Mexico's industrial northland of Monterrey; and Brownsville-Matamoros, with its Gulf of Mexico, near-tropical climate. Clearly, there are considerable differences along the border. Existing studies focus more on the urban regions than what Robert Alvarez calls the "outlands" in a thematic volume on the border.[15] *Presidentes Municipales* and their U.S. near-equivalent mayors sometimes establish commissions through which interacting over common problems and conflicts is possible.

We choose to focus on what others have called the "quintessential borderland" of El Paso–Ciudad Juárez. It is *the* largest population concentration at the border, named an "aspiring global city."[16] Our deep knowledge of this central border region allows us to pursue this pioneering exploration, description, and explanation of cross-border organizing, networking, and binational cooperation. We believe the study explores new theoretical and empirical "territory" that has explanatory implications for borders elsewhere. Yet we would affirm that border spaces are not all like. The contrasts between big cities and small towns are huge.

Ethnographic Moment 1.1: Border Small Towns

In a deserted bit of the desert of northern Chihuahua and southern New Mexico, Palomas and Columbus (remember Christopher!) sit side by side. Nearly a century ago, the area was known for Pancho Villa's military incursion to the United States during the Mexican revolution. In Columbus, a museum and state park celebrate this incursion, with quaint postcards and poster pictures of his band and bounty price. More recently, the integrated communities became famous for how the New Mexico school district welcomed children crossing from Palomas into the public schools. New Mexico taxpayers paid school expenses for Palomas children, including buses to carry them across the border. Our economy and futures are tied together, residents said. The prospects of building a bigger elementary campus, however, deterred Luna County taxpayers from maintaining the welcome mat.

Crossers are still part of the local economy. Just across the border, one encounters a liquor–pharmacy store, with 24 horas 7 dias (24 hours 7 days) on its plastic bags. Prices are marked in pesos, but move the decimal point over once, and one has the U.S. price. Liquor is sold with an automated scanner machine, but if you purchase more (and pay in cash), and engage in a conversational request, discounts are available. Fosamax, prescribed to restore bone density (an affliction faced by 1 in 3 women over 50), is 65 pesos, or $6.50 (with a discount probably available too). The price at U.S. franchise pharmacy is $72.99. Few women in northern Mexico undergo expensive bone density scans, but more do on the U.S. side of the border, especially if they are blessed with health insurance.

An El Paso television station routinely highlights the "pink" place, with its Pancho Villa restaurant on the main drag of Palomas. More like fuschia, with purple beams, the store attracts a motley group of U.S. visitors who buy crafts, eat and drink margaritas (with the peso-dollar price difference of 2:1, not the more than 10:1 pharmaceutical difference above). The average age of crosser-customers is probably 60. Entertainers play songs by request on an electronic piano and as traditional style, in a group with guitars. They are asked to play the Himno Nacional de México (national anthem), but refuse. Some things are too sacred, even for a tip in dollars.

Uncommon Features within Common Zones

A zone implies commonality, but we contest a superficial or romanticized view of that commonality. What makes border zones attractive in the global economy is not only the common spatial location and ensuing transport efficiencies, but also the difference in wages. Mexico's Border Industrial Program offers low-wage enclaves in a common zone. The U.S.–Mexico border, within the North American free trade zone, may be the closest thing to South Africa under apartheid that we know of, given the internal wage inequalities within a common region.

The 2,000-mile U.S.–Mexico border is still leaky in many parts of the uninhabited and hostile desert terrain. Border Patrol strategies over the last decade have pushed unauthorized crossers away from the settled parts of the border zone to this desert terrain. Although the base line for interest in and measurement of "death" counts through crossing the border only began in the 1980s, most observers would agree that this strategic change resulted in increases in annual crossing deaths. Through the pioneering work of those at the University of Houston's Center for Immigration Research, we learned with despair about the hundreds of lives lost attempting the crossing, numbering nearly 500 with official counts in 2000.[17] Borders wreak of human rights problems, but the loss of life is the ultimate abuse of human rights.

We would be remiss if we did not allude to the other border zones that occur on one or the other side of the border. In Ciudad Juárez, approximately 200 neighborhoods or *colonias populares,* complete with names and identities, offer very different living experiences to their residents. In El Paso, the city–county divide is primary when one considers access to basic water and sewer facilities: many *colonia* residents do not have such access. Unplanned settlements give the label *colonias* on the U.S. side a different meaning.

Other borders are also worth analytic attention. Railroad tracks and highways operate like borders to divide people who live and earn in very different circumstances on one side compared to the other. In this book, we also seek to analyze borders like these and how people transcend such lines through solidarity, collaboration, and cooperation.

Border States?

Maps as we can see have neat lines that easily divide states and nations, cities, counties, *municipios* and school districts. Still another way to define and draw boundaries around the U.S.–Mexico border would be through examining matching states. From west to east, border states include Baja California with California; Sonora with Arizona; Chihuahua with both New Mexico and Texas, and Coahuila, Nuevo León, and Tamaulipas with Texas. Governors from these states periodically meet and even establish committees to routinize interaction over common problems and conflicts.

If one counted the population of border states, over 50 million people in the 1990 census, the border's size and significance would

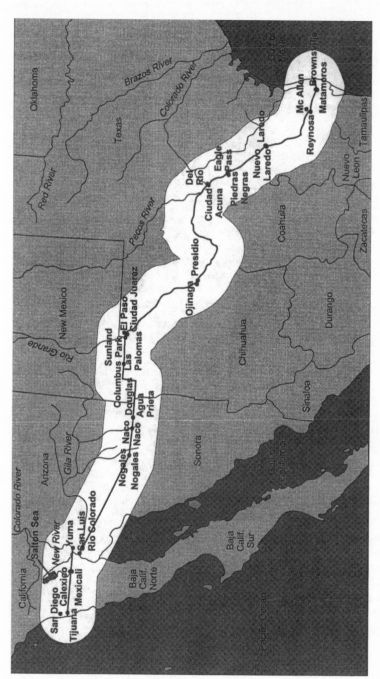

Map 1.1 U.S.–Mexico Border Region and 14 Sister Cities. Source: GAO

surely rise in the minds of officials and residents. According to the 2000 counts, U.S. border states counted 61,673,146 residents, while border states in Mexico total 16,642,676. Approaching 80 million residents, the border state population surpasses France or the United Kingdom. One periodically sees maps of this huge space. Sometimes these maps are one-sided, such as that of the U.S./Mexico Border Counties Coalition of U.S. county officials, beleaguered with the costs of federal immigration laws that burden local governments' criminal justice and medical service systems.[18] Many of the southwestern states in Texas are among the most poverty-stricken in the entire United States. As former Texas state comptroller John Sharp and his staff concluded, after analyzing numerous income and social indicators, "if the border were the 51st state," it would be the poorest in ... " [you name it].[19] Mexico's northern border states, however, tend to be wealthier than central and southern states.

Borders in Foreign Policy Imagination

Still another way to conceptualize the border region is to look at foreign policy agreements. These agreements are the product of deliberation, negotiation, and resolutions that may or may not match realities. For example, the La Paz agreement maps the border as 100 kilometers north and south of the international borderline.

Border states, foreign policies, and metropolitan areas do shape their residents and local governments. However, our book addresses the border zone rather than the state. It is in these zones where significant organizing, networking, and collaboration can occur, with the blessings and curses of personalism, the theoretical framework of this book.

Cross-Border Interactions: On the Rise

We develop and analyze the notion that the transnational focus of regional free trade regimes facilitates cross-border organizational activity.[20] NAFTA provides a transnational institutional umbrella that creates an opportunity structure for civic capacity building. We call this an "institutional shroud." We acknowledge the opportunity that transnational institutions provide for political voice, policy change, resources, and accountability, yet we also would emphasize that those institutions are often more symbolic than real. In the classic meaning of "symbolic politics," those institutions create the appearance of action, and thus can induce quiescence, while in reality, little gets done to address problems.[21]

Thus, we use the word shroud, for its meaning can range from a funeral covering to protective support. Significant obstacles to cross-border activity still remain, many of the same obstacles that deterred people with common interests from acting politically on those common interests over previous historical eras.

Cross-Border Organizational Blockades

In this book, we will address many obstacles to cross-border collaboration, the strongest of which are institutional, economic, linguistic, nationalist, and cultural. Poverty is frequently associated with weak civic capacity, and poverty is in plentiful supply on both sides of the U.S.–Mexico border. Obstacles, like those many listed, have long inhibited transnational peoples from recognizing commonalities and organizing collectively to achieve their common goals.

Not the least of these obstacles is one with two faces: personalism. The rise of much-lauded global and transnational movements is remarkable. History books will record the mobilizations around the World Trade Organization beginning with Seattle, 1999, and others around the World Bank and International Monetary Fund thereafter. These mobilizations occurred, and occurred quickly, through the Internet and electronic communication. People mobilize around justice; they mobilize around hate; they mobilize around making money. Electronic networking itself is neutral to all those with technological resources in a world of unequal digital divides (yet another boundary). While we applaud networking, we caution those who celebrate this new day without recognizing the personal and relational foundations on which lasting networks and organizations are built. In fact, the classic studies of elite networks, discussed in chapter two, are replete with evidence of the influence of personal relationships built on boards, in country clubs, and through alumni associations. Electronic networks without personal connection can be superficial and easily dismissed. Many e-mail users are bombarded with messages they quickly delete.

Borders are the ideal locations in which to ground transnational networking and develop personal relationships in shared space. It is surprising to see the few transnational networks grounded in local border activism.

Of course, personalism has many sides. The negative face of personalism is its tendency to use person- rather than issue-based or ideological criteria in political thought and action. It potentially limits the size of networks, organizations, and alliances. In the next chapter, we draw on theoretical insights from sociology including those on the "strength of weak ties" and on the networks among the powerful—those "who rule." On the surface, these two insights might be viewed as contradictory, until understood in the context of power, money, and control. Personalism, we argue, is endemic in limited democracies.

Yet personalism has a positive face. Person-based criteria often form the basis of relationships and networks, the foundation for collaboration and collective action. Issue-based and ideological mobilizations are hindered in the absence of trust and personal knowledge. In this book, we address a fundamental dilemma faced in many spatial settings, whether borderlands or not: How can personalism be reconciled with the loose ties necessary for strong and effective engagement in public affairs?

Outline of Chapters

This book addresses the two faces of personalism in the contrasting comparative institutional complex of the U.S.–Mexico borderlands, a region of common space and interests beset with obstacles to collaboration. In chapter two, we examine the challenges to collaboration, drawing on theoretical perspectives from sociology, political science, and anthropology. In chapter three, we develop a typology of organizations within and across the U.S.–Mexico borderline. Overlaying those organizations, we analyze the political institutions of each nation-state, and the transnational institutions overarching these institutions. These institutions provide new openings in a changing political opportunity structure at the border.

In the next section of the book, we move to chapters at the heart of people's common and substantive interests that transcend the borderline. The substantive topics we chose allow us to elaborate more fully on a model of cross-border organizing in chapter three, posing factors to answer the question: What facilitates and blocks cross-border organizing? To preview and summarize this model, we examine factors that facilitate and undermine cross-border collaboration that goes beyond rhetoric toward problem-solving actions.

We begin, in chapter four, with a focus on the broad environment of the border: the land, water, and air. We examine transnational, national, and civic organizations that impinge upon environmental sustainability. Binational agreements and institutions have facilitated the visibility of common environmental issues, and the global environment movement strengthens the ability of regional activists to forge common bonds. On the ground, however, environmental organizations produce few outcomes that provide stewardship for the ecology.

In chapter five, we examine business, commerce, and labor at the border. Here too, we find official machinery and institutions that facilitate business and commercial flows. Large-scale capital investments and the possibility of expanded market niches and profits facilitate this movement. The same cannot be said for labor and labor unions, still steeped in national rather than cross-national solidarities and in "justice" systems that do not affirm their interests above or at the level of business interests.

In chapter six, we take up human rights issues, analyzing official actions that range from under-enforcement to over-enforcement and abuse of laws. It is in this realm where cross-border civic actions are the most impotent, compared to environment, business, and labor issues. The toleration of violence against women is callous, and the disappearance of people, including disappeared daughters, merits little action, save activist women whose gender has marginalized them from established power. Immigration law enforcement waxes and wanes with prevailing political winds. The 1986 immigration reform set the stage for amnesty for undocumented immigrants. The border counterpart to racial profiling, immigrant profiling, has long operated, with the consequence of fear and political quiescence. Since the 1993 border blockade, and the 1996 immigration law reform, stricter rules have prevailed, thus undermining the prospect for more "open borders."

In chapter seven, we revisit the theoretical issues of chapter two to integrate our analysis of cross-border collaboration. We then draw action implications from this summary to propose organizing strategies that move the U.S.–Mexico border from asymmetrical interaction to more symmetrical integration toward social justice.

CHAPTER 2

COLLABORATION AT BORDERS: THE TWO FACES OF PERSONALISM

> In Mexico ... you may spend an hour and a half with a client just establishing the personal relationship and then you move on to business. In the U.S., if you get 10–15 minutes worth of personal conversation, it's been a waste of time ... but if your client doesn't like you in the U.S., you are going to have a hard time retaining them.
>
> —"Ricardo," informant

Personalism is alive and well in the business, public, and nonprofit worlds of Mexico and the United States. The timing and cues in both places may be different, and people who are open and sensitive to these alternatives do communicate successfully. The graduate-trained cross-border accountant who shared his insights with us is the quintessential borderlander. His family is from central Mexico, but he was born in El Paso, the family returned to Mexico for a few years, and then returned to El Paso. He describes himself as Americanized, and his peers Anglicized his first name, but he is a fluent speaker of both Spanish and English. Now his business cards list his Spanish first name. His perceptions of personal relationships and their timing in Mexico are widely shared at the border, although many "Americans" seem to mute attention to personal issues in the United States. Personal relationships are relevant to collaboration in the civic, business and public worlds of both countries and especially at the border, as framed and detailed further in this chapter.

Our attention to personal issues, however, is not limited to the business world or to those with resources and talents who may be able to finesse the best of binational work opportunities, sensitivity, and lifestyles. For the majority, there is a caste-like quality to finessing these opportunities, based on class and income, over which a veneer of technological sophistication exists. Mexico assembles advanced technology, automobiles, and medical equipment, yet people working the *maquiladora* assembly line putting together the equipment or computer keyboards may not know how to use them or even be able to afford to buy the technology that is being assembled.

Our key chapter argument is this: If cross-border and transnational movements are to mobilize for a social justice that expands opportunity for far more people in ways that result in a fairer distribution of resources, we must attend to the ways in which relationship are built, fostered, and sustained to lead toward change. Relationships draw on personal factors to develop and sustain themselves. Personal factors like openness, trust and credibility, and cross-cultural sensitivity (including language acquisition) grease the grids of the seemingly mechanistic opportunity structure about which we wrote in chapter one. Ultimately, though, personal relationships ("strong ties") must grow and expand into weaker ties that connect to larger networks and organizations if the border is to develop into a region with equal opportunity and social justice.

By now, global movements and global NGOs are as visible as global corporations and markets. From environmental to feminist activism, global social movements counter, collaborate with, and/or influence industries and nation-states. This activism, at its heart, is about distributional politics in Harold Lasswell's classic sense: Who gets what (including what values), where, when and how?[1] However, the answers are not just national, as Lasswell conceived them, but transnational. By definition, global NGOs transcend national borders.

In this chapter, we move global issues to the local common ground of borderlands. We first consider cross-border, transnational activism as a peculiar variant of local politics. Then we move to theoretical considerations surrounding collaboration within and across borders, focusing especially on *personalism* with all its blessings and curses. If borders are the "hybrid" places about which border theorists write—the zones of difference between nations—then we must grapple with the cultural hybridity that might make personal issues important and thereby infuse politics with personalism, including both its limitations and its possibilities.

Global Movements at Local Binational Borders

"Transnational advocacy networks," say Margaret Keck and Kathyrn Sikkink, are activists "distinguished largely by the centrality of principled ideas or values in motivating their formation." Such networks emerge under certain conditions; they continue when national civil society–government channels are blocked, with political entrepreneurial promoters, and through spaces in which networks can flourish, such as conferences.[2] Advocates seek the openings of political opportunity structures, as discussed in the introductory chapter. We wonder about the personal elements among activists, even the ideological and religious among them.

Many people have written about mobilization against export-processing manufacturing (*maquiladoras*), free trade, and North American Free Trade Agreement (NAFTA).[3] The European Union also provides a supranational institution around which "transnationals" organize.[4] We see a dearth of analysis about the transnational, or cross-border organizing in the common ground of the U.S.–Mexico border, where people share an integrated (if asymmetrical) economy, the same water basins, air, and pollution.

Little ink has been spilled over the organizing challenges posed in the borderlands. However successful global movements might seem to be, measured in terms of United Nations resolutions or virtual communication through electronic mail, if people cannot collaborate across national borders in a fifty-mile radius like El Paso–Ciudad Juárez, how well do transnational and global movements really fare? Global movements must learn from the challenges of transnational organizing within borderlands. Global business and consumption are well organized, even facilitated and subsidized by governments and international organizations, as we discuss in chapter five. Will global movements and nongovernmental organizations ever obtain parity with global business and consumption? Official government subsidies to business do not extend to nongovernmental organizations and global movements.

The focus on global and regional movements provides a welcome antidote to political analysis that stops at a borderline (comparative politics, American politics, Mexican politics, *name-the-country* politics). Politics stops at the border rather than transcends it. The focus also is a relief from attention to high-level foreign policy elites that people study in the field of International Relations. Yet all of these analytical strategies mute attention to the important cross-border organizing strategies that occur *within* borderlands as *regions*. In these spaces, networks can flourish especially well, through kinship, personal friendships, and official coordination bodies (the latter of which often blossom just after elections).

Officially there are several venues that promote binational cooperation. The Border Liaison Mechanisms (BLMs) are coordinated through the American and Mexican consulates as we discuss in the next chapter. Numerous commissions and conferences put binational coordination on the agenda of health service and environmental stewardship. From both sides of the border, public and appointed officials pay lip service to binational cooperation. At the bottom line, however, nations exercise *sovereignty* over their territory; binational actions complicate sovereignty. The idea of "sister cities," warm and fuzzy sounding, resonates well with audiences outside the region. At the border itself, however, concrete results that put these lofty pronouncements and recommendations into practice are few and far between.

Cross-border collaborations respond both to so-called free trade regimes and to regional spaces that share not only common ground, but also common issues that transcend national territorial boundary lines and people who share a common language and Mexican heritage. We are particularly interested in local nongovernmental organizations that respond to the regional and the global: community-based organizations (CBOs), nonprofit organizations/*asociaciones civiles,* unions/*sindicatos* and social justice networks. We wonder about the extent to which they are connected to regional, national, and global movements.

Taking cues from the usual *issue* focus in transnational organizing, we develop issues in subsequent chapters but focus here on transnational organizing in a bordered *space* or place. Cross-border organizing strategies, we argue, are a variant of local politics. Strategists face obstacles and must grapple with the multiple political institutions that shroud them and the resulting accountability complications of contrasting political institutions (that we address in the following chapter). While transnational issue organizing emphasizes the spread of awareness, (as Keck and Sikkink indicate), successful organizing at and around borders generally must move beyond consciousness-raising toward problem-solving. Here at the border, awareness is often quite commonplace, even mundane, with transnational kinship, friendship, and work patterns. Transnational organizing toward problem-solving in a global economy is difficult enough to sustain, but it is particularly challenging in the context of separate, multiple political institutions, of economic scarcity and minimal wages, and of nationalism and mindless jingoism. This complicated context *is* the border.

Collaboration: A Challenge Anywhere

At the most fundamental level, the analysis of cross-border networks and organizations is about collaboration across any lines of difference. The differences range from identities—like ethnicity, gender, and class—to organizations, like unions and lobby groups. The much-vaunted public–private partnerships, between government and business or nonprofit organizations, are also about collaboration. Collaboration occurs *within* legal jurisdictional lines, as in alliances within a city, county, or municipality. Collaboration also occurs *across* jurisdictional lines, as in community-based organizations in different cities that form alliances to strengthen their power in relation to powers they seek to influence. Thus collaboration in a wide generic sense is about crossing "borderlines."

Government downsizing makes collaboration the mantra of turn-of-the century North America. Funders promote collaboration to stretch resources. Funding supplicants seek collaborators to amass real money and in-kind contributions to "make things happen." Collaboration, once a dirty word in war for its suggested complicity with an occupying power, is now the indicator of civic health and effectiveness.[5] A series of organizational-help books, the collective equivalent of individual self-help books, offer recipes for collaboration with little regard for their political complexity. A virtual cottage industry has grown around nonprofit organizational growth, fund raising, and "technical assistance" (TA), a sanitized phrase for actions themselves that generate revenue for nonprofit TA firms.

Collaboration involves people, and the key to strong and effective movements relies on numbers of people generally, strategically placed people, and people with passionate, intense commitments to issues. The heart of collaboration involves building relationships among people. Relationships are inherently personal. To form relationships, some degree of trust is necessary for the time and work to be invested in forming alliances and solving problems together. Personal reputations launch and multiply relationships into networks.

Studies at the U.S.–Mexico border, as well as those of urban neighborhood movements in Mexico, have noted the capacity of people to organize together to demand public utilities such as water and sewer services. *Social capital,* defined as networks and trust relationships for problem-solving, is reflected in such collective organizations. Using the border in a laboratory-like comparison, however, studies identify greater social capital on the Mexico, compared to the U.S. side in low-income neighborhoods and *colonias.*[6]

In the United States, government relationships with low-income communities range from malignant to benign neglect, or even a helping, service orientation. But in communities with sizeable numbers of immigrants, at least one part of government (the Border Patrol and the Immigration and Naturalization Service [INS]) operates with surveillance for occasional removal and deportation. Community residents often avoid and fear government. People are less likely to use the democratic process to press for services or for the kind of autonomy and subsidies that other pressure groups use. Some nonprofit organizations *sustain* that service orientation, plus sustain their livelihoods with grant-writing and fund-raising activities. We periodically hear organizers with an economic, self-sufficiency orientation describe these helper nonprofits as "poverty pimps"—a phrase we abhor, but which we share to draw distinctions among nongovernment organizations.

People could themselves press for services, self-sufficiency, or for autonomy and subsidies like those sought by business lobbies. Some border studies imply, perhaps with more longing than empirical reality, that a transcendent *Mexicanidad* ties people together across the border. In great contrast, the xenophobes are enormously threatened about Mexican identity or loyalty. Radical rhetoricians egg them on with polemics about the new "Mexican Invasion" that counters U.S. invasion of northern Mexico in the nineteenth century, taking half its land. The Mexican invasion supposedly infiltrates quietly, with the steady northward movement of people, languages, food preferences, and customs. In border contrasts, no quiet or strident invasion occurred in El Paso, but it is the largest border city with not merely a majority, but eight of ten residents with Mexican heritage. Spanish is spoken as widely as English. Many jobs require bilingual capability, for public necessity. Yet to reiterate an important point in chapter one, not all borderlanders are alike in their language use, cultural identity, and ideas among other factors.

Personalism: A Social Analytical View

Anthropology and political ethnography address conflict and cooperation, especially at the local level (village, in "anthropology-speak"). The concepts used to analyze politics include attention to clientelism, political machines, and patron–client relationships,[7] which we take up below. Much analysis of Mexico draws on these insights, such as attention to *caciques* as leaders or political bosses, or *compadrazgo* (godparentship), as mechanisms to grow extended families with fictive kin. These are the bases for many political relationships, networks, and loyalty groups called *camarillas*. Of course, even in solidarity groups, like some unions, people use fictive kin terms, calling one another "brother" or "sister." Whole unions have the word "brotherhood" in their names (Teamsters, International Brotherhood of Electrical Workers), though we know of no unions, only feminist or religious organizations, with the word "sisterhood." Insights about personalism are relevant in limited democracies, like the borderlands, as we analyze in the next chapter.

Few political scientists have examined friendships, personalism, loyalty, and betrayal. Indeed, the keyword loyalty on Internet search engines in 2001 hints at what happens to these concepts in advanced capitalism: *consumer* loyalty brings up the most "hits." Yet James Q. Wilson, in his classic study of political organization, compared the different kinds of incentives that attracted those who joined organizations: personal (what he called "solidary" incentives, based on both the status and the pleasure of social interaction); material, like money or concrete goods; and purposive, from single-issue to multi-issue purposes.[8] The many who are attracted to material incentives, like unions, bring a thin commitment to the organization, often satisfied with individual gain. Personal motivations, like faith-based organizing that draws from a congregational base, are potentially unstable until purposive incentives overtake the ever-changing pleasure or status of social relations. Purposive organizing is the ideal of the three, toward which material and personal motivations lead.

To analyze networks and organizations in the U.S.–Mexico metropolitan area of the border, we draw on anthropological and ethnographic concepts, rarely used in U.S. urban studies. And with few exceptions, most political ethnography in Mexico focuses on villages and towns, even though Mexico is a majority-urban nation.[9]

In *Who Rules America?* now in its third edition,[10] William Domhoff argues that a corporate–conservative coalition dominates American politics, challenged by a liberal–labor coalition. He does not merely allege or theorize conspiracy, but examines data on corporate board memberships. For Domhoff, overlapping board memberships—what others sometimes call interlocking directorates—are key to understanding domination. Connected board members work together; they share stake, ownership, and profit in common financial stock. They also play together, on golf courses, in country clubs, and the like. There is a personal quality to these ties—face-to-face relationships—that are deepened with monetary self-interest. In popular parlance, these are what people called "good old boy" networks, but nowadays they are also new and sometimes female but still good for those who benefit.

Elite theorists like Domhoff play little heed to cracks, division, and competition in the monolithic structure they have constructed. A virulent critic of elites, Karl Marx once said one capitalist kills another. Both academics and activists would do well to avoid overstating monolithic controls. In the most authoritarian of settings, people resist, avoid, ignore, or act strategically to pursue their interests. The borderlands potentially offers cracks in the monolith with language nuances and institutional complexities.

Elite approaches, however critical, undermine people's hope and will to collective action and challenges to domination that would change the distribution of power and rewards. We suggest that it is worthwhile to turn this network analysis upside down to examine various organizations, like those in this book, from community-based and grassroots to nonprofit and official, that also have leaders, boards, and members. Some of these people are bound together through personal ties; they also work and play together. Elites are invited to serve on some of these boards, even as their self-interests are not entirely served in organizations with majority non-elites who challenge the status quo. Community-based organizations (CBOs), networks, social movements, cross-border cooperation, and nonprofit agencies challenge corporate-conservatism within and across borders.

Horizontal and Vertical Ties

Modern and post-modern societies are bureaucratic, with rules and procedures blanketing relationships of authority. Max Weber would have us think that modern bureaucratic machinery is rid of personal and patrimonial relations, yet such relationships exist at the base of bureaucratic, public, and private action, relationships that are both horizontally and vertically tied.[11]

Horizontal Ties

Let us first look at *horizontal* relationships among people of relatively equal stature. Among those tied through horizontal relationships, one might expect merit, rationality, and procedures to govern decision-making processes. Still, reputation and personality have bearing on decisions. Take, for example, the boards that govern nonprofit organizations. Board members sign "conflict of interest" statements, which are properly filed away, but personal knowledge, credibility, friendship, and enmity have a bearing on decisions made and actions taken. Take also the example of university decision-making. Great care is taken to avoid the appearance of conflict among married couples and family members making decisions about one another, yet friendship and reputation might be just as personally slanted in decision-making processes. People know, discuss, and even gossip about other people. Anthropologists recognize and write about this in seemingly exotic societies to the south, but analysts hardly deal with it in the north (or if they do, they attribute it to women). As James Scott has said about the "arts of resistance" that include mockery, "gossip is perhaps the most familiar and elementary form of disguised popular aggression... [with] something of a disguised democratic voice."[12] Gossip opens a voice for the mass, although it is a voice without accountability. At the border, sharing *chisme* (gossip) is a pastime in which many participate. In limited democracies like the border region, gossip is the escape valve, but one with potentially damaging consequences.

Can or should people eliminate such personal ties? Hardly! The horizontal, personal ties among people are what make relationships human rather than mechanical. Pity the day that the (in Weber's words) "iron cage" of bureaucratic machinery prevails.

Personal bonds have ripple effects. Friends of friends can bond loosely into networks, short-circuiting the time that it takes to build original trust relationships. These ripple effects have both positive and negative ramifications. When personal factors reign, the enemies of my friends also become my enemies. What seems like a wonderful organizing prospect—friendship networks—also becomes an organizing nightmare, as enemy networks spiral to prevent or damage ties.

Vertical Ties

In hierarchical societies, personal ties are bound to have *vertical* dimensions as well. All societies are hierarchical, but some are more unequal than others and the inequality is ritualized in language use and everyday behavior. Yet one must heed the smile and bow of subordinate to master that is preceded by or followed with mockery and gossip.

Anthropologists have long studied the "patron–client" relationships that bind the less powerful to the more powerful. In exchange for favors from patrons, the client is expected to provide labor, loyalty, and other resources to patrons. Together, many clients' contributions help sustain the patron and the unequal relations. Patron–client ties, as usually conceptualized, are built around people, rather than issues or ideologies.

We use the words "bind" and "bonds" quite deliberately for they aptly paint the double meaning of strong personal ties. In a positive sense, bonds create solidarity and loyalty; surely these are sorely needed characteristics in the strident individualism of post-modern society. In a negative sense, bonds can be like chains. Lots of ties bind people together at the U.S.–Mexico border, from Mexican heritage to Spanish language. At some borders, these ties have been called *Mexicanidad*, suggesting some sort of "bonding social capital" that might form the foundation for the more difficult "bridging social capital" that collaborators seek to build and sustain.[13] The veneer of *Mexicanidad* is belied, we observe, with differences over which bridges must be built: immigration/emigration, with a gulf between those who left and those who stayed in Mexico;

knowledge of Spanish and its pronunciation, to name just a few. Gender also structures differences, gulfs and potential bridges. We often see exaggerated gender difference in public presentation, from dress and body language to speaking style. The Mexican comic books, *Supermachos,* one can still perhaps purchase *semi-nuevo* (semi-new, as it is optimistically called) in public markets, characterize some of the excessive male posturing we observe in organizational and neighborhood turfs, a posturing with its mirror image of gracious chivalry. We have already hinted at and illustrated the extensive personalism we observe at the border. Consider some explanations.

Personalism at the U.S.–Mexico Border

Personalism is alive and well at the U.S.–Mexico border. It has consequences for collaboration within and across borders and for the cross-border networking, organizing, and cooperation in the issue areas on which we focus in this book. Personalism forges ties that could grow into issue networks, but it can also constrain growth, dissemination, and sustained challenge to historical patterns of asymmetry and dominance at the U.S.–Mexico border.

Are the borderlands politics more personalistic than elsewhere? Below, we outline reasons that might explain extensive personalism at the U.S.–Mexico border. Our analyses in subsequent chapters also sustain that view. However, if personalism got greater attention in American political analyses, we suspect that it would become more visible as well.

From the U.S.–Mexico border perspective, the explanations about rampant personalism are sometimes lacking and incomplete. First, we consider the hybridity explanation, drawing on the Mexico connection and communication patterns from so-called "high-context" cultures (refer to cultural distinctions outlined in Table 2.1). Second, we address small-town politics wherein "everyone knows each other," especially the business and governing elite. Perhaps fast-growing El Paso and Ciudad Juárez have not grown and spread their civic capacity in more professional and distant, less personal directions. Of course, personal ties and networks are endemic among members of what class theorists once called a "power elite," as we pointed out in the *Who Rules America?* discussion of the book, again, with its personalistic decision-making behind closed doors. The border has no monopoly on patterns like these.

While the above two explanations add insight to dynamics at the border, we believe personalism to be a relic of limited democracy. Border cities are small towns grown huge in a mere generation. They are populated with majorities who exercise little political power. Personalism, coupled with highly asymmetrical power relations, has been commonplace historically in the El Paso–Ciudad Juárez region as the next chapter develops. Let us look in great detail at the alternative explanations.

Personalism as Mexican or "Cultural"

The border has long been called a place of "hybridity." People cross frequently; bilinguals mix languages; cultural patterns blend and mutate. In border popular culture, we celebrate twice as many holidays, from both nations. One of Ciudad Juárez's main thoroughfares contains a statue of the liberator Abraham Lincoln, and many El Paso walls contain murals of the Virgin of Guadalupe, much revered in Mexico. El Paso has its own Porfirio Díaz street, perhaps the only one dedicated to Mexico's nineteenth-century dictator in all of North America, even in all of Mexico.

At the border, people express pride in "family values" and exhibit—for better or worse—lower levels of marital dissolution and female-headed households, at least compared to the mainstream United States. Extended families are valued. Could hybridity extend into the *public* or civic sphere? Each side of the border takes on characteristics of *el otro lado,* or the other side. El Paso occupies ex-northern Mexico. Many of its earliest residents, people joke, changed nationality when the border changed. Could personalism be a product of Mexican heritage and Mexico's proximity?

Mexican politics has long been characterized as "clientelist," that is, based on vertical networks of ties among unequal people in hierarchical societies. Mexico is the land of many clients and few patrons, an organizing framework for much analysis from anthropology to political science, as earlier noted. In a key classic of political science, comparing five countries, Gabriel Almond and Sidney Verba characterize Mexico as a parochial political culture. Their definition of parochial is not merely private and insular. For Almond and Verba, it is a "lack of" many things present in a civic culture: people are not oriented to the larger political system; people are both ignorant of and pessimistic about both the upward and downward flows of policy making; people lack the sense of self-capacity to participate.[14]

Of course, Mexico since 1980 is in the much-lauded transition to democracy with multi-party electoral competition. It is not the same Mexico as that in Almond and Verba's 1960s-era study. We cannot help but notice the higher electoral participation rates in Ciudad Juárez and the blanket of political campaigning shrouding the city prior to elections compared with the ho-hum attitude of El Pasoans during its many political campaigns. Juarenses wait in line for hours to vote on election day. Of the 350,000 registered El Paso voters eligible to vote absentee a full three weeks prior to election day, it is an unusual achievement if more than 100,000 vote. Just five miles to the south, Ciudad Juárez voter turnout rate triples that of El Paso. Yet civic capacity, measured in terms of organizational strength, continues to be relatively undeveloped in both cities.

In another take on hierarchical inequality, Mexico exhibits extreme "power distance" between people in the workplace. Geert Hofstede's methodical study of 40 countries and over 100,000 interviews identifies Mexico as the country with the highest power distance between dominant and subordinate.[15] This certainly meshes with the patron–client, clientelist ties found in political studies and in both languages and linguistic rituals. In everyday life at the border, people are sensitive to the show of *respeto* (respect). Politicians want proper respect shown (all too often, respect born of fear), but so do ordinary people, individuals who want acknowledgement and greeting. Improper respect is humiliating and uncivilized; it is remembered. Failure to return phone calls is disrespectful enough to undermine organizing strategies.

Spanish and English

The Spanish language embeds within it a range of characteristics alternatively interpreted as graciousness and extreme politeness to institutionalized inequality and excessive respect. Examples include *para servirle* (in order to serve you), or *a sus ordenes* (at your orders) *tú y usted* (familiar and formal forms of "you" that also distinguish the dominant and subordinate), and *Licenciado o Licenciada* (titles that precede the names of those with higher education degrees). Coupled with this is elaborate attention to greeting, handshaking, and hugs (*abrazos*). Interaction *con cariño,* with affection and care, is valued in some public settings.

English, in contrast, is more direct and abrupt. Could Spanish language, as a reflection of culture, deepen personalism? Perhaps. But is this parochial, as Almond and Verba understood it? Probably not. Almond and Verba demonized parochial culture and idealized civic culture without recognizing how the latter buys discretion and space for the politically powerful, if and when the powerless are deluded into thinking they have a voice.

For much of history, ordinary people's perception of their powerlessness matches the reality of who rules. A power-distant political culture creates no illusions about who rules; moreover, rational recognition of power dominance might augment solidarity among the powerless and ultimately strengthen civic capacity. One of the Spanish organizing cries among Latinos, from farmworkers to Alinsky-type organizations (see chapter three) is *Sí se puede!* (yes we can!), as people together shout and convince themselves about hope and possibilities through volume. We do not hear the phrase in Mexico (but in all the Americas we hear and read *ya basta* [enough already]). Disgust seems to transcend national boundaries more than national democratic delusions.

Mexico has no monopoly on clientelist politics. Under conditions of elite rule, the democratic organizational trappings extend to envelop through party and machine-style political incorporation. Patrons selectively distribute benefits to their supplicants in patronage politics based on personal loyalties rather than ideas, issues, and ideologies.

In many U.S. cities, patronage-style, machine politics have long been part of the political landscape in historic and even contemporary times. Sometimes the insider politicians develop purposive issue orientations. Outsiders, like labor union members and women, speak favorably about seeking a "friend in office": he's a friend to women; she's a friend of labor. From Chicago to New York, clientelistic politics are thorough Americana. They flourish in high-immigration eras and locales. Machine-style politics are relics of limited democracies.

Personalism as Small-Town Politics

El Paso is a town that grew up fast to big-city stature. From a population of 130,000 in 1950, El Paso has quadrupled in size over a half century. Migrants made up a critical mass of this population, and a fearful part of the population. Since the creation of the Border Patrol and periodic deportations, whether in the 1930s or the 1990s, immigrants' vulnerability and immigration profiling have undermined people's ability to organize and assert their rights. Many people prefer to maintain a low public profile to avoid surveillance and scrutiny. People generate income through informal means, without regulatory protection. Some families contain people in varying stages of *arreglando,* living and working with partial legality. These differences occur even within one family. Distance from the preying eyes of government protects potentially vulnerable people.[16]

In historical perspective, Anglo male elites have long dominated El Paso's politics.[17] Mexicans and Mexican Americans operated outside networks of influence and officialdom until relatively recently: the first

Mexican American mayor was elected in the mid 1950s; the first Mexican American county judge served in the early 1990s; more than one Mexican American served on large urban school boards only in the 1970s and thereafter. One might label this belated Mexican American participation as the other side of Anglo domination.

Perhaps Anglo domination is the "cultural" problem although we do not believe that seemingly cultural personalism is any more inherently Anglo than Mexican, in contexts of relative equality. But the borderlands are hardly egalitarian places. Anglos ruled government, bigger businesses, and schools. Spanish detention existed in schools through the 1960s.[18] The relatively small elite happened to be an Anglo-dominated elite.

In small-town politics, political people know each other personally, as friends (and occasionally enemies). As El Paso grew, the small-town political networks did not grow and keep pace with population growth and the diversity of that growth. As the former director of El Paso's Center for Volunteerism and Nonprofit Management used to joke, about 300 residents serve on public and nonprofit boards.[19] Without civic capacity growing in parallel with population growth, little semblance of democracy can be maintained or achieved, particularly on an historical foundation of Anglo domination.

Much of El Paso's small, but growing networks of personal politics are characterized by clientelism. What ails El Paso is a weak democracy: low voter turnout, few activists, fear and intimidation about open challenges to who rules and how. What ails Ciudad Juárez is similar, except that voters turn out at very high rates in multi-party elections. In both cities, community-based and nonprofit organizations are growing, and sometimes developing cross-border synergies, but personal bonds tie people together (and occasionally tear them apart) as they "chase" limited resources to achieve their goals as subsequent chapters address on the environment, economy, and human rights. When we compare governance institutions in the next chapter, we analyze how organizational capacity has grown on both sides of the border, but not grown strong enough to mount effective challenges to and solutions for border problems.

El Paso's personalism could be an asset in the growing and expanding opportunity structure at the U.S.–Mexico border. Friendship and kinship can create the basis for political relationships that challenge existing power relations. These strong ties can bind people together. Activists sometimes joke about the small town, even family feel to politics. Some activists develop passionate commitments to cross-border organizing, but those that lack economic resources eventually burn out.

Activists know each other; they sometimes know and like (or know and despise!) one another. These personal, strong-tie relationships could generate ideological and issue-based ties that spin off into looser ties of people who know one another through others or through ideas and commitments. Together, these wider but looser ties provide the resources to mount greater challenges to existing power relations at the border.

For insights like these, we draw on inspiration from Mark Granovetter in the classic sociological article, "The Strength of Weak Ties." Granovetter challenges the seemingly intuitive idea regarding the importance of strong ties to diffuse information and build organizations. Activists with strong ties enjoy assets in networking and organizing: time investments, emotional intensity, mutual confidence, and reciprocity. Yet based on sociometric research, Granovetter argues that "those to whom we are weakly tied are more likely to move in circles different from our own" to *extend* relationships.[20] No one has applied these ideas to cross-border organizing, although Keck and Sikkink make reference to the importance of network strength and density for transnational movements.[21] Density, we agree, is at the core, but strength requires loose ties, especially for those relying on people rather than money to extend their power and ultimately alter power relations. Wealthy people have the money to buy loose ties.

Cultural Context in Communication Styles

Collaborative strategies constitute real strengths compared to the competitive strategies that emerge out of individualistic, marketplace capitalism. Collaboration also meshes well with the culturally sensitive communication strategies in "high-context" settings once attributed to other cultures outside the United States. The United States is often characterized as a low-context culture, but we disagree with this characterization except for its caricature and for its "minority" culture such as privileged white males. Even in the United States, high context communication cultures are quite common among women and at the border. Consider the dichotomies below, adapted from communication studies.[22]

This table is replete with insights for the two faces of personalism. Like any set of dichotomous characteristics, it oversimplifies. Like any set of dual categories, it may over-generalize. However, it is a conceptual tool that advances our analysis. Individualism is prized in mainstream U.S. culture, and individual competition is stressed through many years of education and in workplaces. Yet feminist theorists have often

Table 2.1 Contrasts: high- and low-context communication

High-context cultures	Low-context cultures
Interdependent	Individualist
Externally driven: shame	Internally driven: guilt
Rich language: courtesy	Sparse language: to the point
Language lubricates relationships	Language conveys information
Attentive to non-verbal cues	Oblivious to non-verbal cues
Prize subtlety, nuance	Prize debate, confrontation
History remembered	History a sideline
Personal agenda important	Schedules important
Multiple agendas	Singular agendas

emphasized the relationality that tempers female individualism, from communication to decision-making.[23]

External and internal drivers differ in high- and low-context cultures: in the shame culture, people seek to preserve "face," honor, and harmony. Past humiliations are remembered. In the guilt culture, people prize direct, even blunt messages. The guilt culture focuses on what's ahead, rather than dwells on the past. At the border, people "remember" how and when the United States took northern Mexico; many Anglos, if they know this, wonder what difference it makes for decision-making now and in the future. We offer an example of the Chamizal in Ciudad Juárez, commemorating the redrawal of the international boundary in the 1960s. The Universidad Autónoma de Ciudad Juárez sits on the Chamizal. One of the auditoriums was formerly the *bracero* deportation processing center. In a tour Irasema took, guides said "*esto era de los gringos y ahora le estamos dando buen uso nosotros*" (this used to belong to the gringos and we are now putting it to good use).

Spanish, English, or Both?

On language, our discussion of Spanish and English above affirms the dichotomies. Language is power. In cross-border organizing a lot of effort is devoted to translating materials and meetings. The well-to-do privileged Mexicans tend to either understand English or speak English. In some meetings that Irasema attends in Mexico, one English speaker who does not understand or speak Spanish can influence how the meeting is conducted. The rich Mexicans show off their linguistic skills impressing the Anglos and alienating the poor Mexicans who are made to feel less than the rich because they do not speak English. (Respect is not shown toward the poor.) Every effort is made to accommodate the guest regardless of what the majority speaks in the room.

Female–male communication styles cut across the language line itself; greetings and goodbyes occur with care. Also cutting across language lines is the importance of non-verbal cues in everyday interaction between subordinate and dominate groups; women and other subordinates, historically, watch for facial and body cues.

A U.S. foundation-sponsored study with 42 interviews of 28 Mexican NGOs identified capacity-building needs, including English language expertise. Proposal writing and international conference attendance required English language skills.[24] Not surprisingly, these "capacities" in a Spanish-speaking country work to the detriment of many fledgling NGOs in Mexico.

"Taking on" the Opponent: Confrontation at the Border

Thus far, we have illustrated the importance of personal ties, communication sensitive to context, and language skills. We assumed that interactive style was cooperative, reasonable, and civil. Political struggle often uses other styles, including challenge and confrontation. Some organizing strategies rely on a process that "takes on" those in authority, or targets the enemy relentlessly until concessions are obtained.[25] How effective is this style in the high-context communication of the borderlands?

Confrontation: A Prelude to Collaboration?

Confrontational strategies emerge under conditions under which dominant groups provide no opening to negotiate, relinquish, or change power relations. Much of El Paso's history reflects stuck power relations, but confrontation has been relatively rare, perhaps too rare. We attribute this not only to the fear issue, in places with large numbers of immigrants, but also to the prevalence of personalism. In clientelist politics, clients do not upset existing power relations, however unfair or unequal, for fear of losing minor favors.

Clients may be quiescent, but this does not eliminate anger. Anger, channeled into issue-based organizing or confrontation, can produce a healthy common identity and solidarity. Unchanneled, anger can result in passive–aggressive strategies such as gossip. Gossip is personalism at its worst. Unchanneled anger can also take the form of insulting and rude personal attacks that chill prospects for further organizing, especially in communities that value graciousness and avoid public humiliation—the "high-context" communication cultures at the border. See ethnographic moment 2.1 for its confrontation and collaboration within and among activists in the social justice community.

Ethnographic Moment 2.1: The Voices of Confrontation, Competition, and Consensus: Workforce Training Resources for What and for Whom?

Displaced Workers in El Paso, most of them middle-aged, Spanish speaking women without high school diplomas, have been through the economic wringer. They lost jobs and have little money to no money to spend, a loss to both their households and to the region. Multiplier effects, in this case, had negative spiral effects in all the markets women spent money in: housing, consumption, and food.

Under trade adjustments assistance, many El Pasoans applied and qualified for workforce training and stipends that lasted a year and a half. The overall sum was in no way near the total wage and consumption loss, but it provided short-term compensation and occasional placements, particularly in agencies supplying "temps." Many training programs tried to teach workers English, although they wanted jobs. Few programs placed unemployed workers in new jobs, except those that selectively chose participants with high school diplomas ("creamed" them, said critics).

In dialogue and negotiation over workforce training, workers themselves had little voice. Nor did those at the frontlines of training: the literacy educators. Many programs appeared to be warmed-over versions of longstanding programs whose leaders had chased and competed among themselves for grant monies.

A conference was held in late 2000 to bring together the stakeholders for a two-day conference on displaced workers. Workers themselves participated on panels and in the closing hours focused on action recommendations. Workers cried; a Washington, D.C. staff member was visibly moved; front-line workers heard it before.

Community leaders and activists postured some, reminiscent of the confrontational approaches to organizing. Critics of creaming "took on" other community activists (who themselves "take on" their opponents). They stood with an "in-your-face" posture; they spoke loudly and rudely to one another; they forged no consensus. Meanwhile, the displaced workers wondered about their own desperate situation and what would change from this conference.

Conference organizers had repeatedly invited business and chamber representatives to participate and to present at panels. They did not attend.

They later told other people no one had invited them and they were not welcome anyway.

A year later, another two-day conference was held with a national and local program audience. Speakers lauded the strategic assets of a bilingual workforce. They emphasized the utility of simultaneous job AND language training. Chamber and business representatives sponsored a half-morning panel. Displaced workers' voices, captured on video, could be heard and seen from the TV screen during lunch.

In the face of Anglo dominance, we offer another example. Someone from the school board meeting audience shouts "white bitch" at a trustee. A man achieves momentary victory. More happens than the sear of humiliation in the trustee's soul. Sexism, parallel to racism, rears its ugly head. Onlookers are likely to be of different minds: some are likely to be disgusted with the language with the uncivilized show of disrespect. Others vow to never run for trustee. More important, the issue content is lost in the communication.

The challenge to cross-border organizing is one of channeling anger into political strategies that create conditions for civil engagement and eventual collaboration to make alliances, form coalitions, and stretch resources for problem-solving activities. Confrontation has a place at some stages of this process.

Concluding Reflections

This chapter offers conceptual language for understanding factors that facilitate and undermine cross-border cooperation, networks, and organizations. Our framing continues in the next chapter to address the opportunity structures between both El Paso and Ciudad Juárez and within each city—on each side of the border—that facilitate and undermine civic activism.

In this chapter, we began with the limitations of traditional studies that stop at, rather than cross national borders. We also questioned the high-level, abstract way in which global movement studies occur—a way not grounded like it must be in the peculiar politics of the local, such as at borderlands.

We dedicated this chapter to the consideration of the two faces of personalism, so essential for building relations to collaborate, to build alliances and coalitions, and to achieve outcomes that address the common problems and issues of the borderlands. One side of personalism illustrates the possibilities of friends and kin members utilizing their relationships of trust to work on issues and extend their power in ways to change established power relations. The other side of personalism illustrates the shortcomings of containing issues within strongly tied networks as opposed to loosely tied networks. Strong ties may serve the elite for they can use their economic resources to buy or contract networks or to disseminate information.

In this chapter, we also considered the reasons for why personalism is strong at the border. Border theorists allege "hybridity" but do so largely in literary, linguistic, and cultural terms. We believe there are political and civic dimensions to this hybridity. We outline explanations that draw on the physical location and heritage of borderlands inhabitants, on the language and high-context communication styles of residents, and on the civic demography of small-town politics in high-population areas. In all of these, we find some value, but overarching all this is the limited democracy that has existed for some time in the borderlands region. Economic and government elites have long dominated residents in ways that perpetuated power relations that benefited the few rather than the many. These patterns have begun to change from the 1980s onward, and our book highlights the ways that change has occurred among community-based organizations that collaborate within and across borderlines. Effective change towards social justice requires sensitivity to the high-context communication styles in the borderlands, styles with greater nuance and complexity in the English–Spanish linguistic mix.

CHAPTER 3

POLITICAL INSTITUTIONS, NGOS, AND
ACCOUNTABILITY IN THE BORDERLANDS

[She was asked if she was pregnant, when the last day of menstruation was, sexual activity, and birth control methods.] The nurse gave me a form and said "Sign it." ... She said it was a letter stating if I became pregnant during the hiring period of three months, I would be automatically fired.
—Testimony from National Administrative Office
(NAO) hearings

Mexico's labor laws offer generous benefits for pregnancy and maternity leave for those in the formal economy. Women are to receive paid leave for 12 weeks, and half of their salary for another 60 days within the first year after birth. Yet *maquiladoras* routinely screen for pregnancy. Under a new institution created through NAFTA, the secretary of the U.S. National Administrative Office (NAO), Irasema Garza, consulted with her Mexican counterpart and hearings about a formal complaint were held at the border, from which the epigraph above was taken. Mexico did not send representatives. A 1998 NAO report indicated that Mexico violated its own laws and the International Labour Organization Convention 111.[1] In Ciudad Juárez, year 2001, after the U.S. economic downturn led to layoffs in the *maquilas,* the word on the streets was that the first to be downsized are the women with swelling bellies.

National policies, laws, and institutions are the usual mechanisms of accountability for citizens, residents, and workers. Protests and challenges from nongovernmental organizations, or unions, are the usual mechanisms that people use to press government to follow existing laws or to change laws. Yet for various reasons, governments and NGOs do not act on behalf of their people and constituents. Can transnational institutions substitute? As chapter five will show, the NAFTA-related NAOs are bulky and time-consuming bureaucracies that rarely issue reports with enforcement capability. But they do offer "opportunity structures" across national borders.

In the last chapter, we examined the notion of borderlands hybridity in order to assess the two faces of personalism in networking and organizing within and across borders. Although personalism can strengthen relationships, it requires coupling with purposive, issue-based ties to spread regionally and globally and thereby acquire other resources that would change power relations.

In this chapter, we first discuss the significance of organizations for public institutional accountability. Second, we develop a typology of organizations within and across the U.S.–Mexico borderline, including some of the old and new transnational institutions in the region. We discuss nongovernmental organizations, from those formally registered with national governments to autonomous, homegrown, and grassroots organizations. In our contrast between Mexico and the United States, we illustrate the resource constraints of emergent organizations at the border. NGO staff and organizational homes operate within particular national institutions, so we must, third, analyze the political institutions of Mexico and the United States, including the local governmental complexities therein. These institutions facilitate and hinder NGOs in the changing political opportunity structure of the U.S.–Mexico border. Finally, we conclude with a graph that illustrates the factors that facilitate and block cross-border organizing. These factors enrich the issue and policy areas of chapters four through six in this book.

Why Bother? Institutional Accountability

Decision-making in any institutions should offer open and transparent accountability relationships that make it clear who represents whom, for what goals, and how decisions can be challenged and changed. International trade decisions have long been made behind the closed doors of bureaucracy, albeit through staff and national trade representations with distantly accountable relationships to ordinary people. The protests in Seattle in the late 1990s awakened public quiescence about world trade. Protests against NAFTA have been contained and confined to small groups of labor and union activists, some exhibiting national protectionism and others, transnational solidarity.

With whom or with what institutions do we seek accountability and responsibility for governance, including rights and obligations for actions with effects on society? People have long been conditioned to think of their own national governments (and state and local governments therein). But what about spillovers, not only in borderlands, but in multiple nations in which labor and investors have stakes in multinational corporations? People in border communities are calling upon *maquiladoras* to integrate themselves into the community by supporting nongovernmental organizations, donating to schools, and sponsoring the development of green areas such as parks for children to play. Municipal government has long sought to generate more revenue from the industries to compensate for the huge burden they and their migrant (from the interior) employees place on urban infrastructure. After all, multinational corporations gain a lot from being in the community and increase profits because of the low wage jobs that they provide.

With public engagement, community organizers and activists can tap resources, legitimacy, and leverage to promote their interests. In so doing, they deepen democracy. Activists must diagnose the institutions with which they will engage and what strategies they will use. They make strategic decisions about whom or with what they engage; sometimes, however, the institutions are distant, elite, or non-transparent. Consi-der official institutions that are local, national, and transnational. Institutions exercise *authority* that can be challenged. Official institutions use a *discourse* that can be extended, co-opted, and/or contested. And official institutions *raise, distribute, and/or redistribute* resources that, if threatened and/or redirected, can provide leverage to those outside of government. This book focuses especially on those "outsider," grassroots, informal, community-based, and tax-exempt nongovernmental organizations (whether called nonprofits [in the United States] or *asociaciones civiles* [AC] in Mexico).

For people to make accountability mechanisms work, they must exercise voice and power. This is often realized through informal networks and organizations that include people who share common interests and ideas about issues and ideologies. Usually people organize within *spatial* boundaries, such as within the bounds of a region, a city, or a neighborhood. Governance institutions reinforce that spatial identity with districts and regional units that establish representational accountability to electoral constituencies within spatial boundaries. Boundaries (or jurisdictions) are endemic in public life. At international boundaries, people who span both sides are hard pressed to make institutions accountable to them and their multi-faceted needs. Individuals in this situation often lament, questioning whether democracy can really exist at borders. We think it can, but only with vigorous NGOs that overcome a litany of cross-border blocks, with robust transnational institutions that do more than symbolize a commitment to regional problem-solving approaches.

Cross-Border Organizational Typology

Lots of organizations, governmental and nongovernmental, operate strictly on one side of the border. Few operate across, or on both sides of the border. Cross-border organizations vary in the degree to which they are independent of, tied to, or actually part of a government. Although the hybrid borderlands are fluid, below we develop a semi-permanent typology of cross-border organizations.

Organizations on the left consist of both (1) governmental and supragovernmental agencies themselves, funded and staffed primarily through tax revenues, and (2) nongovernmental organizations that are publicly registered and draw in part on public funds. Those organizations on the right tend to be more independent of government, generating funds from dues, donations, and other private sources. Some of the organizations on the right may also be officially registered to obtain tax exemptions. We list them in three categories that range from, bottom up, locally homegrown to top down, transnationally and nationally, implanted upon the region. After that, we discuss examples of public and private cross-border operations that are developed further in subsequent chapters.

This typology is exploratory in nature, for it includes organizations that are hard to type and assess in funding terms. In the same way, border hybridity makes residents equally hard to type: a question like "where do you live?" (after invoking a response like "why do you want to know?"), might involve temporary and permanent residences on both

Table 3.1 Cross-border organization typology

More public ←——————————————→ *More private*

Transnational/binational	*Transnational/binational*
IBWC/CILA	Environmental Defense Fund
PAHO	Strategic Alliance/Alianza Estrategica
	AMAC
	North American Institute
National, state, local agencies	*National, w/local operations*
Paso del Norte Air Quality Task Force	FEMAP, FAT
Border Liaison Mechanisms	Chambers (*Cámaras*) of Commerce
	Catholic charities
Tax-exempt 501c3/Asociación Civil	*Grassroots organizations*
Community Scholars	Religious: hunger harvests
Los Eco-Locos,	Border Rights Coalition
Rio Grande/Río Bravo Basin Coalition	Casa Amiga, Centro de Crisis A.C.

sides, at least with extended family. We have known people of "dual nationality" long before Mexico authorized this legal reality. Hybridity spills over into organizations. For example, some of the "more private" organizations on the right are tax-exempt and obtain a mix of private and public funding sources; they work primarily on one side, but act on both sides with decision-makers that span the border. Ciudad Juárez's first grassroots generated battered women's shelter, Casa Amiga, reflects the hybridity: it supports domestic violence victims on one side of the border, but obtains a mix of support from both sides, including some public support.

Transnational and Binational Organizations

Transnational and binational organizations have been implanted upon the border, with the source of their authority emanating from capital cities or other distant locales. The oldest of these joins the United States and Mexico with a narrow agenda focused on the Río Bravo/Rio Grande river and flood control, the International Boundary and Water Commission (IBWC)/Comisión Internacional de Limites y Aguas (CILA). Located in El Paso and Ciudad Juárez, its U.S. budget surpasses $30 million annually. Many fine published studies have been done on this official collaboration.[2] Also located in El Paso, the Pan American Health Organization (PAHO) is affiliated with the United Nations. Political appointees lead these organizations, emanating both from national capitals and UN headquarters. Still, these organizations generally employ regional and local staff. The current IBWC appointee is El Paso's ex-mayor, an unusual appointment for the process taps border expertise. Organizations like these generate minimal public participation.

Regional institutions also provide an institutional shroud on the border. Of special interest are those new organizations that NAFTA has generated. NAFTA institutions embrace Canada, the United States, and Mexico. Examples of these institutions include the BECC, North American Development Bank (NADBANK)/Banco de Desarrollo de America del Norte, and chambers of commerce in all three member countries. NADBANK funds borderlands projects, but they have not been joint efforts that require or facilitate more cross-border cooperation.

NAFTA provides a broad space, or political opportunity structure, in which people and organizations can engage for policy change, leverage, legitimacy, and resources. The organizations in this opportunity structure are enormously complex, and their creation results from contentious struggles around the passage of NAFTA. Their symbolic power is enormous, for they respond and partially appease constituencies roused around NAFTA passage. But do they deliver? As we show in chapter four on the environment (NADBANK, BECC), five on labor and business (NAOs), and six on human rights, these unwieldy bureaucracies have made only few concessions to critiques and victims of the new free trade regime. In a section called "NAFTA and Its Creatures," Robert Hackenberg and Robert Alvarez discuss the multi-billion dollar capitalization of institutional messages, but the few certified projects and loans that have been approved.[3]

We also acknowledge occasional national government agencies that operate within and across borders with sensitivity to regional commonalities and differences. We include the Environmental Protection Agency (EPA) located in El Paso and other border cities. The presence of agencies is a far cry from decades back, when El Paso did not meet environmental standards. In the "bad old days," a national official, lunching in a restaurant just meters away from the river and Ciudad Juárez on the other side, pointed to smoking emissions and asked in a patronizing way why El Pasoans did nothing about it. Of course, Mexico governs the sovereign territory just meters away.

Some private organizations are national, but act binationally, such as the Asociación de Maquiladoras A.C. (AMAC). For export-processing industries, AMAC provides a collective voice, collects data, and stimulates more investment in export processing assembly plants.

Local government institutions cooperate together on formal and informal bases. Informal cooperation is easier, given the difficulty of formal contractual cooperation between two sovereign governments (local governments can hardly negotiate that well!). Despite the public outrage expressed if police authorities cross into sovereign "foreign" territory, there is probably more cooperation among police and fire departments than among other agencies; in El Paso, those agencies name liaison officers for coordination. The little published work that exists about official cross-border collaboration is in those areas.[4] In 1993, with help from the Environmental Defense Fund, El Paso and Ciudad Juárez agreed to cooperate over air quality control monitoring, a topic we take up in the next chapter.

Nongovernmental Organizations

In a democracy, mechanisms should exist to hold officials accountable, through representational, electoral, and appointee means. Democratic accountability rarely operates with vigor for women, working-class, and/or the unemployed, but under conditions of strong organized action and/or institutionalized party interest, such vigor is possible. With power exerted from the outside, people can deepen the democracy and make it more responsive to their needs. NGOs are vehicles that deepen democracy.

In the big picture, few NGOs operate across national boundaries in North America, much less Mexico and the United States. In chapter five, we look at labor unions with transnational solidarity. One civic engagement group promotes experiential and service learning. The North American Institute (NAMI) aims to foster community service and volunteerism across national borders in the entire region. A nonprofit organization, NAMI confronts national budgetary processes that require that revenue be spent within, rather than across, borders. For example, the U.S. Corporation for National Service (CNS) funds AmeriCorps members and Vista volunteers throughout the fifty United States of America, but not the United States of Mexico; CNS prohibits them from serving in Mexico or Canada. Likewise, Mexico's *Servicio Social* directs public university graduates to serve in needy communities within the nation.

Few nongovernmental organizations can be placed within the cross-border typology. Organizations often focus on one city, with activists barely achieving their objectives in that city, much less both cities. Why the gap? We consider two key reasons, above and beyond the practical blockages we list at the end of this chapter: insufficient resources and local blinders. Organizations with local blinders do not adopt (or are hostile to the adoption of) a regional conception of their work.

The strategic decision to avoid cross-border work sometimes makes good political sense because activists' target is the local, state, or national government. Women's anti-violence groups in Ciudad Juárez seek attention and justice primarily from their own municipal police and state attorney general. Displaced workers in El Paso seek workforce training, jobs, and/or benefits in El Paso from federal, state, and local funding. Faith-based organizers leverage more state funds for El Pasoans and especially for their own constituents. Their operational funds come from mostly local religious offices.

If the political will existed, couldn't these organizations find resources and regional institutions to bring together constituents on both sides of the border? Sometimes activists do not seek relationships with their counterparts on the other side of the border. The institutional, cultural, and linguistic challenges seem overwhelming. Staff capabilities would be daunting, and the time commitments, enormous. Various social justice organizations, however, have trouble collaborating on one side of the border, much less both: They control "turf" in space, issues, and/or constituents. Externally, they are wary of coalitions, unless they can control them. Internally, they are managed in relatively authoritarian ways (even in the name of collectivist organization); in current parlance, they do not "think outside the box."

El Paso and Ciudad Juárez count a number of local social justice organizations. They include groups like La Mujer Obrera, COMO (Centro de la Orientación de las Mujeres Obreras), and Unite El Paso. LMO and COMO do not collaborate. Unite El Paso was born to build bridges across ethnic borders, within the city, oriented toward providing "fair share" funding from the state government.

El Paso's largest social justice organization is EPISO, the El Paso Interreligious Sponsoring Organization. EPISO claims 50,000 members, a figure that capitalizes on the number of affiliated Catholic church parishes that provide some support for its paid fulltime organizers. EPISO, born in 1981, is part of the Texas Industrial Areas Foundation (IAF), an Alinsky-type organization that develops issue-based leaders trained to dialogue with officials and hold the government accountable for issues important to members. In El Paso, these issues include water and sewer services in outlying *colonias,* workforce training, and schools that engage parents and prepare students for higher education.

Ethnographic Moment 3.1: Industrial Areas Foundation (IAF):

Organizing the Unorganized

Over a thousand parents and some teachers descended upon Austin for a state-wide meeting of the Texas Industrial Areas Foundation during the brief legislative session that occurs every other year in the state. The event was part inspirational, part pep rally, part informative, and primarily an accountability event in which working class people, many of them Mexican and African American, showed solidarity for the state-wide Alliance School effort and the need to increase its state budget.

Tremendous amounts of time and energy are invested into developing leaders and focusing anger on concrete engagement strategies prior to events like Austin. At Alliance Schools, principals, teachers, and parents take parental engagement very seriously. Parents learn leadership skills: they identify problems, negotiate solutions, and maintain pressure on decision-makers to move toward solutions. They develop relationships with one another and with people in power. They raise questions, sometimes awkward ones, to people in power. They plan and time meetings with carefully crafted agendas.

They rehearse meetings ahead of time, and they critique the process afterwards to learn lessons for the next time. They develop winnable goals, and they achieve many of those goals.

For many parents, it is the first time they have joined a social justice organization. The process can be exhilarating, life-changing, and stressful. Initially, the number of meetings seem endless to some. "We meet to decide when to meet." Once parents push their kids and campuses into pathways toward higher education, they rethink their own lives. "My husband works two shifts, and I volunteer at the school. I decided to get my GED and started classes at community college to become a nurse's aid." Overnight travel can also produce stresses in household power relations. "He didn't want me traveling to Austin, but I convinced him we need to do it."

As events began at the dome-like auditorium in Austin, all the IAF organizations shouted their presence and waved their signs around. Delegations from other states not only observed, but also joined in the energy. People started and stopped clapping at the direction of organizers who patrolled up and down aisles. Male experts from the likes of MIT, Rice, and Yale shared their take on the changing global economy, as volunteers translated remarks into Spanish through earphones. Experts' remarks, though, seemed dry and difficult to absorb. Later, participants moved into workshops filled with inspiring personal stories, insightful analysis, and results that offered hope for change.

The next day, delegates from each city phoned their state representatives about coming to the capitol lawn midday to make a few remarks. By that time, the crowd, grouped according to organizational and regional solidarity, swelled to approximately 1,500. Most representatives came out and offered rousing words of support in Spanish and English. An African American representative moved the crowd when he said "Este casa (the state capitol building) es su casa." This house is your house. Mexico's customary warm greetings to guests offered a welcomed return, Mi casa es su casa, (now the stuff of pithy crafts at southwestern fairs), became a statement of public democratic principle. Residents co-own the statehouse and its decisions.

Constituents sought their representatives who did not come down to the lawn. One, hostile to their agenda, met with constituencies in his office. "I don't agree with you, but let me tell you why." Another was busy in committee, and he scolded constituents for their lack of respect. Constituents analyzed comments after each encounter. The cranky patron voted to support Alliance Schools anyway.

Sure enough, Alliance School funding increased dramatically in that session. IAF organizers and Alliance School parents could count on more support for special programs at their kids' schools, including activities that would likely strengthen and deepen their leadership skills.

Groups like EPISO and labor unions are hard pressed to maintain offices, staff, and focus on achievable ("winnable," in their terms) goals for their constituencies, on one side of the border much less both. EPISO relies on paid organizers with middle-class wages, a luxury compared to many organizations that depend on volunteers or meager wages, and occasional weeks without pay. It is quite common for NGOs to depend on volunteers, the latter of whom join for non-materialistic reasons. Yet volunteer-dependent organizations deal with the uncertainties of commitments among their unpaid staff: How much time will they invest in the organization? How can the organization hold them accountable for reasonable or minimum work?

If more funders provided resources for cross-border organizations, the local blinders might be lifted. Some foundations bring a cross-border vision to their funding decisions. The Ford Foundation once funded cross-border policy research that brought academic and community activists together in the early 1990s. Relationships formed during the research, but they were not sustained once funding ended. Even during the funding period, the organization of cross-border conferences was problematic. One conference day was on the Ciudad Juárez side; another on the El Paso side. International bridge traffic always added at least an hour to the trip, sometimes more. And Mexican nationals needed documents to pass, although local passports would suffice (*pasaportes locales* allow cross-border shopping and visiting up to 72 hours). Kathy always noticed far more Mexican nationals who were willing to cross northward than U.S. nationals willing to cross southward for the conferences. Other participants noticed this as well. Nevertheless, academics are open to collaboration, dialogue, and funded research.

The university-based San Diego Dialogue solicits over a million dollars a year of research funding to conduct policy and business research and then to disseminate it through newsletters, working papers, and policy roundtable luncheons.[5] We note that its title focuses on San Diego rather than on Tijuana and San Diego, although "foreign-owned" *maquiladoras* in Tijuana not only fund some of the work, but drive business-related research agendas.

El Paso's local foundations are relatively free from blinders, although their assets pale in comparison to national foundations. In 1995, a binational conference on philanthropy was held in Ciudad Juárez, and the El Paso Community Foundation was a co-sponsor and enthusiastic participant. Also co-sponsor and active in shaping the agenda was the Federación Mexicana de Asociaciones Privadas (FEMAP), whose once-national President Guadalupe de la Vega lived in Ciudad Juárez and led the local chapter. FEMAP's El Paso-based support, the FEMAP Foundation, is managed by people of talent, expertise, and contacts from both sides of the border. Philanthropic efforts redistribute private resources from those with more to those with less; they lean more toward cross-class benevolence than grassroots community organizing to change power relations. For Señora de la Vega, FEMAP's projects and programs that expand women's choices through family planning and microenterprise development empower women as individuals to rid themselves of dependency on abusive relationships and insufficient incomes. Herein, power relations may change, but more with the household than the wider society.

FEMAP is a well-established organization that has operated for almost three decades in more than 40 cities across Mexico. It began as a neighborhood-based family planning organization with volunteer outreach workers known as *promotoras* or grassroots outreach workers. The organization acquired national and international fame and funding. FEMAP established a Maternal and Child Hospital and generates revenue from reasonable fees and quality service that matches or surpasses public facilities. At the hospital, FEMAP estimates that a tenth of its customers are from El Paso, using services they cannot afford in the United States. FEMAP subsequently branched out into other fields, including energy-efficient brick production and microenterprise lending and technical assistance.[6]

FEMAP's operations are so large, and its track record so impressive, that other nongovernmental organizations worry that they can't compete in acquiring regional or national/international support. FEMAP's microenterprise loans are cross-border initiatives, with complicated start-up patterns, as sources like the Inter-American Development Bank restrict activity to Mexico and some U.S. foundations restrict activity within national borders. FEMAP has sophisticated and professional staff who can respond to funders' complex budgetary and evaluation demands. More recently, FEMAP has begun to support the development of other organizations through acting as a fiscal agent, at the request of a local foundation. Small, new NGOs rarely have the cash flow, accounting procedures, and track records to wait for reimbursements or to sustain themselves in between funding streams.

The Paso del Norte Health Foundation has a regional, cross-border mission. To its credit, the foundation sponsors several initiatives that not only work with existing nongovernmental organizations, but that also strengthen civic capacity in new and fledgling organizations located in Ciudad Juárez, southern New Mexico, and El Paso. Members from foundation-supported groups interact frequently and learn capacity-building strategies from each other. Just as with FEMAP, the learning directions are often south–north rather than north–south (the latter, an assumption in much northern-driven technical assistance). The U.S. groups learn much from the grassroots organizing strategies of well-established Ciudad Juárez groups.

Grassroots Organizations

Strong leadership is necessary to piece together funding from several sources that allow cross-border collaboration, even if it means separate funding sources for particular locations. Community Scholars is a home-grown initiative that trains high school youth in web-based policy research and presentation. It operates with strategically placed leaders; a state senator supported its birth and the current first lady of El Paso is its director, a professional journalist in her own right. In its first years, Community Scholars recruited El Paso students and funded their summer salaries through successful grant proposal writing and donations. Students focused on local access to capital and on local and state policies. Each year, they travel to their own state capitol to meet with decision-makers. More recently, Community Scholars tapped local school districts to fund their students.

Community Scholars has an ambitious regional perspective that has now moved to incorporate Ciudad Juárez. It always had representatives from Ciudad Juárez on its board, but moved to triple that board representation in order to foster a regional, cross-border orientation. Most other board members are community-minded and share a regional perspective. Through those board contacts, the Mascareñas Foundation in Ciudad Juárez developed an interest in the regional perspective, and planning proceeded to move from the 2001 pilot program that involved Ciudad Juárez students to a full recruitment of Ciudad Juárez pre-university students in the summer of 2002. A state legislative delegation from Chihuahua City heard student presentations on the policy research of 2001.[7]

Los Eco-Locos is another student leadership group that operates with support from the Rio Grande/Río Bravo River Basin Coalition. The coalition is a broad-based environmental group that not only operates at the border, but across the entire shared river basin, as far north as Albuquerque. In 2000, it hosted a conference in Ciudad Juárez with wide financial support from public and private organizations in both Mexico and the United States, and in the cities of both Ciudad Juárez and El Paso.

Grassroots organizations emerge on both sides of the border, although funds are unstable to nonexistent except from religious resources. The Border Rights Coalition was once a thriving office, with paid staff, meetings, outreach, and a voice in the local press that advocated immigrants' rights and more open border policies. In the 1980s, activists put bumper stickers on their cars that said "Alien on Board" to flout INS rules and to show solidarity with immigrants. It is a shell of its former self.

The local Catholic diocese supports immigration and refugee services, with professionalism and care. It offers a rights clinic to detainees in the INS facilities. The Catholic church's counseling operations offer services to people without regard to their citizenship status or social security (SS) numbers. Such numbers are being used like a national identity card to distinguish those authorized to work from others—a distinction with consequences for health care and other services. Catholic and Protestant churches offer food to the hungry without regard for SS numbers, as is the case in government-supported food distribution. As one activist said, after the 1996 welfare reforms, amid reference to biblical texts about support for neighbors: "Hunger knows no borders."[8] While the church supports community-based organizations like those affiliated with the Industrial Areas Foundation to change power relations, it only does this within national borders. No IAF organizers work across borders, despite the existence of two large affiliates at the border: the El Paso Inter-religious Sponsoring Organization (EPISO) and Valley Inter-Faith in South Texas.

Cross-border organizing is a daunting task, requiring not only a vision and a commitment to think and act regionally, but also creative searches for funding *and* the will to facilitate organizational capacity to fulfill regional vision. Our book highlights cases of successful cross-border organizing in each chapter. The criteria we use to select successful cases include (1) the involvement of activists from both sides of the border; (2) connection to regional, national, or international movements; and (3) open, collaborative interactive process with other organizations coupled with concrete results that address problems. Meanwhile, most NGOs are local or national, operating on one side of the border rather than across the border. We discuss some of these organizations below focusing especially on Ciudad Juárez.

Same-Side (within Border) NGOs

NGOs, or *organizaciones no-gubernamentales* (ONGs), come in a wide range of categories, from those registered with the government for tax and control purposes, to those that emerge and diminish over specific and limited problems and solutions, known as *organizaciones improvisadas* (improvised organizations) in Mexico. In the United States, organizations register with the Internal Revenue Service and the state in which they operate to acquire a tax-exempt status that removes their tax liability on funds they generate. Some of these organizations are democratically organized with members and elections, while others respond to a board, operate professionally as nonprofit organizations, and/or are authoritarian and undemocratic. Some, however, are paper operations, lacking phone numbers or physical locations; others are fronts for other more powerful interests.

To different degrees, organizations range from dependency upon, to autonomy and self-sufficiency from, official governmental institutions for basic operating resources. Many nonprofit organizations consist of professionals who offer services. Even if independent from government, seemingly autonomous civic organizations are all too often dependent on a single funding source. They are "donor-driven" operations that may end after funders lose interest. In El Paso, state-funded efforts to build neighborhood collaborations against alcohol and drug abuse reflect this instability. Other funder-driven operations offer material incentives for neighborhood residents to locate health clients, to sign up with providers of care for indigent and low-income households. These material motivations, rather than the immaterial ideals of purpose and solidarity, leave many nonprofits vulnerable to thin commitment and ultimately, to instability.

There are institutions that have evolved into large entities with the concomitant staff and funding that in many ways become dependent on societal dysfunction. For example, suppose you are in the business of helping poor people in *colonias* receive services and you are doing well personally and financially. What will you do if the problem you work to resolve is addressed because everyone now has services? (Recall our mention of the abhorrent phrase in the last chapter: poverty pimps.)

Over the last twenty years, many nonprofit organizations have emerged to respond to service gaps, as governments cut programs or sought partnerships to "reinvent" themselves as more accountable operations. The growth in international organizations has been spectacular, but it is growth with some costs. As David Korten and others have observed, some NGOs are "people's organizations," while others operate like consulting firms, taking advantage of the opportunities that emerge when governments downsize and tax exemptions are available.[9]

Many NGOs depend on subsidies and grants to maintain and sustain their operations. They continuously apply for grants, and their missions are sometimes distorted as they respond to requests for proposals (RFPs) developed by funders: private foundations and corporations, government and international agencies. If these NGOs have no assets of their own, they run the risk of dependencies and even co-optation.

In Latin America, NGOs faced "identity crises" as they moved from the critical mobilization and resistance postures of the 1970s to "becoming implementers of other people's programs primarily of the state and bi- and multi-lateral donors."[10] With that changed identity come "legitimacy" and "sustainability" crises. Many NGOs are turning to consultancy arrangements, contracted research, and social enterprises, adapting a market and entrepreneurial approach to avoid dependencies. Are they replicating operations they once criticized?

In the United States also, funding from foundations and government provide incentives for NGOs to create Community Development Corporations (CDCs) or collaboratives. The Ford Foundation supported housing and community development collaboratives in various U.S. cities, including El Paso. At that time, in the mid 1990s, El Paso's "small and fragmented" CDCs were not inclined to collaborate on their own, had "few champions at city hall," and overall "little history of community development."[11] Many groups had been dependent on City Hall, specifically Community Development Block Grants. They competed with each other in the desperate chase for funds. The report to Ford notes that "national intermediaries historically were discouraged by the city from coming to El Paso."[12] Not surprising, civic capacity was weak, and collaborative approaches, minimal.

For example, the once radical neighborhood group active in the low-income second ward near downtown, or *segundo barrio* as it is called, La Campaña por la Preservación del Barrio began to mobilize residents to remodel rather than demolish more tenement and apartment buildings in a neighborhood that lost 17,000 units to demolition, the Interstate, and the Chamizal Agreements. The campaign has now become a CDC, but people say of its former leader that she still has the capacity to bring people to the streets.

CDCs, as their name implies, adopt market characteristics. They charge fees for services, borrow and lend money, and/or acquire land and/or property and then develop, rent, or sell it. In so doing, as they have in Latin America, they may take on the characteristics of institutions they, or organizations like them, challenged in the 1970s. In the worst-case scenario, ambitious CDCs become like the absentee monopoly landlords they once sought to displace. In the best-case scenario, they become independent of dependency relations (if once dependent on public funds). They acquire professional and activist/volunteer staff, rather than rely on volunteers or activists who eventually burn out. Power relations may eventually change. Thus, civic capacity is strengthened as organizations scale up and formalize, including the formal capability to collaborate with other organizations in coalitions and alliances.

Levels of Organizing

In both Mexico and the United States, people organize to achieve short-term goals. Their organizations may be temporary and ad hoc, or permanent with strategic plans. Let us begin with *organizaciones improvisadas.*

Improvised community organizing, especially in Mexico, has many dimensions. Residents of neighborhoods (*colonias*) come together to demand a variety of goods and services. Sometimes the organization is improvised for political reasons. For example, if five neighbors are engaged in a conversation complaining about an urban service or the lack thereof, this is now an organization for the purposes of approaching the *presidencia municipal;* after all, there is strength in numbers. In another example, if residents want more frequent piped water delivery service, as was the recent case in Anapra, one of Ciudad Juárez's marginalized *colonias,* people joined forces and took their complaints to city hall (*palacio municipal*), which responded favorably. Other *colonia* residents who want more streetlights, increased police security, or paved roads have demonstrated that they can organize to achieve a short-term goal.

In the United States, this sort of "improvisation" tends to be individualistic. In political science literature, people "contact" representatives and the bureaucracy. In the *colonias* in El Paso, people may be wary of making contact in order to keep a distance from authorities who sometimes serve them, but who also deport and fine people. Faith-based IAF organizations like EPSIO develop leadership among such wary people in order to obtain such seemingly mundane responses as streetlights or such profound public services people in the mainstream United States take for granted, water and sewer services.[13]

This capacity to organize is not exclusive to the poor, but it also is found in middle-class *colonias.* In El Paso, it is the upscale neighborhoods like Rim Road that have neighborhood associations that engage with the city's planning department to negotiate plans for mixed, residential, and commercial land use.

Organizing goes on despite a community's limited resources. Meetings are announced by word of mouth (as people do not receive e-mails or faxes) and leaders keep people informed in similar ways. Budgets are nonexistent and people do not make copies or distribute materials because of the cost. Nevertheless, this type of organizing is useful in achieving short-term goals that usually involve minimal investment or effort on behalf of the government, an easy solution that does not require formal organizing. We acknowledge that the act of citizens coming together to achieve a goal is an important aspect of civil society and should not be minimized, but we now move to organizations that have evolved to another level of organizing.

Organizing: Scaling Up

Scaling up organizations to formalize them with registration with the government takes time and even legal assistance. Many NGOs in Mexico that achieve the second level of organizing tend to get lost in the bureaucratic challenges that the Mexican government imposes on the registration of *asociaciones civiles*. Usually a few people who are close to the organization start by culling their personal resources to create the semblance of an established NGO. In many instances, "offices" are in someone's home; a private telephone line serves as the organization's phone as well; and people invest their time and money into the NGO.

It is a luxury in Mexico to head an NGO and make a living at it. Therefore, many people maintain other jobs and families while they are attempting to bring an NGO to fruition. At this juncture, professional work demands, coupled with family responsibilities at times, force unreasonable demands on organizers who are truly committed and face challenges that sometimes preclude them from giving more time, energy and resources to the organization. Hence, when one sees a list of NGOs in a community directory and finds a contact and phone number, it is not unusual to find that the telephone number is disconnected and that the organization is now defunct. In other instances, NGOs sometimes establish an issue network and join forces or coalitions with other organizations in order to maximize resources. Providing for administrative staff and infrastructure is a luxury that many fledgling Mexican NGOs cannot afford.

In the United States, people tend to focus around one issue and NGOs strategically plan activities around this focus. However, activists in poor communities find it difficult to select one issue and rally around it because there are so many problems facing their communities: economic poverty, lack of infrastructure, poor schools, medical access, pollution, crime, and discrimination, to name some. If we were to ask any mother which issue she would rally around, she would be hard pressed to prioritize and devote herself to only one. People at times organize when there is a crisis or some major catastrophe, address the problem, and then move on from there to another issue.

Organizing Successfully

Successful organizations in Mexico usually receive financial support from a variety of sources: These include (1) U.S. or other foreign NGOs, (2) government, (3) private individual or individuals, or (4) businesses. At this point we must distinguish between the various ways that residents in Ciudad Juárez can organize. We observe *asociaciones civiles, asociaciones religiosas* (religious associations), *cámaras* (chambers), *fundaciones* (foundations), *patronatos, colegios, barras, sindicatos, organizaciones improvisadas* (unions), and *clubes de servicio* (service clubs). More formal organizations try to address every problem that Ciudad Juárez has; however, few of the organizations have achieved the formal recognized status of *asociaciones civiles*. Achieving *asociación civil* status in Mexico is not an easy goal. The bureaucratic paperwork requires time and in some cases a notary public, with powers and skills more like a U.S. attorney, who must be hired or consulted in order to successfully complete the process. Many organizations that reach this point abandon the process due to the hassle, the cost, and the trouble involved and the bureaucratic details. At this point many organizations are overwhelmed with the legal, fiscal, and bureaucratic requirements and opt to work in a less organized manner because they do not want to expend time, energy, and money on the legalization process; they have better things to do. At this juncture many organizations just decline or choose to remain in the informal sector so to speak.

Formally Organized

Organizations that make it, or achieve *asociación civil* status, must have a defined structure, register with Hacienda (the federal tax office), acquire a board of directors, and file the necessary paperwork and appear listed in the *Diario Oficial de la Federación,* which is the official government newspaper published yearly in March. There are NGOs that have achieved this status because a private individual or a small group of people come together and provide the necessary wherewithal and financial support to bring the organization to formal fruition.

In Ciudad Juárez, there are over 400 organizations that have achieved this status.[14] Sometimes the government facilitates the legalization process of groups especially when it is to its benefit and convenience. Formal and established NGOs or foundations in the United States can support Mexican NGOs in their evolution toward formal status. Foundation-supported NGOs tend to favor organizations that have more infrastructure in place, such as office space, telephones, and English-speaking personnel. People in several less organized NGOs expressed concern over the preferential treatment that foundations gave local groups that in their eyes "need the help a lot less than we do." There is the perception that once an NGO receives funding from a foundation, it is more likely that the foundation will continue to fund the same organization in the future.

Most U.S. foundations seem to stick with tried and true organizations rather than facilitate the development of others. Within the NGO community, there is a perception that class differences in society transcend into the structure of organized groups in the community. There are rich NGOs and there are poor NGOs; some fall into the good graces of the government and of outsiders and others do not. Private businesses have also supported NGO organizations especially if they receive media publicity and a tax break in the process. Established NGOs in the United States have been known to support counterpart organizations in Mexico. The issue of whether the funding sources then can influence the agenda or the dynamics of the NGOs is another story.

Once an NGO has office space, administrative personnel, telephone, fax, computers, financial support (regardless of the source) and mechanisms for accountability and it has achieved *asociación civil* status, the government may react in a variety of ways. The NGO may be viewed as a source of competition, as an antagonistic actor making more demands of the government, or as a potential organization that can be co-opted.

Representatives of NGOs feel that the government could do more to help them achieve *asociación civil* status by facilitating the process. The government can enhance the NGO sector by facilitating their creation and evolution and perhaps can share some of the societal burdens and responsibilities with them. On the other hand, some people feel that the more civil society does in terms of social programs, the less government will do; government might expect that NGOs do even more in areas where there is a greater need: substance abuse, street children, housing, and violence to name a few.

The U.S. Internal Revenue Service counted three-fourths of a million tax-exempt organizations around the country in 2001. El Paso counted 715 foundations and tax-exempt organizations.[15] From that number, El Paso's civic capacity seems to be strong, but only about half that number have visible identities, phone numbers, and one or more staff members who advocate for, represent, and/or serve people, neighborhoods, and issues. These are found in the current *Community Links* directory, now produced at the University of Texas at El Paso but once called the *Helpline Directory* when undertaken and produced at the now-defunct El Paso Commission on Volunteerism and Nonprofit Management (an organization that also faced challenges raising funds to maintain its existence).

On the IRS list, many organizations are faith-based, such as churches that seek protection from taxation with their fund-raising efforts. Some organizations are unknown to all but their founders; no numbers are listed in the telephone directory, and their purposes are not immediately evident. On this list, one also finds familiar organizations ranging from the business-oriented chambers of commerce (El Paso has four, all ethnically differentiated) to health and service organizations like the El Paso Diabetes Association and the Child Crisis Center. In the current *Community Links Directory*, less than five percent of the organizations indicate that they have cross-border operations.

NGO Capacity Building

Universities, foundations, and other nonprofits offer workshops for organizations and nonprofits to strengthen their capacity to raise funds, deal with board conflicts, evaluate and document their work, and manage accounts, along with a host of other topics. La Fundación para el Empresariado Chihuahuense created a program titled the "*fortalecimiento para las organizaciones de la sociedad civil* (strengthening for civil society organizations)." In 2000, a series of workshops were held to provide training for NGOs in the community. The workshops addressed financial issues, how to obtain resources, strategic planning and administration of human resources. The Municipio of Ciudad Juárez also provided training through an orientation program geared to "*organizaciones de la sociedad civil.*" The Tecnológico de Monterrey provided a "diplomado (certificate)" for NGOs not only in the community but throughout Mexico and other Latin American countries. The *Desarrollo Integral de la Familia* (DIF) office in Ciudad Juárez initiated a program called Vertebración, whose goal was to bring together com-munity organizations in order to exchange ideas and to support one another's programs.

In El Paso, the state university offers an annual conference on nonprofit management with workshops on capacity-building topics. Leaders and members interact with one another and hear from local, state, and national nonprofit leaders. Additionally, the university's continuing education program offers courses for nonprofit organizations. Texas as a whole sprouted a nonprofit network based in San Antonio. With support from a statewide foundation, it provides networking and technical assistance to nonprofits and training for foundation center libraries. These libraries, located all over the United States, pay annual fees for hardcopy manuals and computer disks with the latest sources of information on fundraising and grant proposals.

Efforts to professionalize NGOs do not go unnoticed. The idea is that NGOs should work smarter and not harder because of the inordinate amount of valuable work that they do in the community. NGOs that take advantage of training obviously have the staff that has the time to do so. Clearly, NGOs that benefit from these capacity-training workshops are higher up on the evolutionary ladder and better prepared to do their work. Therefore, NGOs that cannot or do not want to participate in this kind of training are disadvantaged even more.

The ideal relationship between NGOs, business, and the government would be that of mutual respect and support. The government does more to support private business interests than it does NGOs. In Ciudad Juárez, businesses in many instances prefer to donate money to NGOs rather than the government because of the fear of governmental corruption. Likewise, there have been unscrupulous people that have created NGOs that exploit poor street children, elderly, blind, or deaf mute people for private gain. Organizations established against rape and violence against women, such as Defensa a las Víctimas de Violación and Defensoras de la Dignidad de la Mujer, take a strong anti-government stance because they feel that the government ignores the issues affecting women, especially those who are victims of crimes. "*Nosotros tenemos que crear estas organizaciónes porque el gobierno no hace nada por defendernos y estamos desprotegidos.*" ("We need to create these organizations because the government does not do anything to defend us and we are unprotected.")

Organizations can lose sight of their raison d'être such as defending women's rights and air quality because they focus on what the government does not do. They tend to be against something in this case, against the government, rather than for actions that advance their cause. A common criticism that the government has of NGOs is that they are not prescriptive in their approach. Indeed, problems are acknowledged, but the government does not just need to be criticized but needs to provide creative solutions to problems. Politics is "the competition for ideas"[16] and some NGOs don't plant these ideas in or with government. Citizen participation in NGOs enhances democracy at all levels. But the opportunity structure in which NGOs act is very different in Mexico and the United States. To governmental institutional frameworks we now turn.

Nation-States: Mexico and the United States

As is so obvious in an everyday way to those of us grounded in life and work at an international border, political machineries are different. On the surface, Mexico and the United States are federal, presidential systems of government, rather than centralized and/or parliamentary systems. They both call themselves "federal" systems. They divide authority vertically (national, regional-state, and local-municipal) and horizontally into legislative, judicial, and executive branches. Two or more political parties compete in regular offices for limited terms of office.

Beyond this abstract level of similarity, difference emerges. For example, local government in the United States is highly fragmented (in Texas, into county, city, school, water, and irrigation districts), while in Mexico the *municipio* governs under the heavy hand of Mexico City and state capitols. We offer a "muddied map" of federalism, U.S. and Mexican style.

The government of Texas draws lots of internal borders. El Paso County is divided into county, city, school, village, town, and water districts. A county judge governs four regions, each represented by single-member county commissioners. A mayor governs the city, divided into eight single-member districts with representatives elected through nonpartisan elections. El Paso contains nine Independent School Districts (ISDs), most with seven trustees, elected on nonpartisan bases; the big district trustees represent districts (difficult to add on map), while the smaller districts select trustees elected at large. The city is expanding through annexation (which some outlying residents refer to as its attempt to "*tomar posesión*" (take possession)), but some places have protected their autonomy through incorporation. Many borders exists within borders, and the territorial lines are continuously renegotiated. "Divide and rule" policies could hardly be more complete.

Decentralization proceeds, albeit in limited ways.[17] Local government's ability to raise revenue and to exercise authority ranges from weak in Mexico to strong in the United States. El Paso's city budget (not including the county budget) is ten times the municipal budget of Ciudad Juárez, a city twice El Paso's size. In Texas, locally elected officials run in partisan (county) and often nonpartisan (city) elections from geographic districts, while partisan elections occur in at-large *municipios,* based on

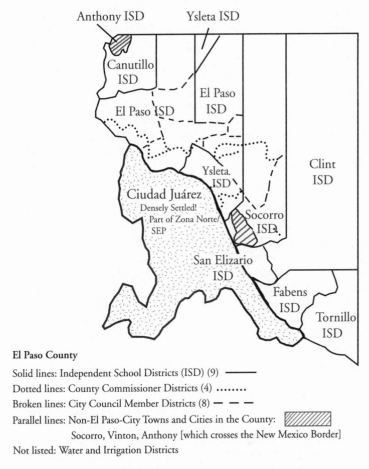

Map 3.1 A muddied map of federalism at the U.S.–Mexico border

proportionality of party vote in Mexico. Even the terms of office vary (two or four years in Texas counties versus three years in *municipios*), with rare coincidental years wherein officials take office. On both sides of the border, however, a single party reigned supreme for most of the twentieth century (Democrats in Texas; Partido Revolucionario Institucional [PRI]) in Chihuahua). In a strange conjuncture in 2000, with simultaneous presidential elections, Mexico's first opposition party president was elected on July 4.

On both sides of the border, national identity and patriotism are infused in civic education (*civismo*) and social studies through which "citizenship canons" are conveyed. Hegemony does its work quite effectively through schools and other means, with youth *Pledging Allegiance,* as a new book is entitled,[18] on daily or weekly bases for nine or more years. In Texas, state identity is fostered through required courses on Texas history and symbolism, with Texas flags at and names for schools. Among El Paso schools closest to the border, we find schools named after Bowie, the Alamo, Austin, and lesser heroes of the Texas "revolution." In contrast to this statism, one of the main streets in Ciudad Juárez is named Abraham Lincoln and a monument honors him as a liberator.

A Framework: Facilitating and Blocking
Cross-Border Organizations

Typically, people engage in the public affairs of their "own" nations around policies framed in ways that promote national group identity and benefits. Historically, mainstream labor unions promoted job protection for U.S. workers, rather than for workers in U.S. multinational corporations or immigrant workers. Labor has been changing its lobbying postures as this book was being written, with leaders advocating amnesty for a potential pool of new union members. Less oriented to nation, capital interests promoted a supposed "freer" mobility of money and commerce across borders. Actually the trade is just differently "managed," given the Byzantine NAFTA and WTO regulations that require translation from lawyers and accountants.

We examine the factors that facilitate and block cross-border organizing. At the top of the organizational "blockades," we must highlight the context of huge wage inequalities between both sides, weak civic capacity on each side, and belated and uneven democracy for the majority of residents on each side. In this chapter, we have focused on the weakness of civic capacity and the confusion of muddied federalism in the United States and highly different political institutions in each nation. Organizing at the border is complex and confusing, perhaps deliberately so.

Workers in Mexico and the United States earn vastly different minimum and average wages. Depending on currency value, per capita income and minimum wages in the United States are five to ten times that of Mexico. A competitive and desperate search exists for decent jobs on one or the other side of the border. (By decent, we mean jobs that pay approximately three times the artificially low minimum wage of $25/week in Ciudad Juárez versus $225/week in the United States.)

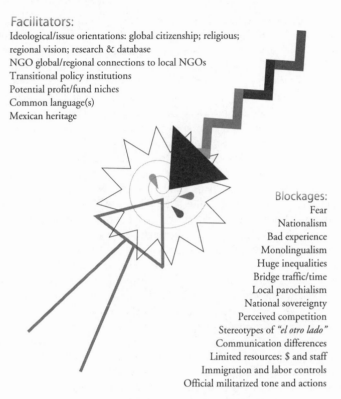

Facilitators:
Ideological/issue orientations: global citizenship; religious;
regional vision; research & database
NGO global/regional connections to local NGOs
Transitional policy institutions
Potential profit/fund niches
Common language(s)
Mexican heritage

Blockages:
Fear
Nationalism
Bad experience
Monolingualism
Huge inequalities
Bridge traffic/time
Local parochialism
National sovereignty
Perceived competition
Stereotypes of *"el otro lado"*
Communication differences
Limited resources: $ and staff
Immigration and labor controls
Official militarized tone and actions

Chart 3.1   Cross-border collaboration: facilitators and blocks

Other daunting obstacles present themselves to cross-border organizers. Organizers need time and resources for partial or full-time commitment to the labor-intensive tasks associated with building civic capacity
and fostering coalitions. Their challenges are considerable on one side
of the border, with huge populations. Organizers' understanding and
connection to constituencies do not necessary transcend borderlines in
culturally and linguistically comprehensive ways, even with cross-border
friendship and kinship. Even the delays associated with crossing the
"bridges" (the heavily enforced territorial line, at least at official crossing
points) deter all but the most committed.

Many foundations and government agencies that fund projects and
programs draw financial borders around their potential fundees and
beneficiaries—borders that mesh with international territorial lines.

Thus, U.S.-based organizers often seek and gain funding from sources that restrict spending to one side of the border. Few cross-border organizations have the grant-seeking capability on *both* sides of the border that can build and sustain action in mutually supportive ways.

Despite the heavy infrastructure of national political economy, complete with national identities, which celebrate themselves versus the "other," borders are the places of "crossing" par excellence. In El Paso–Ciudad Juárez, the crossing works in north-to-south *and* south-to-north directions. People cross or commute to work in authorized and unauthorized ways, with and without border blockades. People cross to visit relatives and friends and to entertain themselves. Student-citizens cross for schooling, with guardians claiming real or contrived residence. Almost 10 percent of the University of Texas at El Paso student body is comprised of residents from northern Mexico, an enrollment that is authorized by the Texas State Legislature to receive in-state tuition rates since the late 1980s. The common ground that borderlanders share, coupled with the common interests associated with crossing, generates shared interests around which people organize from the "big" issues of the environment and human rights to the more mundane.

Cell phones and e-mail ease communication compared to earlier years of unpredictable mail deliveries in Mexico, long distance calls (considerably more expensive from Mexico to the United States), and too few fax machines. Mexico's border think tank, the Colegio de la Frontera Norte, uses a Chula Vista, California, post box for mail deliveries to its headquarters in Tijuana. The Universidad Autónoma de Ciudad Juárez uses an El Paso post box. Time zones can also pose problems. Although El Paso and Ciudad Juárez are now in one time zone, the dates that daylight savings time starts and ends differ, leaving approximately two months of difference. Border traffic congestion means certain delays, however, no matter what the time.

Concluding Reflections

Are transnational tactics operational at the U.S.–Mexico border? Keck and Sikkink identify four tactics for transnational cooperation.[19]

- information politics that generate politically usable information;
- symbolic politics to make sense of "the other";
- leverage politics, wherein "powerful actors" affect situations where weaker actors have limited influence; and
- accountability politics, which "hold powerful actors to their previously stated policies or principles."

When considered in the border context, these tactics do not all work in globally predictable ways. Why? The answer involves the peculiar local version of transnational organizing at the border.

At the U.S.–Mexico border, informational exchange is extensive, from local newspapers with daily coverage of the "other" side to television and radio channels that easily beam across territorial lines as well as relatives and friends who exchange information as they visit and work together. *Informational* tactics are "no big deal," but part of everyday border life. Occasionally, though, striking or misleading results occur. When PAN (Partido Acción Nacional) Francisco Barrio Terrazas ran for governor of Chihuahua in 1986, he was interviewed on El Paso's Spanish language television station for easy viewing during an era of greater PRI hegemony over the media and other institutions. He spoke at the University of Texas at El Paso, as have other candidates from all major and minor parties in Mexico. When the United States changed its immigration laws in 1996, extensive coverage in Ciudad Juárez newspapers provided people with content, though sometimes hyperbolic and misleading. Attorneys in El Paso have a television and radio program in Ciudad Juárez where people can call in and receive "free" immigration advice. One might have gotten the false impression that the Border Patrol raided schools for undocumented children, so enrollment dipped.

Symbolic politics are double-edged swords that both differentiate and bond people on both sides of the border. Nationalist symbols shine and fly freely at the border, with a football-field sized Mexican flag that can be seen from most parts of El Paso. It joined the "other" symbol, the Texas "Lone Star," a lit star at the end of the Franklin Mountains, just before the Rio Grande (Río Bravo) river valley that rises on the other side to reemerge as the Juárez Mountains.

Media attention on Ciudad Juárez evokes fear and "difference," whether on the more than 250 women murdered since 1992 or the suspected drug-related burials headlined in late 1999 to be in the "hundreds," but later reduced to less than a dozen. Yet the portrayal of the borderlands sometimes causes people to pull together over frontier bashing and stereotyping whether from the pen of seeming progressives or "parachutist" journalists. When reporters descended onto the region after the 1999 drug burial story floated, a cross-border group of journalists and activists named these outsiders the new *paracaidistas* in December. Zita Arocha, a prominent Latina journalist who spent an academic year as a Freedom Forum Fellow at the Center for Inter-American and Border Studies at the University of Texas at El Paso, wrote and spoke at great length about the parachute journalists who portray the dark side of the border region based on their one-day junkets.

Leverage and accountability tactics, Keck and Sikkink's final two, need institutional shrouds, but these are few and far in between inside the still-imagined North American Community. And when they exist, it is often capital-derived appointees from Washington, D.C., and Mexico City who make decisions in response to national, rather than local people. The International Boundary and Water Commission is one such example. The Border Environment Cooperation Commission (BECC) and the North American Development Bank (NADBANK) have their regulation-inspired, top-down "steering committee," with occasional means for access. Where are the global human rights organizations on the murdered women in Ciudad Juárez? The United Nations Human Rights leader Mary Robinson did come to Ciudad Juárez in 2001, but there was very little publicity and even keenly attentive cross-borderlanders like us could not track down details. Border places seem to fall through bureaucratic oversight cracks, even though the extent of "civil strife" would seem to warrant attention. As we will see later, local organizing around this gender strife is minimal.

Using sociological concepts from chapter two, we conclude that transnational organizing gains effectiveness from its "weak-tied" quality, while local, cross-border organizing is stymied in long-term sustainability with its "strong-tied" quality. Among problems are competition over scarce resources and resulting enmity between winners and losers, intensely personal friends and enemies that make ideological connections around ideas quite difficult to manage, and burnout or fatigue when too few people attempt to do too much work without compensation or constantly chasing grant monies. Moreover the plethora of societal problems multiply, compound and exacerbate thereby leading to an overwhelming sense of frustration in activists.

CHAPTER 4

INSTITUTIONAL SHROUDS: NATIONAL SOVEREIGNTY AND ENVIRONMENTAL NGOs

La frontera is the back yard ... *no se ve*, (it can't be seen) we can do things there that you cannot do in the front yard.

—Environmental activist

Some come to comfort the afflicted, some come to afflict the comforted.

—Catholic sister

I realize that trust is not a concept that usually springs to mind when Americans think about Mexico. For years, the United States operated on the assumption that Mexico was governed by liars and thieves at worst, or at best, by technocratic authoritarians. Meanwhile, Mexico has long harbored suspicions about its neighbor to the north and acted accordingly. Bad blood and distrust ran deep on both sides of the border, making collaboration on many issues difficult if not impossible. The time has come to make trust the keystone of our agenda.[1]

—President Vicente Fox

The bad blood and distrust that President Fox mentions are indeed obstacles to cross-border cooperation. In border communities, where there is interaction every day of the week, the words of Vicente Fox resonate differently to borderlanders, who in many instances have deep-rooted trusting (and untrusting) relationships with people on the other side of the border. Unlike people at the respective centers of power who deal with bilateral issues from a distance, border people are actively engaged in the binational arena in all aspects of daily life, whether it is for good or bad. Examples of trusting and non-trusting relationships abound on the border. For example, maids from Ciudad Juárez who cross to clean houses and take care of young children or others' elderly parents and enter people's homes and lives obviously have trusting relationships with those who employ them. There are people in El Paso who avoid going to Ciudad Juárez because they are afraid of crime and distrustful of authorities. There are El Pasoans who, despite the fact that they were born in Ciudad Juárez, now report that they "haven't been there in years." Some El Pasoans report going to doctors in Ciudad Juárez "*porque le tengo más confianza a los doctores*" (I trust the doctors more). Cultural affinities and the ability to speak to someone who speaks your language are important factors for deepening trust and understanding. Couple the cultural and linguistic variables with lower costs of medical care and medicine and the appeal to visit doctors in Mexico is greater especially if you do not have medical insurance in El Paso.

Institutional Shrouds: U.S.–Mexico Border Environment

Binational problems require binational solutions, especially when dealing with environmental issues and natural resource allocation and depletion. Natural resource conservation, especially of water, is critical to this border region. The paucity of water has reduced surface water flows, causing serious impacts to water-dependent habitats such as riparian areas and marshes.[2] The Rio Grande/Río Bravo has meandered over time and it has also changed tremendously in its character. Juan de Oñate in 1598 described the Rio Grande/Río Bravo as "having many fish, catfish, bass, white fish." Fray García de San Francisco in 1659 wrote that he saw "apples, roses and vineyards. ... Here they cultivate wheat, corn, beans and sweet plums." Other early settlers described the area as having "vineyards, cottonwoods, oak trees, and in terms of animals antelope, buffaloes, ducks and cranes were abundant." Much has changed since those early days and today the river is hardly a river in some areas, rather a shallow, dry creek bed.[3] As one looks from El Paso into Anapra, one of the poorest *colonias* in Ciudad Juárez, one can see children swimming on a hot sunny day in green murky water. The aforementioned vegetation and wildlife are long gone.

The El Paso–Ciudad Juárez–Doña Ana County metroplex faces a series of environmental issues that clearly transcend borders, both international and with the state of New Mexico. Water quality and quantity issues, air pollution, solid waste issues, transportation of hazardous waste are all salient and important issues in the border region. Environmental problems abound and are compounded with issues of legal responsibility, competency, funding, technical wherewithal and jurisdiction especially in a binational setting.

As Vicente Fox noted, there is a history of distrust that has existed between the two countries that has existed since 1836 when American colonists living in what was then Mexico declared Texas independence and the United States government tacitly approved. However, in spite of the mutual distrust that exists between Mexico and the United States, both countries have attempted to address transboundary environmental issues over time. Agreements, treaties, minutes, annexes, and memorandums of understanding have been signed by both governments regarding envi-ronmental issues, starting with the creation of the International Boundary and Water Commission, the La Paz Agreement, the Integrated Environmental Plan for the Mexican–U.S. Border Area (IBEP), and the side agreement to the North American Free Trade Agreement. The ten bordering states (California, Arizona, New Mexico, Texas, Baja California Norte, Sonora, Chihuahua, Coahuila, Tamaulipas and Nuevo León) have also engaged in cross-border activities with their respective neighboring state. The annual border governors' conference provides a forum for environmental issues to be discussed. This is an area where the institutional shroud is quite heavy. Cooperation in the environmental arena has been rather extensive at all levels of government, unlike immigration, human rights, drug enforcement, and labor issues. Notwithstanding the formal mechanisms that have been established to address environmental issues, this is an issue area that will require far more collaboration in the future. At a time when competition for water resources in this arid region becomes more intense, air more polluted, and the population growing and exerting more pressure on natural resources, it is very important to capitalize on existing institutional mechanisms and the binational efforts of NGOs. It would stand to reason that if so much institutional cooperation has taken place in the environmental arena, then these problems would be addressed. However, that is not the case. In spite of the heaviness of the institutional shroud in the environmental arena, these problems still abound and lend themselves to mistrust and misunderstanding among neighbors and friends in the border region, especially when trying to find the culprit(s) of air pollution, water contamination and depletion, toxic spills, and clandestine solid waste dumps.

The focus of this chapter is to set forth some of the binational environmental problems on the border, including the formal institutional mechanisms that exist in the environmental arena starting from the federal level down to the grassroots level, and to provide and highlight nongovernmental organizations in the region involved in environmental issues, such as the Joint Advisory Committee for the Improvement of Air Quality in the Paso del Norte Air Basin, (JAC), Environmental Defense, and The Rio Grande/Río Bravo Basin Coalition. We will depict the heaviness of the institutional shroud of the environmental arena. Last we will present the perceptions of different actors involved in both the government-sanctioned institutions and the NGO sector regarding obstacles, challenges, and successful examples of cross-border cooperation.

Air Quality

While environmental problems abound on the border, in this section special focus will be given to two important issues: air quality and the solid waste issue of tires. The binational dimensions of both problems will be highlighted to demonstrate the complex nature of environmental issues.

Air quality issues have been a source of contention for many years in the border region. There are many variables with varying degrees of explanatory power that help to explain and understand bad air quality in the community. However, we contend that more binational scientific, climatological, and geographical research needs to be conducted in order to better inform binational policy making in the community. Air quality is of concern throughout the border region.

> Air pollution is a growing problem for the California-Baja California border region. Air pollution comes from different sources, but ultimately is linked to growing human populations in the region. The exact transborder linkages of air pollution are not well understood. It is not clear to what extent San Diego's air quality is affected by pollutants transported from Tijuana sources and vice versa. At the same time, it is not clear how pollutants generated in the Imperial/Mexicali valleys move back and forth across the border. Also, air pollution sources outside the region are important. It has been documented that a significant part of the failure of San Diego to meet minimum air quality regulations for a certain number of days each year is caused by the transport of pollutants by winds and air currents from the Los Angeles basin. This may also affect Tijuana.[4]

The complexity surrounding air quality research in the El Paso–Ciudad Juárez region is just as challenging as in the San Diego-Tijuana metroplex and other sister cities. Additionally, diesel trucks waiting in lines to cross the border pollute the air; however, it is difficult to determine the exact amount and how much of it can be attributed to privately owned vehicles. What is important to note is that the trucks idling away in long lines at the border are carrying goods for the entire nation, not just border consumers. Fresh fruits and vegetables grown in the state of Sinaloa find their way to U.S. markets via Nogales, Arizona. Finished products assembled in *maquiladoras* also enter through other border cities. Heavy truck traffic and subsequent pollution impact border communities adversely, yet the entire nation (and Canada) benefits from the availability of tomatoes, melons, televisions, medical equipment, and other products at reasonable prices due to low labor costs in Mexico. There are many variables that help to explain the inordinate border traffic and subsequent air pollution that occurs at the border.

> ... Meanwhile, the U.S. Customs Bureau contributes to both traffic congestion and air pollution by not opening all 15 lanes at the Bridge of the Americas. Thus, El Paso residents and public officials are forced to surrender local control of key issues to federal agencies located thousands of miles from the Border which do not work together and often make far-reaching decisions without regard to local needs.[5]

The communal and aggregated vox populi blames air quality problems on Ciudad Juárez; however, there are other factors that come into play that people tend to ignore. The general public contends that Ciudad Juárez has too many cars that are old, do not run on unleaded gasoline, are not well maintained, and contribute to air pollution. Certain segments of the El Paso community fail to see that the old cars sold to residents of Ciudad Juárez are usually U.S. vehicles that otherwise would be have to discarded creating a landfill problem in the United States. What would happen should Mexico decide that these old cars could no longer be imported into Mexico? What impact would that have on the United States? For sure, used car sales dealers in the United States would be very upset and probably be put out of business. Where would the United States dispose of all of these cars that now go to Mexico? A short trip to the area of Ciudad Juárez where the *yonkes* (comes from the English word "junk") are located gives an indication of the amount of solid waste that would be created in the United States.

Additionally, when those aforementioned old cars wait in line, sometimes one to two hours, to cross the international bridge, they are idling and contaminating the air. Never mind that these folks contribute substantially to the El Paso economy, either by working, shopping, entertainment or seeking services. There are approximately over half a million cars in Ciudad Juárez traveling on a road system that is less than half paved.[6] A Partido de la Revolución Democrática (PRD) activist in Ciudad Juárez suggested that only 30–35 percent of all streets in the city were paved.[7] In spite of the estimated difference in the amount of paved streets, it is clear that dust also contributes to the air quality problems of the community. Furthermore, many people in Ciudad Juárez use wood and coal for home fuel in order to keep warm in the winter. Wood and coal burning also negatively impact air quality, practices that are common in Ciudad Juárez. Brickmakers in Ciudad Juárez also use alternative fuel sources such as garbage, used tires, and wood scrap (often impregnated with toxic resins, laminates, and varnishes) to burn in their kilns thereby creating more air pollution.

The Ciudad Juárez Brickmakers Project established in 1990 by FEMAP with the collaboration of binational private and public sectors attempted to promote the use of clean-burning propane. However, by the late 1990s many of the brickmakers have reverted to burning debris due to a variety of factors, including lack of public support, compliance costs, and the voluntary nature of the program.[8]

One of the areas where binational cooperation has worked well at the local level is that in October 1999 Ciudad Juárez and the City of El Paso ensure that gasoline stations only dispense oxygenated fuel in the winter months. This has helped reduce air pollution in the region. The oxygenated fuel program was enacted due in part to the binational efforts of the JAC, an organization that will be highlighted in the next section of this chapter.

Lack of infrastructure is common on both sides of the border. The fact that there are unpaved streets in *colonias* in El Paso County that also contribute to the dust and air pollution of the region does not go unnoticed.[9] However, inhabitants north of the political boundary very seldom mention or even acknowledge this urban amenity that is taken for granted. Residents in *colonias* in El Paso County complain vehemently about the dust in their neighborhoods due to unpaved streets. However, many of them would rather have water, sewer, and natural gas infrastructure in place before the streets are paved, a preference that obviously makes economic sense in the long run.[10] The plight of the more than 340,000 *colonia* residents in Texas has often been a topic of state and national concern, in part because the scattershot settlements are characterized as pockets of extreme poverty on the southern edge of one of the wealthiest nations in the world.[11]

A "Tired" Border

Likewise, the inordinate number of tires from the United States that find their way into Mexico are subsequently used for a variety of things such as flower beds or embedded on hillsides to avoid erosion. The problem of tire disposal crystallized in 2000 when the Mexican government stopped trucks heading into Ciudad Juárez with old tires.

Evidently, there was a small group of people from Ciudad Juárez who made their living by going to El Paso businesses and receiving payment ($1 per tire more or less) to take the tires into Mexico. When the Mexican government stopped the importation of tires, then Mayor of El Paso, Carlos Ramírez stated that the landfills in El Paso would not be able to handle the amount of tires and that it would create a problem for the community. The tire problem also posed a health hazard in certain areas of the border region because they became breeding grounds for mosquitoes and are the main culprits in the transmission of dengue fever.[12]

While there are official and formal mechanisms that address certain environmental problems, there is a thriving NGO community that is promoting more binational cooperation in this arena. Though it is difficult to actually quantify the number of environmental NGOs in the community, what is important to note is that in the community the spirit of binational collaboration is valued highly by borderlanders. The environmental NGOs in the community are some of the best-organized communities in the region, with a classic example being the El Paso, Ciudad Juárez, Doña Ana County Clean Air Coalition. Texas National Resources Conservation Commission (TNRCC) official Diana Borja, who hosted a public meeting in El Paso in the spring of 2000, remarked that "the people in El Paso were upset that we were starting the meeting without their Mexican counterparts present." She went on to say that in her opinion the environmental NGO community in the El Paso–Ciudad Juárez demonstrated great sophistication and knowledge of the binational dimensions of environmental issues and most importantly were acutely aware of the need for cooperation in this area. Last, she commented that she had attended similar meetings in the border region and that the environmental NGOs in El Paso–Ciudad Juárez "had its act together in terms of working binationally."

Environmental problems on the border are not a new phenomena; rather, the attention that they are now finally receiving from federal, state, and local governments coupled with the demands and exigencies of an empowered citizenry in the region are the new phenomena. It seems that there is a lack of connection between people's environmental problems and the institutions that are supposed to serve them. In some instances it is intimidating to go to a public hearing of the TNRCC or the Environmental Protection Agency (EPA) and express your concerns regarding waste-water in your *colonia* and it is another thing that someone will follow up and address your concern. The accountability factor is missing from the equation. After all, who is responsible for waste-water issues in *colonias,* the county, the state or the federal government? Another important factor that must be taken into account is that poor and minority people in communities such as El Paso–Ciudad Juárez are plagued by a host of issues: poor wages, inadequate housing, limited access to medical care, transportation concerns, quality of education. Because of this host of issues, environmental problems might not be high on peo-ple's personal or political agendas, especially if they are unemployed, or sick. The same conditions exist in El Paso and are exacerbated by limited English speaking skills and legal status. The plethora of concerns that people contend with daily could be overwhelming and may preclude people from becoming more involved with environmental institutions. In the next section, an overview of the institutions that are mandated to address border environmental issues will be presented.

The Evolution of the Institutional Shroud

Seven different institutions, agreements, plans, and boards comprise the environmental institutional shroud: The International Boundary and Water Commission, Mexico–United States Border Environmental Cooperation Agreement, The Integrated Environmental Plan for the U.S.–Mexican Border Area, North American Free Trade Agreement–Border Environmental Cooperation Commission and the North American Development Bank, Border XXI, United States Environmental Protection Agency and a variety of local, county, *municipio,* and state entities. All will be discussed in the following section.

International Boundary and Water Commission (IBWC)/
Comisión Internacional de Limites y Aguas (CILA)
This venerable institution, which has served the border region well for more than one century, is a model of diplomatic binational cooperation at the federal level. Created originally in March 1889, the International Boundary Commission's purpose (along with its Mexican counterpart, the *Comisión Internacional de Limites*) is to address physical boundary issues. These are two separate entities that work jointly. In 1944 water sanitation issues became part of their mission, hence the name change to the International Boundary and Water Commission, and the *Comisión Internacional de Limites y Aguas.* Officially housed at the Department of State and *Secretaría de Relaciones Exteriores* (Ministry of Foreign Relations) the IBWC/CILA have provided binational leadership in the environmental arena. Traditionally, the IBWC/CILA addressed issues of

international boundary preservation and demarcation, water allocation, border sanitation and maintenance programs for the international bridges. IBWC/CILA's modus operandi is one of treaty writing and passing of minutes; in essence a major part of their work is one of diplomatically addressing problems through a series of negotiations with their counterparts.[13] The IBWC/CILA has been criticized for its lack of citizen participation in their decision-making process.[14]

The IBWC is attempting to address the issue of citizen participation, as we will discuss this later in this section. However, from the Mexican perspective, CILA is a closed entity due to the high level diplomatic negotiations that they engage in without the inclusion of local citizens. An example of this is the critical situation encountered in the Colorado River Delta. The IBWC's main concern is the allocation of water between the two countries, both at the Colorado River and the Río Bravo/Río Grande. Mexico "owes" the United States 1,024 million acrefeet of water (1,263 million cubic meters) from six Mexican tributaries to the Rio Grande specified in a 1944 Treaty. The deficit occurred over time during 1992–1997 at the height of a serious drought that afflicted the region. Farmers in South Texas and regions in Northern Mexico were adversely affected. The deficit pitted the two countries against each other. Although a diplomatic and negotiated agreement was reached in 2001 by IBWC/CILA, it is yet to be seen whether or not Mexico will "pay back" the water that it owes the United States. Notwithstanding the negotiating powers that the IBWC/CILA share, there is a lack of enforcement authority on either side, just a lot of diplomatic goodwill that may or may not come to fruition. In reality, it can be said that the IBWC/CILA minutes do not have any enforcement mechanisms or sanctions.

This lack of enforcement of environmental laws on the border is a perpetual problem due to the regulatory nature of environmental institutions. Industrialization taxes the environment and its resources and subsequently, pollution and degradation are by-products, or negative externalities of capitalism. However, some would argue that pollution is a necessary evil that we can only attempt to regulate and cannot really prevent.

A Mexican national who both belongs to an agency that is part of the environmental institutional shroud and is closely linked to the activist community in the Baja California/California region relayed the following example of the limitations of the IBWC/CILA and also highlighted the lack of *confianza* (trust) and secretiveness of the organization:

> Approximately, 150,000 farmers in the Mexicali Valley rely on water from the Colorado River for agricultural use. The U.S. proposed channeling

the "excess" water to the All-American Canal[15] thereby denying the farmers in Mexico the use of this resource that they have been using for several generations. The channeling of this water is a violation of the 1944 Water Treaty and Mexican NGOs in the past have put up posters in Mexicali using the typical Uncle Sam picture, stating "*Tío Sam quiere tu agua*" (Uncle Sam wants your water).[16]

Additionally, several agricultural growers and NGOs have requested a seat at the negotiating table with the IBWC/CILA, which under the shroud of secrecy, diplomacy, and high-level government negotiations, has traditionally excluded people. While this water controversy is not new to the government negotiators, what is distinct is the way that an increasingly sophisticated and active NGO community on both sides of the border increasingly demands participation in the decision-making process. Community reaction has been rather sophisticated, with Mexican citizens writing to the Mexican Congress with documents attached that demonstrate that in 1994 the U.S. Bureau of Reclamation published a report on the environmental impact of lining the All-American Canal. In this report, the bureau proposed transferring 200,000 acre feet of water classified as excess, claiming that it would not affect Mexico. (The water would be transferred from the Imperial Valley to the Los Angeles–San Diego Area). In page 8 of the document one can read:

> Reclamation has complied with the E.O. by informing the USIBWC of the Project and by providing technical support to USIBWC for the consultation. USIBWC has kept the Department of State informed of the process and has received guidance from that agency. USIBWC also counseled Reclamation regarding the diplomatic sensitivities of the issues involved, and advised Reclamation to limit dissemination of information regarding Project impacts to Mexico to avoid jeopardizing the consultation and diplomatic relations with Mexico.

This is an explicit recommendation to withhold information from Mexico, an example of the lack of openness that exists in this area. "We do not trust the CILA to do the right thing because as you know they are all political appointees. We Mexicans have a hard time with them. But can you imagine that the U.S. government is withholding information from Mexico at this high level?" denounced a community activist in the region.

Over time, the traditionally treaty-mandated duties of the IBWC/CILA have been challenged by new realities and more complicated environmental problems such as hazardous and toxic waste issues. With the signing of the NAFTA, the IBWC/CILA became part of a new environmental regime on the border. IBWC/CILA were included in the Border Environmental Cooperation Commission (BECC) as nonvoting members.[17] The IBWC staff helped to organize the NAFTA-created BECC, and subsequently became members of the board of directors. In the Ciudad Juárez–El Paso region, the commissions organized for the United States and Mexican consulates a community development work group to support the consulates' Border Liaison Mechanisms (BLMs). The BLMs bring together people from both sides of the border to discuss issues affecting the communities such as traffic congestion, environmental issues, and trade among other issues.

The IBWC/CILA has demonstrated that it has the potential to be flexible and adapt to new realities. Still, some people doubt their effectiveness since no accountability mechanisms exist. Whether or not the IBWC/CILA does its job right or not is not important; what is significant is that it continues to exist as an institution.

The post-NAFTA IBWC/CILA is more visible in the public arena. It is expected to address more complicated and substantive issues. The IBWC/CILA is studying and collecting data on new pipe and power lines that cross the border and examining hydraulic and environmental studies, current flow data on the Rio Grande, flood control, and salinity control. The growing population on both sides of the border, the demand for more water and wastewater infrastructure development, coupled with the recent drought that has affected the region, all pose challenges to this organization. In spite of its limitations, the IBWC/CILA have been touted as a model of binational cooperation in many international forums. It is clear that this institution has the experience, technical expertise, and the capacity to address in the traditional sense many of the environmental problems of the border. In the information section of November 12, 2001 *El Paso Times,* for example, one can read:

> The Rio Grande Citizens' Forum of the U.S. Section of the International Boundary and Water Commission will meet on Nov. 28 at 6:30 PM at the Chamizal National Memorial. The commission's Rio Grande projects near El Paso and Las Cruces will be discussed.[18]

According to an IBWC official, they have hosted a series of public meetings in order be more accessible and open to the public; they hope to establish a citizen advisory board in the near future. After 100 years of existence, this is seen as a novel and timely idea. As problems become more complicated and competition for natural resources increases, especially for water in the border region, it is uncertain whether the IBWC/CILA can adequately address these problems. What is needed is a mechanism for institutional accountability as well as responsiveness to border citizens on both sides. CILA is not as open as the IBWC to citizen participation.

The IBWC/CILA clearly is a positive role model for binational cooperation and has provided stability and leadership in this area over time. While it faces future challenges in its dealings with the complexity and severity of border environmental issues, it can benefit from working with other agencies in various states, NGOs, and other stakeholders in the region.

La Paz Agreement

Another example of the heaviness of the institutional shroud in the environmental arena is the La Paz Agreement. Presidents Ronald Reagan and Miguel de la Madrid signed the La Paz agreement on August 14, 1983. This bilateral cooperation agreement established that the United States and Mexico "cooperate in the field of environmental protection in the border area on the basis of equality, reciprocity and mutual benefit."[19] Among many other things the La Paz Agreement defined the border as 100 kilometers north and south of the political border, created six work groups (air, water, hazardous and solid waste, contingency planning and emergency response, pollution prevention, cooperative enforcement and compliance). Additionally, it prohibited the location of nuclear waste dumps in the border region. The La Paz Agreement has on occasion been touted as *the* fundamental environment agreement between the two countries.

The La Paz Agreement can be interpreted as an arrangement between the two countries to meet and discuss the important issues. But it did not adequately address the how to, the when, and the concomitant funding streams needed to address these border problems. One long-time border resident from Mexico described the early meetings of the designated officials attending the La Paz Agreement meetings as suffering from *juntitis* (meetingitis). "They loved to meet and meet, and in nice places, but they really never got anything done."

In the early 1990s when the community of Sierra Blanca, Texas, located 75 miles east of El Paso and 16 miles north of the Rio Grande/ Río Bravo, was proposed as a possible site for the location of a low level nuclear waste dump, activists from both the United States and Mexico were quick to point out that the La Paz Agreement prohibited that kind of siting.

Representatives from the state of Texas never referenced the La Paz Agreement in their press releases regarding the proposed siting nor did officials from the Mexican government. According to a Texas state official, "There was an agreement struck between the two governments, one was that we would not mention what was going on in Salamayuca, Chihuahua, a nuclear waste dump that was clearly not meeting legal requirements and they would not mention the proposed site at Sierra Blanca."

The La Paz Agreement was about to become lost in the upcoming NAFTA debate. Although it remains viable and legal, it is seldom referred to by community members or activists, nor is it invoked by government officials as a mechanism for sound environmental management on the border.

Integrated Environmental Plan for the U.S.–Mexican Border Area (IBEP)

Sandwiched in the middle of La Paz Agreement and the NAFTA was the short-lived IBEP. In 1990 President George Bush and Carlos Salinas de Gortari met in Monterrey, Nuevo León, to discuss the potential economic benefits and environmental effects of trade liberalization between the two countries. The two respective federal environmental agencies were tasked to address the issue again since NAFTA was looming around the corner. The goal of the plan was to protect human health and natural ecosystems along the border. The plan had four specific objectives:

1. to strengthen the enforcement of environmental laws
2. to reduce pollution
3. to increase cooperative planning, training, and education
4. to improve the understanding of border environmental problems.

The introduction of the document in 1992 clearly describes environmental problems in a binational context. The problems of the northern Mexican border are clearly articulated: rapid industrialization had led to the creation of jobs in northern Mexico leading to the migration of people and the subsequent inability of local governments to meet the infrastructure needs of a growing industrial base and labor force. Later it was discovered that this binational plan was written by a firm in Massachusetts and was handed over to the Mexicans right before it was released. "This was the only way to get this done in a timely fashion. If we would have written it jointly and haggled over the details this would have never been done. There was a lot of political pressure to get this done because of NAFTA. The Mexicans were given drafts to comment on" (USEPA official).[20]

The negotiations and controversies surrounding NAFTA led to a growing awareness of the border region. All of a sudden the border was a place where national and international television crews were documenting border realities as if they were a new phenomena. Border residents were surprised and astonished that infrastructure deficiencies, health problems, inadequate living conditions in *colonias,* and other issues and concerns that they had lived with for years were now becoming the focus of the media and of the discourses of politicians. Of course this hyperbole was well received by border residents who perceived this attention to be a validation of their existence. In some instances, people's expectations were raised that politicians were now going to address border problems. Some touted NAFTA as the ultimate solution to the ills of the border region. Others felt that NAFTA would only compound the existing problems and put more pressure on natural resources. They also felt that expanded trade would cause more traffic congestion and that jobs would be lost thereby exacerbating poverty in the region.

At this point intense opposition to NAFTA was brewing especially in regards to the labor and environmental accords, and both governments became heavily involved in the stretching and widening of the institutional shroud vis-à-vis the environment at all levels of government including citizen advisory boards. IBEP was perceived as not going far enough in terms of environmental protection.

Good Neighbor Environmental Board (GNEB)

The GNEB was created in 1992 as a federal advisory committee to advise the president and Congress on how the U.S. federal government can effectively promote good neighbor practices in environmental infrastructure projects along the border with Mexico. Membership on the 24 member board is diverse and comes from the four bordering states of California, Arizona, New Mexico, and Texas. In addition to geographic representation, the nongovernmental sector, academic, private, tribal, and governmental stakeholders are represented. Representatives from eight federal government agencies also attend the meetings and provide an added dimension to the discussion on their agencies' border-region program. Over time, the GNEB has produced four annual reports that include recommendations to policymakers vis-à-vis the border environment. This bilingual report is widely disseminated in the United States and Mexico and is posted on the official website of the EPA. Several board members have extensive binational linkages due do their civic engagement or professional obligations. Once a year the GNEB meets with its Mexican counterpart group Consejo Para el Desarrollo Sustentable Region I (Consejo) (Region I Council for Sustainable Development). The binational meetings have been more symbolic than substantive though a joint communiqué was issued after a meeting in Reynosa, Tamaulipas, in 1999. One of the concerns that border residents from both the Consejo and GNEB had was that Region I included the states of Baja California Norte, Sonora, Chihuahua, Coahuila, Nuevo León, Tamaulipas and non-border states Baja California Sur, Sinaloa and Durango. Some felt that the group was too large; over 100 members on the Mexican side precluded meaningful discussions on specific border issues. The Consejo advised the Secretaría de Medio Ambiente, Recursos Naturales y Pesca (SEMARNAP) (Ministry of the Environment, Natural Resources and Fisheries). When Vicente Fox was elected president, the name of this ministry was changed to the Secretaría de Medio Ambiente y Recursos Naturales (SEMARNAT) Ministry of the Environment and Natural Resources). During Secretary Victor Lichtinger's visit to Ciudad Juárez, Chihuahua, in October 2001, he announced the creation of the Consejo Para el Desarrollo Sustentable para la Frontera Norte (Council for Sustainable Development for the Northern Border). The creation of a border-specific *consejo* was well received by border residents as well as by members of the GNEB who are very interested in pursuing a binational environmental agenda. It is expected that the binational work with the *consejo* will evolve into the elaboration of reports to each respective government as well as a joint report in the future.

The GNEB meet three times a year in different border cities. The binational meeting with the *consejo* is held in the United States on one year and in Mexico the next year. These meetings also serve as a forum for public participation since the meetings are open to everyone. Various organizations ranging from those in the private sector, to human rights and environmental groups have presented their work and concerns before the GNEB.

The GNEB is the only federal advisory committee whose sole purpose is to analyze conditions along the U.S. border with Mexico and recommend how the federal government can best apply its resources.[21]

While the GNEB only has advisory power, it has gained recognition over time. In recent meetings held in Brownsville and Laredo, Texas local media, newspaper, radio, and television stations provided coverage of the meeting. The annual report is the most important vehicle that GNEB has to disseminate its recommendations.

According to the members of the GNEB, the board has evolved over time and has become more vocal. The annual reports are increasingly more succinct in their recommendations (the first report had over 150 recommendations) and members have had briefings on Capitol Hill in order to elevate the visibility of the board's work with the hope that members of Congress will be better informed about border environmental issues.

The North American Free Trade Agreement BECC/NADBANK

> In a few moments, I will sign side agreements to NAFTA that will make it harder than it is today for business to relocate solely because of very low wages or lax environmental rules. These side agreements will make a difference. The environmental agreement will, for the first time ever, apply trade sanctions against any of the countries that fails to enforce its own environmental laws. I might say to those who say that's giving up of our sovereignty, for people who have been asking us to ask that of Mexico, how do we have the right to ask that of Mexico if we don't demand it of ourselves? It's nothing but fair.
>
> —President Clinton, September 14, 1993[22]

> ... banks will never make a loan to a community without the capacity to repay....
>
> —former NADBANK official

During the NAFTA negotiations, the La Paz Agreement became obscure. Government officials were quick to note that NAFTA would address past environmental problems and avoid future ones. The environmental and labor accords were to address both sets of concerns. As the institutional shroud again was thickened by another agreement, the environmental concerns still remain an important fact of border life seven years since NAFTA was implemented. With the signing of NAFTA, everyone's (from the average resident, policy makers, and activist) expectations were raised. The question still remains: Is the border environment better off than it was in the past?

Ethnographic Moment 4.1: Pre and Post-NAFTA "Smell" on the Border

At a meeting in February 28–March 1, 2001 the Texas National Resource Conservation Commission (TNRCC) in Austin invited people from bordering states to discuss the role of the states in environmental policy making. I, Irasema, was invited to sit on a panel along with other representatives from the border states who would present their best practices vis-à-vis environmental binational cooperation. An activist attorney, also on my panel, from the Arizona Center for Law in the Public Interest, Vera Kornylak, made a presentation of her efforts to sue the city of Nogales and the USEPA because the wastewater treatment plant of Ambos Nogales did not meet environmental standards. Vera went on to say that she was in the process of suing the city of Nogales, Arizona, and the USEPA for their non-compliance of the National Pollution Elimination Discharge System standards from the waste water treatment plant discharges that failed to meet minimum standards. According to Vera, community residents are complaining about the "smell" and they have demonstrated concern for the impact of this plant on their health. While I, Irasema, was heartened to see the passion, concern, and expertise in the environmental arena that Vera demonstrated, I could not help but laugh and cry at the same time. I was happy to see someone as knowledgeable and committed to people's environmental health as Vera taking on the culprits so to speak. Likewise, I was saddened and angry because as long as I can remember or as people in Spanish say, desde que tengo uso de razón, (since I have use of reason) the wastewater treatment plant in Nogales, Arizona, has always been a problem. Memories of my parents and siblings driving by and pinching our noses and holding our breaths so as to avoid the "smell" of the wastewater treatment plant warmed my heart. However, I thought to myself, this was well over forty years ago and today people are still smelling the same stench in Nogales, Arizona. Many questions raced through my mind: Has the border environmental infrastructure improved? Why is the wastewater treatment plant still a problem in Nogales, Arizona? Have the NAFTA-created institutions worked?

At the height of the NAFTA negotiations, environmental activists, policy makers, and academics at the border region were concerned with the impact of enhanced trade on the environment. More trade meant more trucks crossing the border and more air pollution. Expanded opportunities for commerce would also promote the creation of more *maquiladoras* that would create more jobs and lure more people to northern Mexico and in turn would put more pressure on water resources and wastewater infrastructure. As much opposition as there was against NAFTA from the environmental and labor communities both in the United States and Mexico, it nevertheless was signed into effect in 1994.

NAFTA also created false expectations in many border communities. Among certain sectors of the population, there was the expectation that the border region would become an important economic enclave and would prosper from the passage and subsequent implementation of NAFTA. More trade would also allow for the development of a broader tax base and subsequently more revenue that would be used to provide the financial wherewithal for badly needed environmental infrastructure projects. Others expressed concern that border cities and towns would lose business because American companies and merchants would be allowed to go into Mexico. The long standing tradition that U.S. border communities are the favored destination of Mexican shoppers looking for American products would be lost because these businesses would be allowed to relocate into the interior of Mexico. The entire NAFTA debate provided a window of opportunity for border environmental issues to be put on the broader national political agenda. Environmental concerns have plagued border communities for years; however, with NAFTA, issues such as wastewater treatment plants, solid waste issues, air pollution, and the shipments of toxic chemicals, were being discussed openly in the U.S. Congress. President Bill Clinton exclaimed that NAFTA was the "greenest trade agreement" ever signed and the institutional shroud was again broadened with the creation of two new border-specific institutions.

The NAFTA produced two sister institutions, the Border Environmental Cooperation Commission (BECC), located in Ciudad Juárez, Chihuahua, and the North American Development Bank (NADBANK) located in San Antonio, Texas. BECC and NADBANK were officially created on December 27, 1993. The idea (in a nutshell) behind these two institutions is that the BECC would certify projects that would address water and wastewater problems and would have the support of the community. Once the project was certified, the NADBANK would provide the concomitant funding. BECC and NADBANK would fund projects 100 kilometers north and south of the political boundary. One of the main goals of the BECC is to certify projects that meet sustainability criteria. Additionally, the impact of the project on the border or the transboundary effects had to be analyzed and taken into account in the approval process. While these two institutions have evolved, they have nevertheless experienced growing pains and have come under public scrutiny. Larger communities that have the technical expertise on their staff to write proposals are at a greater advantage to get their projects certified and funded. Smaller communities that do not have grant writers and engineers are obviously at a disadvantage. Although technical assistance programs have been developed to address this situation, there have been limited resources provided to address the magnitude of the lack of environmental infrastructure on the border. Presently, there is talk in the higher echelons of government about expanding the mandate of the NADBANK. Expanding the mandate could possibly mean two things: one, that the NADBANK would lend money for other projects that have a border impact; or else, that they would fund them outside of the 100 kilometer limit. Community groups have expressed concern that the funding would go to "subsidize private businesses" that would build nuclear or hazardous waste dumps, for example, or allow for *maquiladoras* to borrow money to build wastewater treatment plants. Poor and unorganized communities would therefore have to compete harder to obtain BECC certification and NADBANK funding.

The NADBANK's resources amount to approximately $304 million dollars, of which only $11 million dollars has been lent to border communities. Lending solely for water, sewer, and trash projects has proved difficult, bank officials say, because those services generate little income that poor communities can use to repay the loans.[23] Communities report problems with NADBANK loans, the main one being high interest rates at market rate, 12 percent, while mortgage rates are 6.5 percent. Poor communities cannot afford the high interest rates. Steep interest is coupled with the fact that some of the major infrastructure water and wastewater projects are very expensive and there are only a few users to divide the costs among themselves. For example, the cost of a wastewater treatment plant in a community of 100,000 people is more easily absorbed than a community of 10,000. A community in Texas can obtain a Texas Revolving Loan for wastewater treatment that is only at 2 percent interest rate. President Vicente Fox has proposed the idea that NADBANK funds be used for infrastructure projects in the interior of Mexico. The concern about the future of the NADBANK centers around the fact that the U.S. Congress may decide to defund it. After all, they have been in existence six years and have made very few loans all this time. The NADBANK is not in the business of giving away money. Poor communities are reluctant to borrow money and the bank is not interested in lending money that cannot be repaid. Lowering the interest rate on loans would be a welcomed option, though it is unclear whether this action is a policy decision or if it requires an act of Congress. Perhaps, by design, the NADBANK was created to fail.

During the public comment session in October 2001 in Laredo, Texas, regarding the NADBANK/BECC expansion, we learned that several people were extremely happy and pleased with both institutions. Obviously, communities that had received technical assistance and subsequent funding were more content with the institutions than those

that haven't. However, representatives from communities that had benefited from NADBANK/BECC were critical of the certification process.
Critics commented that it was not specific enough, it was too slow, and
procedures were complicated. It was interesting to note that the public
comment session was well attended and that several representatives from
communities in Mexico took advantage of the opportunity to express
their concerns regarding the aforementioned institutions. In public,
people said things like "We have to come here because they are not
going to have hearings on our side."

Over 20 people from the states of Nuevo León, Tamaulipas, and
Coahuila took the time and trouble (security measures enacted after
September 11, 2001 seriously impacted the international bridges; some
people reported waiting up to two hours to cross) to present their recommendations vis-à-vis the NADBANK/BECC to three U.S. government
officials who attentively listened to the translation of people's comments.[24]

Border XXI Program

The Border XXI Program was established in 1994 and builds on the
efforts of the IBEP and other previous environmental agreements (La Paz)
and expands the scope of previous environmental agreements to include
environmental health, natural resources, and environmental information.
The Border XXI program, a joint effort by the United States and Mexico,
can be seen as another layer of the institutional shroud that is constantly
thickening and unfolding on the border. The mission of Border XXI is:
"To achieve a clean environment, protect public health and natural
resources and encourage sustainable development along the U.S.–Mexico
border." The major goal of Border XXI is to promote sustainable development in the region. Three major strategies were set forth to bring this
to fruition:

1. Ensure public involvement
2. Build capacity and decentralize environmental management
3. Ensure interagency cooperation

This program can be described as yet another referendum of both
countries' commitments to collaborate in the environmental arena.[25]
Border XXI has been described as an excellent vehicle to promote state-
to-state, federal government-to-federal government cooperation.

Three new working groups were created to augment the six original
work groups that were created by the La Paz Agreement. The new
groups are: natural resources, environmental health, and information

resources. Border XXI was seen as a deepening of the environmental agreements to date because for the first time the commitment to develop binational environmental indicators to determine the quality of the environment were put into place. Subsequently, these environmental indicators would be used to measure whether or not the environment had improved over time.

In the summer of 1999 Carol Browner, administrator of the USEPA; Julia Carabias, secretary of the Secretaría de Medio Ambiente, Recursos Naturales y Pesca; Albert C. Zapanta, president of the United States–Mexico Chamber of Commerce; and Javier Cabrera, general manager of the BECC, signed the "US/Mexico Business and Trade Community: The Seven Principles of Environmental Stewardship for the 21st Century." The seven principles that comprise this agreement were developed through a public/private partnership to promote sustainable development in the U.S./Mexico border area in furtherance of the goals of the Border XXI Environmental Framework. The seven principles included a commitment to sustainable development and improved environmental performance through policies that emphasize pollution prevention, energy efficiency, adherence to appropriate international standards, environmental leadership, and public communications among other things.

While this example is yet another fold in the environmental institutional shroud, these principles did not have any teeth to them nor was there an accountability factor included. This is a fine example of symbolic politics at its best that just made both governments and businesses look good.

United States Environmental Protection Agency (USEPA)

While the USEPA is the lead agency in the nation regarding environmental policy, it has nevertheless fallen short when it comes to addressing environmental problems on the U.S.–Mexico border. The United States Environmental Protection Agency (USEPA) is divided into regions; Region 6, headquartered in Dallas, is responsible for the states of Texas and New Mexico. Arizona and New Mexico fall under Region 9, headquartered in San Francisco. It would probably make more sense if one region were responsible for the border area. In many instances, USEPA employees from both regions work on similar problems in different geographic areas.

Border residents are well aware that binational environmental problems require binational solutions; and clearly, USEPA does not have jurisdiction in Mexico. In spite of the formal agreements, treaties,

minutes, and NAFTA, the environmental issues of the border are difficult and costly to address. For example, in 1998 BECC certified and the
NADBANK approved funding for wastewater treatment facilities in
Ciudad Juárez, Chihuahua, to the tune of 31.1 million dollars. These
plants would benefit 1.2 million people and have been touted as a great
success story. It is important to keep in mind that the population growth
rate of Ciudad Juárez is 3.7 percent annually.[26] It is estimated that
10 percent of the city does not have sewer infrastructure and therefore
the problem of untreated raw sewage still persists in the community in
spite of the wastewater treatment plants. Politicians, however, capitalize
on the development of infrastructure and fail to recognize that in spite
of these limited successes, there are people whose basic needs are not
met on both sides of the border. Conservatively speaking, 5 percent of
the population of Ciudad Juárez do not have running water and 10 percent do not have access to sewer.[27] Lack of wastewater infrastructure is
not exclusively a problem in Mexico. On the U.S. side the numbers vary
from 1,500 to 5,000 people in El Paso County living without basic
water and wastewater services. On both sides of the border many people
use septic tanks, cesspools, and private water suppliers in order to meet
their basic needs.

Ethnographic Moment 4.2: An Important Binational Meeting

*Christine Todd Whitman and Victor Lichtinger sat at the head table with
two of their assistants next to them. In the middle sat the governor of the
state of Chihuahua, Patricio Martínez. Governor (as she is still referred to as
according to staffers) Whitman's visit to the region included a visit to a colonia in El Paso County, a visit to an elementary school, and to a wastewater
treatment plant in Ciudad Juárez. The top ranking environmental officials
met in Ciudad Juárez and scheduled meetings with various stakeholders,
tribal leaders, representatives of the states, and the like. This part of the meeting in a popular hotel was scheduled for public participation. Mostly nongovernmental organizations were invited and then were asked to sign up to
speak.*

*Representatives from NGOs throughout the border region on the U.S. side
attended. People came from California, Arizona, New Mexico, and Texas to
present their concerns to both Christine Todd Whitman and Victor Lichtinger.
Various issues were raised in a rather succinct and timely manner since participants were given only a few minutes to speak in any language with simultaneous translation provided.*

A representative of an Austin, Texas, NGO raised the water debt issue. She lamented that she was concerned about the rhetoric surrounding this problem in South Texas where farmers were complaining about the debt. An activist from Ciudad Juárez stated emphatically that his community was becoming a dump for the United States, "tires, old cars, everything is sent here and then it becomes our problem." He also mentioned the problem with the hazardous and toxic waste used in the maquiladoras as well as the risk associated with the transboundary movement of these substances. A tribal member from California reiterated that he and other tribal members were happy to participate in a meeting with such high-ranking officials and stated that there were five tribes in the same watershed who were concerned with air quality issues and that they were being engulfed by urbanization.

The Colorado River in the California–Arizona–Mexico border region was mentioned as an area of concern due to the quality and quantity of water that Mexico was receiving. Over time, several themes emerged. Some of the prime concerns involve the need for cross-border cooperation in order to address environmental problems, the lack of regional environmental education on both sides of the border, and the importance of public participation in environmental policy decision-making. Several comments were directed at the NADBANK and BECC reform: more grant money should be given rather than loans, merge the institutions, leave them as they are, make the BECC more efficient. One participant offered results from a research project where people who were actively engaged and interested in BECC and NADBANK issues were surveyed.

At the end of the meeting, governor Patricio Martínez made a long speech regarding the history of the region, from indigenous history to the present day. The governor mentioned that he had been on the telephone with Texas Governor Rick Perry about the water debt. "We agree that we owe water to our neighbor based on the 1944 Treaty. Chihuahua does not have water. International Law states that no one is obligated to do what is not possible. We live in a desert and all the farmers should be aware of that and change to crops that use less water or "que se dediquen a otra cosa" (dedicate themselves to do something else) stated governor Martínez.

He also mentioned that there was a lack of "cultura" (cultural awareness) regarding environmental problems and that many people littered the highways with soiled diapers unaware of the long-term consequences. The meeting closed and the officials were then taken to another room to meet with representatives of state governments to discuss the future of the Border XXI Program.

Afterward, during the unofficial debriefing outside the meeting room, participants complained of being limited to two minutes to provide their comments while the governor, as one participant put it, "hablo hasta que se canso" (spoke until he was tired). Activists stated that they were invited at the last minute and wished that they would have had more time to prepare. Others questioned aloud "porque invitaron a tan pocos?" (why were so few people invited?). One woman in the group felt that it was "maleducado" (rude) to serve the "funcionarios" (government officials) cappuccino during the one-hour meeting while the audience was left "con la boca abierta" (with one's mouth open). Last, a man and woman commented that the EPA administrator was writing notes and snickering to her assistant during the governor's speech.

In spite of the criticism, this was one of the few opportunities that border environmental activists had to share their concerns with such high-level government officials on the U.S.–Mexico border.

Notwithstanding the formal institutions and treaties that exist, the USEPA has been one of the most important agencies in the environmental arena that has worked with its counterpart institution in Mexico. It is interesting to note that former Secretary of the Interior Bruce Babbitt had a close working relationship with Julia Carabias, former head of the SEMARNAP. Officials from both institutions report that they would on occasion go camping together to discuss these issues. Additionally, they report that former EPA administrator Carol Browner did not have as close a working relationship with her counterpart, Julia Carabias.

In October 1994 the USEPA established border liaison offices in El Paso, Texas, and San Diego, California. The role of the USEPA border offices is to respond to community needs and concerns, provide program updates, technical information and grant announcements, conduct open houses as well as public meetings to discuss local environmental issues, and to work with the nine Border XXI workgroups to coordinate effective communication with the community and other government agencies.[28] Policy decisions are not made at the border offices but they serve as a vehicle for outreach and participation on the border.

Community activists were very complimentary about the outreach efforts undertaken by the El Paso Border Liaison Office. The border offices have worked well and have provided several services to the community—the most important of which is having a physical presence in San Diego, California, and in El Paso, Texas. The USEPA border office in El Paso organizes a monthly Border Forum where guest speakers from various organizations in the community make presentations on environmental issues. For example, in November 2001 the principal engineer with the IBWC, Debra Little, discussed "Binational Coordination and Water Resources Planning: The USIBWC Experience." Other speakers have included members of nongovernmental organizations, professors from the University of Texas at El Paso and representatives of local, state, and federal agencies. This forum is well attended usually by 20 or 30 people who are interested in the topics discussed.

In October 2001 EPA administrator Christine Todd Whitman and SEMARNAT director Victor Lichtinger met in Ciudad Juárez, Chihuahua, a monumental step forward in promoting binational and bilateral cooperation in the environmental arena. This, of course, had an element of symbolic politics to it but at the same time this meeting provided an opportunity for border residents to express their concerns.

The EPA has a pretty tall order to fill in regards to its mandate and responsibilities. Certainly, environmental issues have been addressed although some people criticize the EPA for only regulating the polluters and not stopping the production of pollution, which of course is a natural by-product of our industrialized and capitalistic way of life. Could EPA do more in terms of addressing environmental issues on the border?

Other Levels of Government

Local, county, *municipio,* special districts, state and federal governments all have a plethora of institutions and organizations that address environmental issues on both sides of the border. However, little is known of their interagency cooperation agreements and of their legal ability or willingness to work with each other. On the Mexican side, the State of Texas interacts with four different states: Chihuahua, Coahuila, Nuevo León and Tamaulipas and every Mexican state has a set of actors addressing environmental issues. Clearly, this presents some interesting challenges to policymakers from Texas who interact with officials from different states, political parties, and economic realities.

Access to information is a key element to helping solve and address environmental problems. If institutions are not forthcoming with air quality data, or rates of diseases, or if the financial support does not exist to collect the data in the first place, border environmental problems cannot be readily solved. It is easy to say that the Rio Grande/Río Bravo is polluted; however, decision-makers need to know exactly how many parts per billion of fecal choliform is in the water. The old adage "if you can't quantify and measure the problem, then you don't have one" is very true in the border region. Institutions in the United States do not share information with each other as readily as they should and likewise in Mexico. In both cases, the cost of data gathering is costly.

Binational Cooperation: Obstacles, Challenges and Successes

The basic structure and function of government and political systems condition people to work in a specific manner. In theory, democratic nations with transparent and open institutions tend to promote public participation, and inclusion in their decision-making process. An empowered and engaged citizenry is beneficial to both sides of the border and helps to move political agendas forward in a positive manner.

In regards to obstacles of participation, the political culture of each country plays an important role. In the United States employees of agencies like the TNRCC and EPA are civil service, career employees, although there are people who have political appointments in government institutions. Changes in administrations at the state and federal level obviously lead institutions into new directions; however, the basic structure remains the same and personnel remain on staff that have a historical memory and hands-on experience in dealing with binational environmental issues. In Mexico the situation is different and it is common to replace personnel in key decision-making positions in institutions every three or six years based on electoral terms of office depending on the level of government. Although there are career employees in Mexican institutions, they tend to be at the lower end of the hierarchy. New political appointments are made when elections take place, leaving power vacuums as well as voids in the continuity of certain binational efforts in all areas. Within the context of the U.S.–Mexico border, the differences in political systems affect how representatives of formally recognized institutions interact with one another.

On the U.S. side, a representative of the TNRCC noted:

> the *Mexicanos* do not understand that we have certain limitations as a state agency, they also do not understand the role that the water districts have in some of these water issues. They are used to high-level authorities making decisions and then everyone going along with them. This is not how it works here. For example, the governor can say that he/she will work with Mexico on water issues but in reality it is not really his/her call; there are other institutions that deal with water issues: the IBWC, the water districts, etc. They (*Mexicanos*) do not understand that we have a system of checks and balances and different levels of government.

Mexicanos who are used to an authoritarian and personalistic political system of government have a difficult time understanding that the U.S.

local, county, and state governments and special districts have in many instances more legal authority to address an issue than the federal government or the state governor. A Mexican affiliated with the BECC shared the following observations regarding the Mexican political culture: "Vicente Fox took the PRI out of Los Pinos but it is more difficult to take out the "*pequeño priista que llevamos dentro porque es parte de nuestro perfil*" (the little priista that we all have inside of us).[29] He added that all Mexicans alive today know only one form of government.

> We are used to corruption, *prepotencia* (arrogance) it is part of our culture. If we approach a government agency, we are not used to following policies and procedures because we are used to or conditioned to pay bribes to *agilizar el proceso* (facilitate the process). If an institution is now more transparent you do not know how to work within the system. In the past you did not make demands of bureaucrats because they only slowed down the process. We create our own obstacles and need to learn to work with transparent institutions.

This of course requires capacity building within communities and the NGO sector. It is difficult to negotiate any bureaucracy, and groups need to learn how to effectively channel their energy and resources.

An academic from Mexico stated:

> There are people in Mexico who like the old way of doing things; it was easier because you could very easily pay a bribe to get things done. Now you have to do things the right way, simple things like registering a car, you now have to have things in order and have the necessary paperwork. Before, you just paid your money to someone *de confianza* (of trust) and they would deliver the necessary paperwork the next day.

An EPA official stated that she had been working on organizing a binational meeting and that the public notice had gone out on the federal register as required by law and with as many details about the location of the meeting as possible—who, what, when, where, why, agenda items. Details about public transportation, access for handicapped people, all have to be listed in the register.

> One day they call (officials at SEMARNAT) and ask that we change the meeting because one of the high-ranking Mexican officials could not come on the date and time that had been agreed upon. They wanted me to change the day and I explained to them that it was not possible because of the requirement that the meeting be posted in the federal register. They made me feel like I was not accommodating to them, they

could not understand why we just could not change the day. This is a requirement that we have to comply with at all times, for any public meeting (U.S. government official).

This example crystallizes how people on both sides of the border have different rules and ways of working that can prevent or hinder cross-border cooperation and lead to misunderstandings. As we mentioned in chapter two, personalism can constrain growth, dissemination, and sustained challenge to historical patterns of asymmetry and dominance. The U.S. government official frustratingly stated that "on a personal level it is no big deal to change a meeting day, but I could not, because that was not my call. Even if they called the higher ups we still could not change it because of the regulations that we must follow." Once this situation was explained to the Mexican government officials they understood that this was not a decision that any one person could make. "After I explained to them they understood and it helped to clarify that for future meetings" the government official stated. Clarifying the situation was useful in future binational planning until personnel changes took place in both agencies.

Mexico has recently attempted to decentralize its governmental authority and this poses challenges to policy makers at the local level who are used to acting at the behest of people higher up in government. Moreover, one of the complaints that Mexican officials have expressed at the local and state level is that while the Mexican government has decentralized and devolution is taking place, the concomitant funding is lacking thereby stymieing their efforts at the local level.[30]

Binational Cooperation in a Binational Organization

There are various ways of working together and promoting binational cooperation: the best approach would be collaborative, and integrative, and holistic. Even conflictual or confrontive methods can work especially if environmental problems can then move up on the bilateral agenda of both countries. In the environmental arena, unilateral action is not conducive to solving problems. For example, when addressing air quality problems in the El Paso/Ciudad Juárez region, it is possible that unilateral action could probably ameliorate one aspect of the problem, but that working together can better address the problem.

Representatives of two institutions that are mandated with binational cooperation in the environmental arena shared their insight with us regarding their experiences within these two organizations. We were interested in how binational these institutions really are and how both Mexicans and Americans worked together to bring cooperation to fruition. We asked the representatives of these organizations to share with us the obstacles, challenges, and successful examples of cross-border cooperation that they experienced or observed in their daily work.

One respondent spoke candidly of his first moments as an employee of the BECC.

> I thought that I knew Mexicans, but I was totally wrong. It is almost an art working with the Mexicans, because they are so sensitive. One word, or the way that you say the one word can offend them. The Mexicans are very formal, in a way stuck-up; they do not appreciate your talking like the people. I do want to say that it is an arrogance or superiority—it is an elitism.

When the respondent was asked to describe the obstacles to cross-border cooperation, he said that he saw hurdles instead and that one of the major impediments was language.

> We are all supposed to be bilingual. Some people do not speak English or Spanish well. Mexicans tend to elaborate; Americans are more to the point. I stepped on a lot of toes. I was too blunt for them and even hurt them. Language can be an impediment because every word has a meaning. Simple statements can be pretty loaded for Mexicans. Sometimes what you don't say means a lot more than what you do say.
> —former BECC employee

The high context vs. low context communication issues clearly manifest themselves in binational efforts. Verbal and non-verbal communications subtleties and nuances obviously become important challenges to working in a binational setting.

"*Esperando la linea oficial*" (Waiting for the Official Party Line)

Authoritarian regimes tend to dictate policies from the top down and have minimal regard for public participation. Within the BECC, the hiring processes and modus operandi of the two countries affect human interaction at the ground level. "On the Mexican side, BECC personnel were appointed based on their political connections. Many times the higher ups would not make a decision because they were "*esperando la linea oficial.*" "You see in Mexico these are very well paying jobs so everyone wanted to make sure that they did what was expected of them by the higher ups in the government" stated a former BECC employee.

Public participation in a binational context also poses some challenges. BECC/NADBANK public sessions allow the public a forum to present their concerns regarding the environment. One of the major divisions reported by staffers at the BECC was the *Mexicanos'* response to public participation. People involved in planning binational meetings expressed that the Mexicanos were uncomfortable with public participation sessions at their meetings. A BECC employee stated:

> There was an elitist attitude (on the part of the *Mexicanos*) about the NGO activist participation. Mexican officials who sit on the BECC board of directors were uncomfortable with the level and intensity of public participation at their meetings. They just didn't like it. You could tell that they were not used to this and did not really like it. At times the (Mexican) higher ups would look at the NGOs and wonder aloud who invited the *chusma* (rif raf) to come here. They were inattentive at times and would be glad when they left. Some of the NGOs were really happy to be able to participate in the meetings and felt somewhat protected by the US groups that were present as well as by the US staff.

This of course led to differences between the Mexican and U.S. staffs and members of the board of directors at the BECC.

In the United States public participation is welcomed and even solicited by local, state, and federal agencies in some instances because it is genuinely desired or because it is required by law. Usually, there is a requirement that the agency or institution announce ahead of time the time and place where the public can provide their input. Different attitudes vis-à-vis public participation, coupled with legislative requirements on one side of the border and an elitist attitude on the other side, can lead to misunderstandings and tensions.

In the BECC certification process, public participation is required for any project to move forward. Therefore, in many ways this requirement has helped to open up democratic spaces for citizens. A Mexican affiliated with the BECC remarked that "the Americans think that they are democratic but they are not. It is hard to work with them because just one person so easily lures them. They had their own agendas that they promoted and it is clear because so many U.S. projects were funded."

A true test of binational cooperation would be to determine how many truly binational projects have been presented before the BECC. For example, have the City of El Paso and Ciudad Juárez jointly submitted a proposal that would address water or air quality issues? The projects that have been presented are usually presented by respective border cities, not joint ventures. Perhaps the BECC and NADBANK can encourage the elaboration of joint projects by border communities.

Successful Cases of Cross-Border Organizing Efforts

While we are aware that there are many cross-border organizing efforts, it is difficult to highlight all of them. Just because they are not mentioned here does not mean that they do not exist. Many organizations promote cross-border collaboration, among them, the Texas Center for Policy Studies (TCPS), in Austin, Texas; the Southwest Center for Environmental Research Policy (SCERP) in San Diego, California; the Interhemispheric Resource Center in Albuquerque, New Mexico (publishers of *Borderlines*); the Coalition for Justice in the Maquiladoras in San Antonio, Texas; the Southwest Environmental Center in Las Cruces, New Mexico; and the Center for Environmental Resources Management (CERM) at the University of Texas at El Paso. However, we want to focus on cooperation at the most local level in the El Paso–Ciudad Juárez region. We do mention numerous organizations throughout the chapters that epitomize cross-border cooperation in diverse regions only because we want to crystallize a point. We contend that cross-border organizing at the local level poses some serious challenges that need to be fully examined if we are to successfully address the binational problems facing the border region.

*Joint Advisory Committee for the Improvement of Air Quality
in the Paso del Norte Air Basin (JAC)*

The Joint Advisory Committee for the Improvement of Air Quality in the Paso del Norte Air Basin (JAC) was formed in response to local grassroots efforts of the Paso del Norte Air Quality Task Force. The task force started meeting in the early 1990s with the support of then governors Ann Richards of Texas and Francisco Barrio of Chihuahua. This binational political support led to the evolution of the task force. Subsequently, people with serious "credentials" were appointed to the board: academics, a medical doctor, a representative from FEMAP, and government officials working on environmental issues on both sides of the border. From Mexico, people who worked with or had experience with environmental agencies at the federal, state, and local levels were appointed. Since its inception, the task force looked at air quality issues holistically to include Doña Ana County, the greater El Paso and Ciudad Juárez communities. The TNRCC was very supportive of this effort and established an office in El Paso at that time. The JAC was established in May 1996. The JAC is a binational, 20-member, diverse, multi-stakeholder advisory group that makes recommendations to the Border XXI Air Workgroup. The advisory group members are appointed for three years and can be reappointed no more than five times. There are two co-presidents, one for each side of the border. The EPA El Paso Border Office provides on-going support to the JAC; hence they have official support from a government entity and therefore have a solid support infrastructure in place. The JAC also receives support from the U.S. State Department and the Secretaría de Relaciones Exteriores (Ministry of Foreign Affairs) in Mexico. On May 6, 1996 at a binational cabinet meeting, an agreement was signed that created the JAC with the acknowledgement that the air shed, (a region that is affected by the same air quality) was broader than the limit that the La Paz Agreement designated as the 100 kilometer limit.

The JAC meets every three months, alternating on both sides of the border. Meetings are open to the public. The JAC is not a 501c3, (non profit organization); rather it is a voluntary community organization. Their strategic plan includes promoting public transportation, facilitating the crossing of vehicles, and inspecting automobiles' exhaust systems, among others. The JAC is successful because it has government support coupled with highly qualified people whose organizations promote their participation in the organization. In the fall of 2001, the JAC received the Governance Institution Border Environmental Merit Award at the 29th meeting of the U.S.–Mexico Border Environmental Cooperation Commission in Mexico City.

Environmental Defense

Environmental Defense (ED) is a leading public interest group. A staff person with ED describes his job in the following way: "I work on projects having to do with the atmosphere with a strategy that entails community participation, the scientific community, social institutions, local foundations, governmental offices and through the years they have been able to make both governments realize the need for international participation." According to this staff person this past year he has been able to form a coalition of local institutions that work on air, water, health issues and also in getting organizations to collaborate on strategies that will bring economic growth to the area. He describes how his work in this arena evolved in the following way:

> In the beginning when I tried to get cooperation from governmental and non governmental organizations, I had to convince them that this was an urban metropolitan area. Of course there is a borderline and a political geographical line exists between the two cities on a map, but for this office after 10 years of existence, this is an urban metropolitan area that is affected by what is done on both sides of the border in regards to global

warming. Infrastructure projects also need to be developed to make water more cost-effective for both sides. When these projects take place and are completed, then both cities will be impacted positively. At that moment, the Paso Del Norte region's health will benefit from it.

ED works with other organizations in the community on natural resource issues. A staff member from ED has been invited to other regions and academic institutions to share with them how to replicate what has been done in this region regarding binational environmental protection. When asked to explain why ED as an organization has been successful in the binational arena, the staff member listed a variety of variables including:

1. the ability to distinguish between both governments, both sets of laws, and both sovereignties;
2. an academic stance (he has a Ph.D) that helps people take him as a staffer seriously;
3. long-term focused projects (an air quality agreement took over three years to develop and sign);
4. works from the bottom-up in reference to finding cooperation from other organizations;

Personally, the staff member feels that he has no academic, social, governmental, or professional level impediments because he works for an established internationally recognized environmental organization. He went on to state that:

> There are more proactive leaders, participants, advocates in border communities and those that by birth can identify themselves with the local community are those that will make the effort to better the natural resources that are needed in his or her community and will realize that resource problems do not have borders and that involvement is necessary for the region. They must tell themselves that the involvement has to be shared between both cities because if Ciudad Juárez has air quality problems, then we will and vice versa.

One of the distinct characteristics that Environmental Defense utilizes is a bottom-up approach to projects and planning; projects must start at the local level. According to our source:

> The most serious problem that the border faces is global warming. Water and air contamination are very serious. The U.S. Congress and the state governments see the southern border as a low income and low economic

growth area, high unemployment, little infrastructure, and low educational statistics. The politician's point of view is what damages our border because they do not see the potential for our city; they don't know what's out here. We don't have to go to the top for all of our projects; we should start locally. There are many organizations that are making changes happen. There is not one solution to our problem. The most cost-efficient solution is for the community to come together but both governments and diplomats must allow binational cooperation.

The obstacles that both governments impose on binational cooperation at the local level represent a challenge to nongovernmental organizations on the border who are committed to working together on environmental issues. Unilateral action on one side of the border, although it may help ameliorate air or water quality problems, cannot have the profound and lasting effects of joint action. One of the challenges faced by border residents is lack of information. According to an ED staffer:

> It is very important for citizens and institutions to have access to information along with an educational program or outreach program that will teach citizens to become active in the community in regards to air, water, global warming which will better the quality of life. If we have governmental offices that will give us the tools to do this, we can have more cooperation.

The work of ED has received recognition in Mexico. One of their staff members received the first ever Individual Border Environmental Cooperation Commission Award at the 29th meeting of the U.S.–Mexico Border Environmental Cooperation Commission (BECC). ED was lauded for its collaboration with other organizations and institutions on both sides of the border.

The Rio Grande/Río Bravo Basin Coalition or the Coalición de la Cuenca Rio Grande/Río Bravo

The importance of coalition building in the region is of utmost importance to the environmental well being of the region. This aforementioned coalition is described by one of its members in the following manner: "We are a community organization; we don't work in one community, but work in different communities." The Rio Grande/Río Bravo Basin Coalition or the Coalición de la Cuenca Rio Grande/Río Bravo is another fine example of binational cooperation in the environmental arena. One of their major projects is the Día Del Río (Day of the River), which is celebrated throughout the entire river basin during the month of October. Día del Río is celebrated from the headwaters in the state of Colorado to Brownsville/Matamoros, where the river flows into the Gulf of Mexico. Over 25 local communities on both sides of the border organize different events that promote an appreciation for the river and promote conservation. Activities vary from picking up trash along the river, planting trees, sponsoring lectures about the river, to river festivals, to watching movies about the river, art and music contests and other festivities—all to raise awareness and demonstrate solidarity with the river and its inhabitants both upstream and downstream.

This partner-based coalition is funded through private foundations mostly and its leaders say it doesn't receive a significant amount of funding from the state. At the moment the coalition has approximately 50 partners who pay dues. The coalition is focused on raising awareness about the state of the river. One of their staffers explains their modus operandi:

> We are not very radical, or confrontational, or we don't take things to litigation. We try to find solutions, and different ways of doing things with all stakeholders. We do very little lobbying, only as the opportunity arises. It is a very little fraction of the work that we do.

Promoting the river through binational local community involvement has yielded positive results for this organization though they do acknowledge that this collaboration is challenging and rewarding. One of their staff members observed that organizing in Mexico was different than in the United States.

> Non-profit work is different and is not easy to come by in Mexico. I found that people can't really dedicate themselves to this type of work; I'm not saying that there aren't any professional non-profits, because there are certainly a great number of them. I feel that the need is greater over there, so it is more fulfilling for me to work down there. The non-profits get their funding from grants, and U.S. foundations give them their funding. There are many foundations that are based in Mexico as well. It's just harder to get the 501c3 status in Mexico. I was working with a lot of people that had full-time jobs that do not involve activism or organizing communities. There isn't time to write grants or to visit people for donations. It's common knowledge that there isn't a gift giving culture in Mexico. It's a different atmosphere. Here it's pretty common for people to give $100 to their favorite organization once or twice a year; it's not as common over there. You also have a lot of organizations like ours that help our brothers and sisters across the border.
> —Staffer, Rio Grande/Río Bravo Basin Coalition

Solidarity among people in the border region is strong among certain environmental groups and the aforementioned examples indicate that a true bond exists between people when they are united for one cause. Financial support is secondary to the promotion of cross-border solidarity and gravitating around an issue, in this case the river, that both unites and divides this border region.

A unique characteristic of this organization is that it has offices on both sides of the river in El Paso/Ciudad Juárez and a satellite office in Laredo. One of the staff members describes her experience working out of the Laredo office in the following manner:

> I was the only person down there, and was one of the only bilinguals, so I did a lot of work trying to recruit people on appreciating the river. When I first started working here, they gave me a list of communities and told me it was my job to try to recruit them, so I worked for the U.S. section and some of the communities they gave me were in Mexico. I like working across the border more because there's more potential and people are different in Mexico.
> —Staffer, Rio Grande/Río Bravo Basin Coalition

In her opinion, language can be an issue that precludes cross-border cooperation. She suggests that people who are involved in binational work should: "Certainly speak the language, you will be crippled if you don't speak it. You can't expect others to accommodate you." However, it is interesting to note that she is able and willing to accommodate others. This staff person indicated that she admired how hard Mexicans worked who were involved with the coalition. She added that:

> I'm a big person for taking things in context. I think that I have never had to work with someone from Mexico and feel as if they are not pulling their weight. I'm rarely in that position, if I can accommodate them it's not a problem for me.

When asked to describe the challenges and barriers of cross-border cooperation, she stated the following:

> There are a lot of barriers. One that comes to mind is different ways of working. For example, in the U.S. we have a listserv where we post things and my name is on there because I post a lot of things and my name is read hundreds of times. Well people in the U.S. feel that they know me, that there's a connection there because of that. When I finally meet the person they say, oh I know you; you're the girl that sends me that stuff, or good job. I could work with them over the phone because they feel there's a connection. I don't have to meet and in Mexico there needs to

be more of a connection than that. And it gets really hard. When you meet them, then the works gets easier because they've met you and had coffee with you or something. They can relate more to you when you meet them and you can work with them better. There needs to be a more solid connection.

—Staffer, Rio Grande/Río Bravo Basin Coalition

According to this staff member there are many other obstacles to cross-border cooperation.

I think that a pace needs to be set at a federal level to improve the quality of life and to a certain extent I am not satisfied with what has been done by both presidents. Right now both presidents have this camaraderie going on and they talk about certain issues, but they talk about repaying a water debt. But as an environmentalist you want them to talk about conservation and structures of the river that are completely ignored and abused and you would like for them to talk about water management and what could be done, but you can't always have what you want. I would like for it to be set in terms of what's good for the river and the water, but our president doesn't do that in the boundaries of our own country so that's going to be hard. We are not in an environmentally progressive state; we are in a ranching, conservative state; we need to work at a local level. We are a community organization; we work and respect all levels. Issues that El Paso and Las Cruces have are not issues that other cities along the basin have. Certainly you would like that federal, local and state levels were in sync. You see little bits of it at every level, but you wish it would move faster. I can't see that we are completely ignored at the federal level, or that the local community is not doing anything because it's not true. I'm not saying that everything would be ok if President Fox and President Bush were talking about the river.

—Staffer, Rio Grande/Río Bravo Basin Coalition

Sovereignty is another issue that impedes cross-border cooperation according to this staff person.

In the U.S., there is the question of sovereignty. I see U.S. agencies that need to work with Mexico on certain things, but don't because they don't want to step on Mexico's toes. You can just go in and not respect the border, but people don't want to bother with them. When I worked in Laredo, there was an organization that was giving away their computers and equipment to an organization in Mexico. It was very frustrating to see that their authorities would not allow them to cross the gifts without paying for them (import tax) and having the necessary documentation. Their bureaucratic process and having a border between the two countries is terrible. The act of giving to a Mexican organization is compounded by having to do it across the border.

—Staffer, Rio Grande/Río Bravo Basin Coalition

Hence, there are impediments on both sides of the border mandated by federal laws that impede good will and cooperation at the grassroots level. Obviously, government dynamics are very different than social dynamics. The organizing skills of the Rio Grande/Río Bravo Basin Coalition are a fine example of cross-border cooperation among people who have a common interest and need to protect the Rio Grande/Río Bravo.

Conclusions

If the political boundary did not exist, environmental issues would be dealt with at the local level, community to community. Because of the political boundary, environmental issues become foreign policy issues and escalate to the higher level of government, one that is less connected to local communities. If El Paso and Ciudad Juárez were two major urban centers in the interior of the United States or Mexico, environmental problems would be solved differently and locally, much like greater Phoenix or the Dallas-Fort Worth urban areas—international boundaries do not run through these areas and they address their environmental problems collectively. While all of the aforementioned efforts to promote binational cooperation in the environmental arena have provided useful and fruitful results, there is much room for improvement. JAC's success can be attributed to the formal and institutional support that it receives from agencies in both countries. ED is successful because of the credentials and vision of its staff. The Coalition has had a broad reaching impact on the entire River Grande/Río Bravo basin. People have rallied around the issue of the "river" and the Día del Río is now an event that has helped to bring people together from border cities in a meaningful way. Día del Río is celebrated by school children in Piedras Negras, Coahuila, environmental groups in Las Cruces, New Mexico, and community college students in Laredo, Texas. What is important about the impact of this organization is its geographical integration of border people around the issue of the river. This kind of integration is a way of promoting solidarity among people in the region; perhaps this can spread into other areas such as labor and human rights. We laud all efforts that promote the well being of the region on both sides of the border.

The environmental institutional shroud continues to wax and wane in the border region. While some tangible results are evident such as the waste-water treatment plants in Ciudad Juárez, it is necessary to address part of the problem but is not sufficient to meet the needs of all citizens. Long-term neglect, the growing population coupled with poverty, the harsh economic and social realities afflict the quality of life of border residents negatively. It requires an inordinate amount of time, resources, energy and knowledge to access these environmental institutions and make them accountable to the region. NGOs need to make their presence felt by setting time limits as well as accountability mechanisms on the environmental institutional shroud.

Despite the critique of the institutional shroud, it seems to facilitate cross-border collaboration to some extent. The fact that upper-level government environmental officials are meeting on the border and working together to address these issues is a huge step forward in the bilateral agenda. Border citizens crossing the international line to attend meetings on both sides of the border to present testimony and collaborate with other NGOs are positive signs that there is a will to work together. Unfortunately, the aforementioned barriers, linguistic, cultural, economic, are now coupled with heightened national security concerns and that too has had a major impact on cross-border activity.

CHAPTER 5

CROSS-BORDER TRADE: AN INSTITUTIONAL MODEL FOR LABOR UNIONS AND NGOS?

"Buy American!"
—nationalist slogan, appropriating the word *American*
for the United States rather than the geographic Americas

We are all tied up in the same emerging political and economic system.
We [in the U.S.] cannot understand that system without understanding
how it works in Mexico.
—Dale Hathaway, author

In chapter five, we examine business, commerce, and labor at the border. Here too, we find official machinery and institutions that facilitate business and commercial flows. Large-scale capital investments and the possibility of expanded market niches and profits facilitate this movement. The same cannot be said for labor and labor unions, mostly steeped in national rather than cross-national solidarities. Competition also underlies these relationships, both among business and labor.

Historically, both workers and capital have crossed the U.S.–Mexico border using official, formal, and informal channels. Workers and capital both cross the border in north-to-south and south-to-north directions. "Foreign" investors move capital across borders, whether the source of that capital is American investing in northern Mexico, or Mexican investing in the southwestern United States along the border. In the late twentieth century, both a large, high-profile El Paso bank and hotel were run by an investor group from the state of Chihuahua in Mexico. "Foreign" workers also move across borders, whether their movement is authorized or unauthorized by immigration laws. *Maquila* managers live in large numbers on the U.S. side of the border and work in enclaves on the Mexican side. Workers, ranging from professionals to maids, live in northern Mexico and work on the U.S. side.

In this chapter, we compare the business and worker cross-border and collaborative models. The factors that facilitate success are great for business, but many obstacles confront cross-border actions among workers, nonprofit organizations, and community-based organizations that represent workers. At the heart of this chapter is a case study of successful cross-border collaboration among progressive unionists who are threaded into the cross-border NGO, the Coalition for Justice in the *Maquiladoras* (CJM).

We address the strong personal ties that mushroomed into loose ties that expand the strength of collaborations in the heartlands of North America. In the not-so-successful examples of common interest without collaboration among unorganized workers, we also illustrate the weak legacies that that personal enmity sustains. We close the chapter with the still-delayed free trade in health insurance in systemic ways that would address access for the indigent and working poor.

Business Succeeds, Workers Stymied

In this section, we contrast the seeming success of business in developing cross-border relationships with that of workers. Much of this success is explained by the historic and contemporary institutional frameworks that legitimize, subsidize, and facilitate cross-border cooperation. Public policies operate from the local to the state, and national levels (the latter of which is known as "foreign policy," "international commerce"). Private institutions further this activity, deepening it and supplying it with services, contacts, and models. This impressive range and display of institutions is part of global capitalism, a hegemonic idea of free trade that powerful people have absorbed and educators have taught as natural, the outcomes of which have spread to and engulfed many countries, not the least of which are Mexico and the United States, two major trading partners in North America.

Contemporary global capitalism draws on the long-standing economic principle of comparative advantage: countries have advantageous qualities, such as expertise, labor of a particular cost, and/or natural resources, that together can be joined to maximize profits and reduce consumer costs. Corporations transcend national borders free of dissonance with national patriotism. Nationalism among workers and consumers, however, serves as an obstacle to cross-border solidarity. Here on the border we can see how this is played out among working-class people. According to a labor organizer we interviewed who is active in the region, many workers in the United States understand globalization and how that has led to the movement of goods and services and their jobs abroad: "At first, the workers here were angry at the Mexican workers; now they know it is not the worker they should be mad at, but the greedy company." Corporate officials and chief executive officers earn more than 50 times what they pay workers, the Mexican minimum wage. U.S. engineers and managers, living in El Paso and earning $5–10,000 monthly, live in huge homes over 3,000 square feet while those they manage earn less than $200 monthly and live in two-room concrete block homes. *Electronic Business* reported in 1998 that the CEO of one company that we know has *maquiladoras* earned the following: Salary $1,110,000, Bonus $11,861,652 and other compensation $144,067.[1]

The slogan, "Buy American," maintains the mystification of a global production process that fragments the division of labor across national boundaries. A supposed U.S. auto manufacturer may draw on more "foreign"-produced parts than a non-U.S. auto manufacturer who draws on U.S.-produced parts.[2] It is difficult to know what is a "national" product anymore, unless one knows formulas and percentages of production.

If hegemonic, transnational global free trade is the overarching idea that binds together many nations and corporate lobby groups, lesser attention is given to the subaltern concerns for transnational fair-value wages and reasonable labor standards. World capitalism predates workers' unions and international labor solidarity by several centuries. Only in the eighteenth century did modern labor unions emerge as we now know them.

In 1919, the International Labour Organization was born, later affiliated with the United Nations. ILO brings together three major stakeholders—labor, business, and the state—and it sets forth conventions on labor principles to which many countries adhere, at least on an abstract or policy level. Principles operate *within* countries, not transnationally. These principles are quite consistent with two countries, side-by-side, wherein *minimum* weekly wages are $25 (Mexico) on one side contrasted with $200 weekly (U.S.) on the other side. But even ILO conventions are unmet when state-level enforcement is lax. For example, although child labor is officially banned for those below age 15 in Mexico, girls work in *maquiladoras* with cheaply acquired documents asserting their adulthood. Several assassinated girls (see chapter 6) forfeited their lives after leaving second-shift *maquila* jobs where they worked as "adults." Many Juarenses are loath to talk publicly about the murders for the shame they believe it brings to their country. Such shame undermines prospects for national political accountability, despite international ILO leverage.

Unions tend to be organized on local and national bases, a long historic tradition. Idealists then and now call for international solidarity among workers, but national patriotism and national producer and consumer interests get in the way: workers in rich countries like the United States often seek to "protect" high-paying jobs and cheap goods, cheap at the expense of low-cost labor in other countries in corporations without accountability to the national-level democratic institutions that regulate labor and wage conditions. Democratic nation states offer concrete accountability for people in contrast to the diffuse United Nations system and World Trade Organization.

Yet regional institutions provide some umbrella structures of accountability, more diffuse than nation-states and more dependent on legal, bureaucratic, and foreign policy officials than ordinary politics in a democracy. Compared with the European Union's employment standards and social policies,[3] the NAFTA institutional shroud is weak, yet it nevertheless provides the policy, legitimacy, and potential accountability to transnational business and worker relations. (Chapter 6 deals with migrant workers.)

One of the NAFTA side agreements, the North American Agreement on Labor Cooperation (NAALC), established a National Administrative Office (NAO) in the United States, Canada, and Mexico to investigate labor rights violations. From 1994 to 2001, 23 complaints have been filed against employers across national boundaries. Coalitions of organizations file complaints; hearings about these complaints may result in documented findings with remedies that range from the weak (holding seminars, intergovernmental consultations) to the strong remedy of economic sanctions by one government against another.[4] Strong remedies have never yet been adopted under these rules, yet the mechanism and ensuing process move cross-border solidarity considerably beyond consciousness-raising activities and mutual support.

Mexico and the United States come together in a free trade arrangement that facilitates capital investment across borders and the cross-border provision of goods and services. But most workers from both countries have yet to cross the borderlines of solidarity that would challenge transnational capital. National patriotism, however contrived and ritualized in sports and educational settings, separates workers as much as free trade joins global capital. The institutional frameworks in which workers make claims are relatively new, weak, and not readily transparent and accountable. But the frameworks provide accountability tools that make complaints and findings visible and amenable to organizing around strong policies and remedies for unjust practices.

The Business Model

Capital crossing has sometimes occurred with the blessings, financial incentives, and subsidies of both federal governments. Labor crossing has occurred through temporary worker programs, work permits, and lax enforcement of border crossing guards. Mexico and the United States have long been important trading partners, and the relationships were augmented with three huge benchmarks: (1) Mexico's Border Industrialization Program in 1965 and corresponding U.S. incentives for business to invest in export-processing factories, known as *maquiladoras,* with limited tariffs; (2) Mexico's entry to the GATT, or General Agreement on Tariffs and Trade in 1986, in the move toward global free trade; and (3) NAFTA in 1994, an agreement to reduce tariffs over a decade.

Local governments also bless and subsidize businesses, including cross-business collaboration. El Paso is home to four Chambers of Commerce, ranging from the Greater Chamber with its many divisions and programs to the Hispanic Chamber, champion of small business, the Black and Korean Chambers. The chambers are tax-exempt, non profit organizations. They are adept at obtaining funds from their own members and grants that enhance the profitability of their members and free-riders in business generally. They have been successful recipients of funding from sources like the Community Development Block Grant, the Empowerment Zone, school districts, and the city's Economic Development Department. Chamber leaders are well represented on many public and nonprofit boards. There is little devious or partisan (if by partisan we mean the Republicans and Democrats) politicking in this pro-business, receptive climate. A widespread belief among El Pasoans is that "we need more jobs and better paying jobs." Election polls confirm this, as does campaign rhetoric.

Even in the hotly contentious, officially nonpartisan El Paso mayoral elections of 2001, candidates differed in the kinds of pro-business strategies proposed, primarily around who gets access to capital—big versus small, local versus out-of-town capital.[5] All the candidates, from the initial six to the run-off election among the final two, spoke positively about cross-border collaboration. In El Paso, politicians who speak the language of social justice and redistribution look to wider access to capital and business growth to solve border problems.

In Mexico, the commerce and industrial chambers, known by their Spanish acronyms of Cámara Nacional de Comercio (CANACO) National Chamber of Commerce and Cámara Nacional de la Industria de Transformación (CANACINTRA), have long been associated with the state, but not as tightly controlled as the labor, peasant, and middle-class sectors.[6] The state was once nearly synonymous with the Partido Revolucionario Institucional (PRI), (Institutional Revolutionary Party) but PRI's monopoly ended at the state and local levels in northern Mexico during the 1980s. Businessmen associated with the Partido Acción Nacional, or PAN, (National Action Party), plus some who exited the PRI, triumphed in local *municipio* (municipality) elections from 1983–1986, and from 1992 and beyond. After a probable PAN guber-natorial victory in the 1986 Chihuahua elections, not recognized by the Federal Election Institute, PAN went on to win the 1992 elections, but then lost in 1998. *Norteño* businessmen have had an uneasy relationship with official parties and with the extreme centralization of power in Mexico's peculiar federalism, one that extracts and appropriates local resources.[7]

In the 1998 election for the Municipal President in Ciudad Juárez, an ex-CANACO *lideresa* (leader, feminine) ran under the more radical and left-oriented Partido de la Revolución Democrática (PRD). In Ciudad Juárez, too, business-oriented politicians use social justice and redistribution rhetoric. There is a link between elected officials and the business community, especially the *maquiladora* industry. Owners of industrial parks are often supportive of politicians who promote the *maquila* industry. Likewise, owners of industrial parks pass themselves off as providing jobs and opportunities for people who would otherwise not have them.[8]

Is Business a Model for Collaboration?

We began with the question of whether business offers any collaborative models for replication in the labor sector. Business collaboration enjoys facilitators to cross-border organization, ranging from the sheer profits to be made to the subsidies business receives for such collaboration. Local, county, *municipio,* state, and federal governments on both sides of the border promote cross-border cooperation among businesses. The state and local governments in Chihuahua, for example, are in the busi-ness of luring more companies into Ciudad Juárez and the region. Elected officials and business leaders in El Paso believe that residuals from that investment will trickle into the local economy. Bilingual billboards in the region announce "factory" space for lease in Ciudad Juárez, and there are usually two telephone numbers provided, one in the United States and the other in Mexico. El Paso's Greater Chamber of Commerce has a person whose title is Economic Development and Binational Development Vice-President. This individual is in charge of activities related to Mexico and visits Ciudad Juárez frequently to attend meetings with the Cámara Nacional de la Industria de Transformación (CANACINTRA). The person in this position promotes the region (broadly defined) for economic development and to improve commerce, generate jobs, new industries, and attempts for local business to expand. The government of Chihuahua has a Secretaría de Desarrollo Industrial (Secretariat of Industrial Development) and has people responsible for promoting economic development in Ciudad Juárez: "One of my main functions is to attract foreign investment in the region, principally the city," as one of our informants said proudly.

While governments and chambers of commerce are attracting business and promoting cross-border activities, why is it so difficult for human rights organizations, environmental, and labor NGOs to do the same? In the case of business and commerce, the institutional shroud is very well developed and extends widely on both sides of the border. Coupled with financial resources, it is easy to see how business can operate on both sides of the border with great ease. We know of no government officials in charge of cross-border civic capacity building.

High Business Stakes

On the eve of NAFTA, opportunities seemed ripe for expanded markets and new profits. According to 1994's *The Arthur Andersen North American Business Sourcebook,* North America was a $6.5 trillion marketplace. These figures were stated repeatedly throughout the 621-page manual, in bold heading and regular text. Wages in Mexico also featured prominently.[9] In 1993, a *New York Times* article touted "America's Newest Industrial Belt," not coincidentally using the word America to describe northern Mexico as "an almost 51st state," (remarks that would make most nationalist Mexicans cringe). The article contains a bar graph contrasting top-paid skilled workers at Ford Motor's plants in Mexico and the United States: $2.87 per hour versus $20.21 per hour respectively.[10] What business concerned with costs of production and profit return could afford to ignore such startling facts, in a context of growing globally organized production?

Collaboration
Businesses are willing to pay to facilitate collaboration through membership fees, a tax-deductible business expense. In exchange for

steep annual membership fees of $250–$1,500, and honorary contributor designations of $2,500 to $10,000, members of the World Trade Center El Paso/Ciudad Juárez are promised business assistance programs, online global communications, networking opportunities, conference rooms, and publications with a secret password to its full website. Solunet is an El Paso business with an easy-access website, that sells an annual edition of *The Complete Twin Plant Handbook,* with an Internet promise of unlocking the $70 billion per year *maquiladora* market.

To promote transnational investment, public international institutions like the World Bank and International Monetary Fund (IMF) have advocated supportive climates for business growth and development. They have done so in the name of good governance, legal transparency, efficient government, and accountability.[11] Investors analyze "political risk" factors, such as corruption, that add to investment costs.

Both Mexico and the United States have trimmed government operations over the last twenty years, but much work would need to be done to synchronize local government building and fire codes. Increasingly, though, local governments become less relevant given the emergence of insurability and regulation standards provided in the private sector. For example, ISO standards are used for many business accounting, construction, and operating practices.[12] Businesses incorporate these standards for transnational insurance, real estate value maintenance, and resale considerations. Private trainers and public universities provide training in various ISO standards. With these standards, it matters less to international business whether local governments are out of date, inefficient, or ineffective. Although there are social accountability standards, we know of few global standards for environmental stewardship and employment or on nonprofit registration. The United Nations regularly offers ILO-type business and labor guidelines and standards that sovereign governments are free to adopt, ignore, and/or implement.

Competition
Businesses do more than collaborate with or sell services to one another. They also compete with one another. Like anywhere, the border is littered with failed businesses and bankruptcies. The Marxist dictum— "one capitalist kills another"—is not an encouraging model for other non-business civic, union, and other organizations. The focus on competition in the business arena is contrary to the focus on cooperation that other sectors strive for. For example, in the environmental arena, cooperation is always a key word in any government document or treaty, and within human rights agendas as well. Businesses seem to cooperate only in order to strengthen their competitive positions.

Competition is not what NGOs seek to model or emulate. However, in communities with limited resources, organizers compete with one another for the limited public or private foundation funding unless they cast their funding requests in a wider pool that is regional, national or international. Those that operate with local blinders face finite sums: when one gains, another loses. Such has been the fate of organizations in the Community Development Block Grant process in El Paso and other cities. The chase for funds engenders a sometimes ruthless and personalist competition among nonprofit and grassroots organizations. The competition for resources is intense simply because the need for funding is so great and the amount of grant money available is so little. On the surface, businesses seem self-sufficient, although government subsidies belie that superficial interpretation. Nonprofits are generally not self-sufficient, but rather dependent upon the benevolence and availability of funders, unless they can generate membership dues and fee-based revenue.

Unions are divided into numerous "locals" with different names and numbers. Each has its own due structure, sometimes burdensome to members (who may shop around for lower dues or leave to join the chronic "free rider" problem of unions—people who benefit from gains without contributing to the costly process of achieving those gains). While some cities nominally unify unions through Central Labor Union Councils, these councils may offer more symbolic than real collective power. For example, political candidates affirm support during elections and on important holidays, but in between such events, labor union councils primarily hold their own in an economy with steadily declining union members as proportion of the labor force. In the United States in general and El Paso specifically, unions collaborate more with one another than with other NGOs.[13]

Ethnographic Moment 5.1: Annual Labor Day Breakfast, El Paso

Around three hundred people attended El Paso's annual labor breakfast in 2001 at the city's only union hotel. Organized labor leaders from the fragmented array of task-oriented unions attended: sheet metal workers, postal workers, building and construction trade workers, among them. Of course, many belong to labor federations, like the AFL-CIO, and the El Paso Central Labor Union sponsored the event.

Many politicians attended, including judges and candidates for judge. A 36-page booklet contained the agenda on page 19, topped with U.S. and Texas flags, surrounded by advertisements from union councils and pictures of politicians and lawyers who call themselves "friends of labor." We saw no organizers of the non-union workers, such as the Asociación de Trabajadores Fronterizos, La Mujer Obrera, or EPISO, although the front table contained three priests, one of whom was one of EPISO's many "co-chairs." The keynote speaker, the late Msgr. George Gilmary Higgins, known nationally as "the labor priest," chided the breakfast audience for waiting until almost lunch time to let him speak (after introductions of many politicians) and for the non-existent coalition with IAF groups (like EPISO). Labor–IAF coalitions are typical in other parts of the country. Higgins represents that part of the Catholic Church which stresses "preferential work for the poor." His remarks were pro-immigrant, both for reasons of humanity and for their potential presence in organized labor. We saw none of the Border Prayer Network people who have a strong presence in the maquila-driven *Strategic Alliance.*

Each of the round tables in the room made a border and North American regional statement with their centerpieces of four decorative and colorful flags: U.S., Mexico, Texas, and New Mexico. The event began with the presentation of national colors. Several youth marched solemnly to the front, carrying flags. The Master of Ceremonies noted afterward how this "makes you proud to be an American." Everyone stood to sing the (U.S.) National Anthem and put their hands across their hearts reciting the Pledge of Allegiance. As breakfast began to be delivered, music filled the room, with De Colores at the lead. The song is associated with Cesar Chávez and the United Farm Workers. A member of El Paso's state delegation, Norma Chávez (unrelated) worked hard in previous years to have Chávez recognized as a state holiday.

A highlight of the day involved a brief but passionate speech in Spanish from a Mexico City-based leader of Mexico's independent union, the Frente Auténtico Laboral. He spoke about solidarity across national lines around the free trade agreement, which needs drastic revision or repeal, many in this crowd would agree. We saw no labor leaders from Ciudad Juárez.

The morning closed around lunch with an emotionally delivered rendition of the song, God Bless America. It was sung after the Benediction, just as the National Anthem was sung before the Invocation.

Workers can also be in competition with one another for jobs. The U.S.–Mexico border has been described as a region of Bantustans (reminiscent of apartheid South Africa's territorial enclaves).[14] Despite low wages and per capita incomes in the U.S. borderlands, workers' wages are five to ten times those of workers in northern Mexico. El Paso's local unions, representing only five percent of the workforce, worry about protecting jobs. El Paso holds a dubious distinction: it has the largest number of NAFTA-displaced workers compared to other U.S. cities. Most of those displaced workers did not belong to unions, and organizers in non-union groups fault unions for attending to their own members rather than to workers generally.[15] For example, garment factories have a bleak future in El Paso, Texas, and the United States generally, yet some community-based organizations seek protection for these industries because their constituents are at least getting paychecks for now. Workers like these are "overpaid" in the United States, according to business thinking, and will eventually lose out when firms move to Ciudad Juárez or elsewhere.

Nonprofit and union organizations exhibit some similarity, including competition among them, but the obstacles nonprofits encounter in cross-border organizing are much greater than business. There is no "market" niche to be developed, advanced, and profited from, for civil society tends to operate within countries, engaging for accountability with national or subnational institutions. Business marches to national and international drummers, both consumers and investors, to whom they are accountable albeit in a regulated economy. Business controls far more resources, including subsidies from the government, and gains official support through national policies that facilitate free trade. While national governments usually do not prohibit cross-border civil society organizing, they do not subsidize it, facilitate it, or encourage it through official policies and incentives. If couched in economic development, however, governments do promote cross-border activity for business. Civil democracy is a far lower priority than the economy.

An example of how business cooperated in the border region with the blessings of both governments is the establishment of the Dedicated Commuter Lane (DCL) in the El Paso–Ciudad Juárez community. One obstacle frequently mentioned as an impediment to cross-border cooperation is the inordinate amount of time that people must wait on bridges to cross into the United States. The Dedicated Commuter Lane permit is available to people who meet certain requirements, pass a Federal Bureau of Investigation background check, pay an application fee to the INS, and pay the fees to the office of Caminos y Puentes Federales (CAPUFE) (Federal Roads and Bridges). The El Paso Foreign Trade Association has all the necessary documentation available online for people who want to have the Dedicated Commuter Lane option. The fees total $129 to the INS and $268 to the Mexican Department of Transportation. Congressman Silvestre Reyes (D-TX) issued a press release in January 2001 in response to a Mexican government announcement that the cost of the DCL lane would be increased. Congressman Reyes immediately contacted the Mexican embassy and Secretary of State Madeline Albright.[16]

"The goal of the Dedicated Commuter Lane is to ease congestion, long lines, and pollution at the international bridge," continued Reyes. "Increasing the fee for users of the DCL will not only lead to further congestion along the bridge, but the manner in which this was decided is contrary to the spirit of binational cooperation. It is not our role to mandate how much the Mexican government charges their citizens; however it is in the best interest of the United States, Mexico, and the communities along the border not to make these decisions unilaterally.

It is interesting to note how quickly the congressman responded to this modest increase. After all, those most affected by the increase are the people who can probably afford to pay. One wonders if the congressman is apt to respond to other unilateral actions so quickly. DCLers are an elite group of people who can afford to pay the fees as well as meet certain requirements. Why can't this privilege be extended to other border residents for a nominal fee?

Distant decisions, such as the one just described, are made about transnational trade, whether in national capitols or in the headquarters of corporations and unions. The monetary opportunities and potential gains loom large in business, but are murkier in labor given the discourse of protection and loss. Distant decisions are also made in lobbying efforts and priorities. National chambers and unions are not always ideologically congruent with those at local levels.

On the eve of NAFTA, local businesses in El Paso were hardly poised to take advantage of the impending change. One study drawing on a El Colegio de la Frontera Norte (COLEF) study of 800 small businesses in Ciudad Juárez and Nuevo Laredo and 700 small business chamber members in El Paso, Laredo, and San Antonio found that small firms with Mexican-heritage owners did not have the technology, contacts, capital, and networks to finesse growth in the impending era. In El Paso and Laredo, small businesses had focused on retail and wholesale trade, taking advantage of what was in principle "unfree trade": Mexicans crossed to purchase in the United States with little investment and advertising.[17] Local business, without loose but potentially resource-rich ties to the regional, national, and global levels are also at some disadvantage in the changing free-trade regimes.

Thus, when business is analyzed, we must differentiate among local, national, and international; small, medium, and large. Such differentiation is also required for NGOs. Yet even with an acknowledgement of such diversity, the opportunity structures and facilitators for business far surpass those for cross-border organizational activists. Civil society could try to model itself on business, but organizations are structurally disadvantaged and gaps exist between business and NGO capacities to operate on cross-border bases. Still they try. Below are examples of successes and failures, focusing on workers, whether unionized or not. We conclude with attention to portable cross-border insurance both for workers and small businesses, many of the latter of which are unable or unwilling to offer health benefits to employees.

Cross-Border Organizing Cases

Below we examine labor organizing across borders, highlighting our conceptual criteria of personal ties that are connected to regional, national, and international ties. We also note how leaders come from both sides and bring linguistic and cultural expertise to their collaborative processes. Given the enormous challenge to cross-border organizing for social justice outcomes, we would hardly call these cases final successes in terms of achieving goals. We consider them to be pursuing pathways toward success, inspiring models for other cross-border visionaries.

FAT–UE: Successful Collaboration

In Mexico, few labor unions are independent from political parties and tainted pacts with government to keep wages low. A major exception is the Frente Auténtico del Trabajo, (Authentic Labor Front) or FAT. The FAT works in cross-border solidarity with the United Electrical Workers, a U.S. union, at local and binational levels. We analyze the strong, personal origins of these ties, solidified in institutional and loose ties, and concrete manifestations of both strong and weak ties.

Both unions have a long history that predates cross-border collaboration. The United Brotherhood of Electrical Workers was born in 1949 (formerly part of the Congress of Industrial Organizations or the CIO), and the FAT was born in 1960, in a declaration committed to "Christian Unionism." From its inception, leaders gave priority to worker education, or what was called *formación*—formation that went beyond information conveyance to transformation that would[18]:

> convert workers who have been shaped in an abusive world of limited expectations into workers who fully realize that it is their right as

human beings to be able to live a life of dignity in a fully democratic environment.

This philosophy underwent transitions toward the principle of *auto-gestión,* or "workers' democracy through self-management," similar to what U.S. unions call rank and file unionism,[19] although U.S. unions range considerably in their top-down management styles. The FAT took on both national and international businesses and corporations, a primary obstacle of which involved process, or the ability to organize freely.

Personal relationships birthed cross-border relationships. At a General Electric plant in Ft. Wayne, Indiana, worker Tom Lewandowski visited Polish workers in Solidarity (the worker-opposition movement) and sister-city relationships, a visit that spawned a visit to Indiana from workers in Poland. Just a few years later in 1993, Lewandowski and a FAT organizer exchanged visits, creating ripple effects of contacts that reduced the nationalist xenophobia. In the first border field experience, U.S. workers took a "Visit Your Jobs" eastern border tour near Reynosa, and Matamoros, (in Tamaulipas state) border cities to McAllen and Brownsville, Texas, with a unionized TV crew that produced a half-hour show.[20]

How is cross-border solidarity facilitated? What evidence exists of its accomplishments? Recall our critique in chapter two of global solidarity movements that involve consciousness-raising disconnected from action. The successful cross-border collaboration highlighted in this chapter goes well beyond the limitations we critique. It operates in the heartlands and in the borderlands. In the national heartlands, UE–FAT solidarity is documented in action: mutual support through picket lines, sharing resources for striking workers, and bilingual assistance to organizing drives among Spanish-speaking workers in the United States. With the legal machinery now available under NAFTA, organizers make claims to the NAO offices in North America, although the enforcement and change mechanisms are still weak, as examples below illustrate.

NAFTA, originally formed to facilitate business transactions, passed the U.S. Congress with side agreements that focused on labor and the environment, as outlined earlier. One of the first tests of the institutional shroud that legitimized workers' rights was the attempt to form an independent FAT metalworkers' union at the Hyundai auto parts Han Young plant at Tijuana, in the state of Baja California Norte at the westernmost border. The plant violated Mexico's unenforced labor laws, and alliances across borders made illegal practices visible with publicity, pickets at Hyundai dealerships, and a formal complaint with the National Administrative Office. Most abuses are filed with the NAO against plants in Mexico (11), then the U.S. (7), and last, Canada (2), and result in studies, seminars, and interministerial consultations. The NAO in 1998 found that Han Young had violated Mexico's laws. This finding did not end Mexico's toleration of continuing illegal actions against organizers and plant workers thereafter. With the pattern of weak enforcement, both nationally and transnationally, Dale Hathaway concludes that the NAO has not protected workers' rights.[21]

Legal machinery needs to be strengthened, if workers' rights are to be protected. Currently, transnational corporations are free to fire worker activists and blacklist activists, with little more than an investigation. Corporations and businesses are free to pursue practices, and it is the exception wherein complaints are filed rather than the rule. It is almost impossible to register new unions in some cities. Corrupt unions continue, and thugs intimate organizers and pack organizing meetings. Reports like these come from the hard and electronic copies of *Mexico Labor News & Analysis,* a UE-supported effort that provides careful and methodical documentation and reports and is widely distributed through listservs—comprising in and of itself an example of regional and international loose ties.

Locally, strong and personal ties maintain and solidify connections. For example, worker-exchange visits continue on at least an annual basis. Union activists visit one another from afar and close up, among borderlands residents. In July 2001, UE brought a group of union and student leaders to the border for field experiences and visits with workers at the FAT education center known as CETLAC, or the Centro de Estudios y Taller Laboral, an NGO. One of us interacted extensively with the delegation, as well as engaging in preparatory conversations. Locally, UE and FAT organizers know one another, attend one another's events, and show solidarity.

The obstacles to free and fair union organizations are far greater than the competition and alliances formed among businesses. If the terms of NAFTA are to be changed, workers' organizations in North American countries must exercise proactive change and vigilance in national capitals, just as their business and corporate counterparts have set precedents for. Publicity must be generated for illegal deeds, beyond electronic listservs such as *frontera, Mexico Labor News & Analysis,* and other activist fronts. Cross-border solidarity has spread to the national heartlands, although pro-worker advocacy faces uphill battles.

The Coalition for Justice in the Maquiladoras

Fortunately, other organizations operate in alliances as well, adding the strength of loose ties. To illustrate attentiveness to worker justice, we use the Coalition for Justice in the *Maquiladoras* (CJM). The CJM consists of over 100 coalition members from Canada, the United States, and Mexico. Their 30-member board of directors is rather diverse: a newspaper publisher from Nuevo Laredo, a lawyer from Mexico City, representatives of religious orders, and activists. Importantly, leaders of CJM overlap with leaders in other cross-border organizing successes, including unions. Of the 30 board members, 15 are from Mexico, two from Canada, and thirteen from U.S. groups. The modus operandi of the CJM is multifaceted.

They organize workshops for workers addressing issues such as sexual harassment awareness and toxic chemicals. They host events such as the "Public Forum for Freedom of Association" which more than 300 people attended in the gathering of union leaders, political leaders, and academics that took place on the border in support of workers rights.[22]

A person, part of the CJM, has shared how they encourage religious orders and others to invest their money in corporations that have *maquiladoras* in Mexico. Once a certain number of shares has been purchased, the shareholder is invited to attend the shareholder meetings and vote on resolutions. This kind of economic/political activism is limited to those who have money to invest. Once a person has reached that level, resolutions can be introduced and the rest of the shareholders can vote on the measure. While not all resolutions that they have introduced have been well received and passed, (after all we are mostly talking about potential voters who want to maximize their profits), the CJM has been effective in bringing about changes in *maquiladora* working conditions.

Consider this example. A CJM staff person described a situation where workers from a *maquiladora* went to meet with the CEO of a company at their headquarters in the United States. The meeting was originally supposed to take place in Texas, but the CEO was unable to make the meeting. Subsequently, he sent his private jet for the CJM staff member and the workers who had been invited. Workers expressed some of their concerns ranging from lack of toilet paper in restrooms to recent work-related injuries. The CEO was perplexed because this particular company had maintained an injury-free record for quite some time. The workers indicated otherwise. The CEO asked for the injury report files for that plant for the week. When he received the report (almost immediately) there were absolutely no injuries reported on the days the workers had indicated and of course the plant had an injury-free record because the injuries were not reported. Quickly he called the plant directly and asked for an explanation regarding the injury reports and at the same time requested that the restrooms be stocked with supplies. Subsequently, the responsible party was fired for not reporting the injuries.

The CJM also has addressed issues of sexual harassment in the work place. *Maquiladora* women are asked to provide a soiled sanitary pad to prove that they are not pregnant. This practice is shameful and humiliating, but surprisingly widespread in the *maquiladora* industry.

Many *maquiladoras* have medical staff at their place of work. While this is an extremely nice benefit to have on site, their reasons for being there were not all altruistic. Birth control was "pushed" on the women by the medical staff in some plants. Work injuries were treated on site and this prevented the worker from seeking treatment at the Instituto Mexicano de Seguro Social (IMSS) (Mexican Institute of Social Insurance). The work-related injury was never reported and subsequently the company monitored the worker on the worksite. IMSS is rather lenient in giving workers time off to recuperate from injuries and therefore the company must continue paying the worker. Having a medical staff at the place of work avoided this from happening. There have been instances where the workers were told to not go to IMSS lest they would lose their jobs.

The CJM is a fine example of economic/political activism that has had some impact on the well-being of workers. CJM staff members also visit local schools and raise awareness about the labor practices of multi-national corporation abroad and how those practices affect the price of items that students wear. For example, CJM staff members ask students what brand of tennis shoes are they wearing and how much they cost. The link is then made between consumer goods, corporate profits, and exploited workers. This is a good way to socialize people into thinking about their consumption patterns.

Besides education, CJM accomplishments can spawn ripple effects. It produced methodical studies on living wage standards in northern. Mexico, a living standard that equals at least four times Mexico's minimum wage. It has also produced, in Spanish and English, occupational safety guidelines and *maquiladora* standards of conduct,[23] reminiscent of Reverand Sullivan's standards for foreign industries under apartheid South Africa. Cross-border activists need not reinvent these wheels, but rather build on a purposeful base with its networks to move awareness toward problem solving and social justice.

Within other Unions?

Where, readers may wonder, are other unions who represent the bulk of rank and file members? And what about the unorganized workers, or those who belong to community-based organizations? The AFL–CIO is a large union with many international alliances. During the Cold War, it allied with Latin American pro-government, anti-communist unions under the umbrella of the American Institute for Free Labor Development (AIFLD), supported with U.S. governmental funds. Pro-government unions had a weak track record for representing members' interests.

John Sweeney assumed leadership of the AFL–CIO in the mid-1990s, moving the union beyond its national protectionism position. Major unions supported the political party that promised the least harm to workers under NAFTA. The Clinton-negotiated side agreements of NAO and training for NAFTA-displaced workers did little to change the structure of transnational business operations in North America. The new face of the AFL-CIO nationally points toward more internationalism, organizing drives among unorganized workers, and support for immigrants, such as the 2000 declaration to support another amnesty for immigrants.

The AFL–CIO co-signed, with other North American workers and labor lawyers in organizations that total 18 million members, a letter to President Vicente Fox about the violation of labor rights and freedoms in Mexico on March 28, 2001.[24] Co-signers asked the President to respect the pledge he made during the campaign to support the document, *20 Commitments to Trade Union Freedom and Democracy.* The freedom to organize, with secret ballots free of threats from thugs, continues to be an issue. Canada and Mexico engage in Ministerial Consultation over these matters, with Canada's NAO exercising the strongest leadership among the three countries.

Locally, the AFL–CIO focused on organized workers and participated in El Paso's Central Labor Union Council. Its narrow focus on the already organized, amid the tragedies that beset unorganized workers with garment factory closings and NAFTA-related displacement, is remembered with some bitterness on the part of CBOs representing displaced workers. Even though the AFL-CIO has shifted nationally, local shifts are not so evident, both on the part of local leaders and wary CBO leaders. With the lens of personal strong ties, one sees personalism do its destructive work in maintaining the memory, not of solidarity, but of nonsolidarity. Such memories undermine collective power among those with common interests and maintain divisions among them that forestall collaboration.

Ethnographic Moment 5.2: Generic Radical Organization (GRO)

They started over twenty years ago, at a time when no one cared about the exploited people for whom they advocate. In the early days, organizers went for weeks without any income, but somehow they managed to scrape by with help from friends. Now they generate some revenue for the organization and their modest sustenance, but they work at least sixty-hour weeks and often more. It is their whole life, but a lifetime of stress and absolute commitment. Some of their colleagues just burn out and leave.

They remember the founders with reverence. They also remember those who ignored and betrayed them and their people. "And did the unions ever support us?" leaders ask with cynicism. A certain bitterness and persistent suspicion informs their work. Potential allies are scrutinized carefully and often rejected out of hand. In coalitions, one cannot control the partners.

They've been burned before and are unwilling to submit themselves once again in collaborations and coalitions. When outsiders contact them about new coalitions, they wonder: "what are they really up to?" No words are to be taken at face value. "How are they going to try to use us this time?" They maintain their "critical" stance with rudeness, sarcasm, and provocative questions. The questions are good ones; questions like these need to be asked. They demand responses that can never be achieved in their lifetimes. Each time they achieve no "success," it supports their dismal worldview.

They believe in collective decision-making. Decisions consume enormous amounts of time, and factionalism prevails within the organization. Once a decision is made, only the jefe/jefa (boss) speaks the consistent line. No one else should speak to outsiders. How ironic that these democratic people's organizations seem so authoritarian.

Those for whom they advocate [we will call them advocatees] are sometimes fearful of the wrenching personal attacks that precede and pervade decisions. Advocatees instead watch from the wings, careful not to get too close to one faction or another. They dare not speak to outsiders; a safe strategy is to report all contacts to the jefe. Advocatees respond to leaders' strategies as best they can, appearing at demonstrations, but not always privy to the reason and rationale behind actions. Some say, "As soon as we're on our feet economically, we're out of here." Others remain, grateful for advocates' sacrifices. But they cringe at the language and rudeness.

How might one characterize these organizations at the border? Are they cacique (political boss) driven? Are they Stalinist? Whatever, they are authoritarian, even as their rhetoric is collective democracy.

This is an exaggerated, generic case. Organizations like these exist in most big cities. They can follow one of several paths. First, they fall by the wayside, for others find them impossible to work with (including to fund) and their members eventually judge their circumstances to be unbearable. Second, they form different fronts, maintaining their "radical" edge with one and pursuing other strategies through other(s). Third, they become non-profit organizations, a bit top-heavy, or heavy-handed in management style. They may undergo "transitions," akin to China's cultural revolutions, to renew their missions and achieve partial internal democracy.

Cross-border business alliances have been the most fruitful and most intense of all interactions on the border. It is clear that individuals are motivated by economic incentives help to promote business opportunities across borders. Local, county, *municipio,* and state governments also facilitate this intense border business interaction because they are interested in fomenting economic development as well as establishing a potential tax base. It is easier to install a *maquila* in Ciudad Juárez than it is to establish a cross-border human rights organization. Thus cross-border interaction has traditionally resulted from actors pursuing their own interests and establishing relationships to satisfy their own short-term economic objectives.[25] Clearly, the short-term economic objectives have not become long-term ventures.

Workers' Health Benefits

As a metropolitan area of more than two million people, residents of El Paso and Juárez confront problems of access to affordable and responsive health care. Poverty itself aggravates health care problems: people may not have the money or insurance to pursue wellness, preventive, and primary care. Behaviors like these may delay people's contact with medical providers until it is too late for remedies and crisis care is tapped in hospital emergency rooms. Environmental problems may trigger health problems, such as pollution and unpaved roads, amid the dust and wind of the high desert, aggravating respiratory and asthmatic conditions.

Contrasts in the health care systems of the United States and Mexico could not be greater. The U.S. health care system is a hodge-podge of market-based, government-subsidized, and individual health care. No public commitment to meet the health care needs of the U.S. population has ever existed. People with money and insurance have the best access to health care. Mexico has a public commitment to meet the health care needs of its population, but it is a paper and rhetorical commitment given the scarcity of budgetary resources. For example, in Mexico the IMSS provides coverage to workers who are employed in the formal sector. In the state of Chihuahua in the year 2000 the IMSS reported that 771,585 people were insured, leaving many uninsured,[26] reliant on private care, an under-resourced public health system, and charity for medical services. Due to the nature of the Mexican economy, many people work in the informal sector and subsequently cannot avail themselves of the IMSS services.

El Pasoans have a high rate of uninsured residents, or 37 percent according to a 1997 study. Local health providers estimate that 70,000 El Pasoans, or approximately 10 percent of the population, fall into the category of "indigent." Juarenses technically have access to public and private hospitals and clinics, but often the waits are long and the technical facilities lacking. Juarenses with money cross from south to north, tapping facilities in El Paso and other parts of the United States. Hospitals even have special staff to interact with Mexican consumers who may extend their stay along with other family members who need motel and other accommodations in El Paso. El Pasoans with limited money cross from north to south, tapping the Mexican medical and dental providers, along with hospital and pharmacy facilities. El Pasoans even tap veterinarian providers in Ciudad Juárez, and informal pet passports emerge to deal with possible difficulties at the international ports of entry. The costs of care are dramatically less in Juárez. In the mid 1990s, approximately 60 percent of households in a near-downtown and a *colonia* neighborhood cited that at least one member utilized services in Ciudad Juárez. According to a private hospital in Juárez, ten per cent of its users are El Pasoans. Medical providers on both sides of the border have yet to develop documentation or tracking systems of cross-border medical care.[27]

Publicity periodically surges over one controversial aspect of cross-border care: crossing to birth and thereby to create citizenship for an infant. Citizenship by birth is an historical legal principle from the 15th amendment to the U.S. Constitution that protected the citizenship of ex-slaves after emancipation. Among low-income Juarenses, crossing to give birth would occur in either the public hospital or in one of many midwifery clinics, for Texas is one of a few states that license midwives.

Stories abound on this cross-border birthing practice, but concrete data on trends are lacking.

There is anecdotal evidence that people who lack insurance in El Paso and do not want to end up with a major medical debt deliver their babies in Ciudad Juárez for a much more nominal fee. This is more common if one parent is an American citizen and immediately registers the birth at the American consulate as a "child born abroad of an American citizen."

People who tap medical providers recognize the extensive documentation requested for treatment, from social security number to details about insurance, residence, and employment. These questions, invasive for tracking and repayment purposes to citizens and residents alike, are threatening to legal immigrants (known by the acronym as LPRs, or Legal Permanent Residents) and to undocumented residents. LPRs may worry that subsidized treatment may put them in the "public charge" or indebted category and thereby endanger the citizenship application and its ever-changing rules. The public hospital treats ER patients. Border counties are hard pressed to cover the needs of both their property-tax paying residents and border crossers. In the summer of 2001, the Texas attorney general issued a policy that undocumented people should not tap health care in Texas, but local health care providers and hospital officers challenged that ruling based on historical court precedents.[28]

Various institutional shrouds exist to promote binational discussion (but little action) on health care, from international to national bodies and national and binational NGOs such as the U.S.–Mexico Border Health Association. The United Nations located its Americas field office, the Pan American Health Organization or PAHO, in El Paso in 1942.

Nevertheless, the dream remains to provide seamless care on both sides of the U.S.–Mexico border. Such care would provide a database on each patient that caregivers would consult so that patients' medical histories would be taken into account. The privacy of such databases would be crucial, should evidence about citizenship (or lack thereof) endanger patients if such evidence got into the hands of law enforcement authorities, including those who police the border. Such care would also have a network of providers who met good-enough standards of care. On both sides of the border, one would likely find providers with care that is not good enough. Finally, such care would be available in both Spanish and English. A third-party insurer, to use health-care lingo, would reimburse costs to providers. At bottom line is the question: who will fund the third party, how much will it cost, and who bears the burden for raising these funds, if not the consumer of health care?

The Case of Portable Health Insurance

We choose to focus on a legislative case, albeit a failed case, to illustrate the difficulties and dilemmas of cross-border, binational approaches to health care. In the 2001 Texas legislative session, a bill was introduced that would provide, again using the lingo of health providers, "portable insurance" that could be used across the border. One El Paso representative promoted this idea, and another criticized it, questioning the "standards" of medical care in Mexico. The bill was considerately transformed itself from introduction to hearings and finally in session when HB2498 ended with the promise to "study" the matter in between the biennial Texas sessions.[29] What was behind this failure?

For almost ten years, El Paso's claim to Texas was that it had never gotten "fair share" funding. This is social justice, redistribution-oriented language. The state generates revenue from all its residents, but does not spend it fairly, according to the claim, resulting in poorer services and fewer jobs with living wages and benefits. Technical formulas allegedly masked discriminatory funding patterns. A special Court of Inquiry during the 1990s fostered a process whereby more transportation money was spent on El Paso's highways. More recently, fair share issues once again got raised over the reimbursement of medical providers. El Paso providers' reimbursements were less than those of medical providers elsewhere in the state for the same services.

Medical providers in El Paso already are challenged in earning the spectacular salaries elsewhere in the United States. Many depend on Medicaid, Medicare, and other government reimbursements. Some nonprofit health organizations generate enough revenue to sustain themselves through these reimbursements. High-profile medical specialists have left El Paso in well-publicized departures. Medical doctors and hospitals are organized into associations and lobby groups in the region and the state. Their voices are heard in the political process—louder voices than the uninsured.

Knowing this context, what are the likely consequences of "portable insurance?" If U.S.-based insurance providers covered treatment in Mexico, it would be a logical extension of free trade. Barriers would be reduced to products and services across national boundaries in a way that would benefit not just consumers in retail stores, but also patients who are direct recipients of preventive, primary, and surgical medical and dental care. This has appeal to many, not including many U.S. providers who might view this is a cheapening of health care services and an expansion of competition (unfair competition, think some, given Mexican medical doctors' mere four years of higher education, in contrast to nearly double that amount in the United States). Lawsuits are not the mechanisms for accountability in Mexico as they are in the United States. Thus some worry for other reasons about standards in Mexico. The medical and hospital communities are predictably opposed to portable insurance. Their market niche would diminish.

As in any legislation, the devil is in the details, in popular parlance. Some health care advocates worried that the insurance would benefit, but also isolate and identify undocumented and legal immigrants. Documentation and tracking of these consumers would make them vulnerable to removal, should records be shared. The public charge label might also make immigrants vulnerable in citizenship applications.

The working poor in El Paso lacks access to health insurance, for many businesses either do not offer benefits or do so with plans far too expensive for workers to obtain. All sorts of people, citizens and immigrants alike, need affordable health insurance, but the national will to provide such coverage is not yet present.

Other advocates felt constrained about public advocacy for portable insurance, given their dependence on private doctors and hospitals for assistance in charitable cases. Preventive and primary care for the undeserved does not include surgical care, and clinics must rely on personal connections and good will to encourage already busy doctors to help their patients. To paraphrase one health provider interviewed, "if I need a favor, how can I turn to doctors whom I may have alienated with support for a measure which they oppose?"

Under the conditions of scarce resources, and in El Paso and Ciudad Juárez there is extreme scarcity, personal relationships have two faces, to draw on the discussion in chapter two. On the one hand, personal relationships and connections allow medical advocates to gain favors and assistance, so essential in charitable cases. On the other hand, connections can be undermined and go sour. Public policy, without regard to income or borders, would eliminate the sort of dependency that constrains free voice and comprehensive solutions to regional, binational problems.

For those with money, plenty of medical care is available, even for cosmetic concerns. In the yellow pages of the El Paso telephone directory, medical doctors in Ciudad Juárez advertise to North Americans who seek different kinds of medical care, such as plastic surgery, including breast augmentation, reduction, liposuction, reconstructive surgery, droopy eye lids, to name a few, and eye laser surgery, to correct one's vision. Numerous dentists and orthodontists also list their services in the yellow pages. While many North Americans can avail themselves of what one could call a luxury medical procedure, many people in the community do not have basic health services. There is a cadre of doctors in Ciudad Juárez that caters predominately to Americans who pay in dollars; they advertise on the Internet as well as the yellow pages of the telephone book in El Paso.

In the same yellow pages one can see the long list of plastic surgeons in El Paso who will provide the same services as those in Ciudad Juárez, obviously for a higher fee. It is lamentable that the city of El Paso does not have one pediatric surgeon yet at the same time over 20 plastic surgeons can provide cosmetic surgery. There is a growing medical tourism industry flourishing where certain medical clinics advertise that they can provide certain medical service for a nominal fee in a reputable clinic where they speak English.

The poor in Ciudad Juárez resort on occasion to the "doctor of the poor," the local pharmacist who may or not be trained, to obtain medical care. Pharmacies in Juárez now sell individual pills because some of the prohibitive expense of some medicines that the poor cannot afford. (This reminds us of vendors who sell cigarettes by the sticks or single eggs.) In one pharmacy in Ciudad Juárez, you can have a person begging with the prescription in their hand to buy medicine for their sick child, an elderly North American person buying medicine that is more affordable and Medicaid or Medicare will not cover, and others buying diet pills or steroids. According to the Sharp Report, one in four U.S. tourists visiting Mexico comes home with a pharmaceutical products.[30]

Some people from El Paso go to Ciudad Juárez for sonograms, laboratory tests that are more expensive in the United States On some occasions, doctors in El Paso will ask patients: are you going to go buy this prescription here in El Paso or in Ciudad Juárez? Doctors will then prescribe accordingly and warn patients about differences in dosages. Dosages vary greatly, and in some instances patients and doctors report that medicine sold in Mexico does not have the same potency.

There are people from El Paso who cross to Ciudad Juárez to avail themselves of medical services at the FEMAP hospital and clinics as was mentioned before. People who cannot cross the border legally are the ones who anguish over medical care availability and costs; they must go to private providers in El Paso and pay for the service and prescription on their own. Undocumented people tend to stay away from clinics lest they be asked to provide documents that they do not have. Basic health care should be a right afforded to every human being. Here on the border it is a luxury that very few people have and many more cannot afford.

Concluding Thoughts: Toward Human Rights

In this chapter, we have examined the business model for cross-border collaboration and found many factors that facilitate its success. Businesses draw on government cues and subsidies to connect across borders. Moreover, with subsidies they develop businesses and business-oriented NGOs that generate revenue and tax savings off the further facilitation of those connections. Yet the ties are mostly weak and built on the expectation of material gain, rather than on principles and purposeful commitments. NGOs enjoy few of these facilitators. They tend to work within national frameworks from which they seek accountability and resources.

When NGOs cross borders to organize, they draw on personal ties and purposeful commitments. These connections are enhanced when local strong ties are matched with regional, national, and international looser ties. In some cases, the distant looser ties bring locals together with resources, programs, and projects. The next chapter moves toward the most challenging of cross-border organizing efforts, connected to human rights. If borderlanders earned better and more equal wages on both sides, these rights might be respected more. But a poor record of human rights is matched with overall poverty and little economic wherewithal to correct the human wrongs.

CHAPTER 6

HUMAN RIGHTS AND HUMAN WRONGS

> Like the girls that were murdered and raped, they are said to be dispos-
> able girls, the girl is poor and is a Mexican girl, so what the hell. I want
> those bastards to say in public [referring to the attorney general] that
> every one of these girls has a life that is as valuable as my mother's, daugh-
> ter's, as my wife's, as my sister's. Their lives are not more important than
> theirs, but not less important either.
>
> —Human rights activist

> There are groups that protect the Mexican spotted owl but not the Mexican.
> —Federally certified court interpreter

> At one time after I had arrived in the U.S. [illegally], I was afraid to leave
> my house because I thought, what if the Immigration takes me away
> while my children are at school. What will happen to them? As time went
> on, I realized this is no way to live ....
>
> —Undocumented woman, mother, activist[1]

> The Juarenses rolled their eyes back in outrage as [U.S.] speakers discussed
> the murdered worker-girls. "Why do speakers humiliate the nation?"
> —Participant observer at a panel discussion for El Paso City Council
> Candidates, Spring 2001

The vision of social justice is best put into practice among those with an
ideological commitment that frames their work. We see all too few
activists of this kind, both on global and local bases. Rather we see
people impelled to organize across borders for material reasons; the most
prominent among them are business people. Union support is typically
driven with this kind of thinking as well, although we saw in the last
chapter that the cross-border activists and even labor day celebrants
infuse their rituals and events with religious symbolism and meanings.
Material incentives also impel those who organize around poverty,
whether it is impoverished participants who need resources or, alas,
the "poverty pimps" who use circumstances to raise funds for their
nonprofit organizations. Recall from chapter two, the three incentives

that drive organizers to organize: material, purposive, and solidary. The latter, solidary, is a reminder of the personal element that motivates people to join organizations and to sustain their involvement.

In the best of organizing worlds, organizational sustenance occurs when purposive incentives expand upon the solidary ones. Purpose, whether ideological or religious, does not replace the personal. It adds reason and logic to the effort and provides the rationale to maintain commitment even if and when personal relationships change or go sour. In material terms, border inequalities are so exaggerated as to be obscene. The differences between the have and have-nots on the border are stark, both across the border and within boundaries. Mexico's wealthy compared to Mexico's poor is the epitome of a paradox: one can compare the homes in the *Campestre* area of Ciudad Juárez, with those of any *colonia popular* and see the vast differences. This, too, is evident in El Paso, where mansions on top of the mountains contrast sharply with trailers in poor *colonias*. Researchers attempt to understand why poverty exists, but very few ever ask why the rich are so rich. Social justice, a mantra of the PRI, has never been achieved in Mexico, and in the United States; in spite of redistributive policies, there is also grave inequality in the distribution of incomes and services.

In chapter six we take up human rights issues, analyzing official actions that range from under-enforcement to over-enforcement and abuse of laws. It is in this realm where cross-border civic actions are the most impotent, compared to environmental, business, and labor issues. Law enforcement is weak on matters relating to violence against women and the disappearance of people, including disappeared daughters. Yet enforcement is virulent to the point of racial profiling and its border counterpart, immigrant profiling. We have a broad, all-encompassing and holistic view of human rights and include education, freedom from want and poverty, access to health care, meaningful and well-paying employment that includes fringe benefits, decent housing and human dignity in its definition. Unfortunately, many of these things are not present on the border.

In this chapter we will focus only on immigration, the plight of the disappeared, and women's rights and labor concerns. The human rights abuses that we will present revolve around the enforcement of immigration laws in El Paso, unsolved crimes, murders, and rapes in Ciudad Juárez, and low wages and employment vulnerability.

This chapter unfolds in the following way: first we discuss the non-existent human rights shroud through a discussion of U.S.–Mexico relations within the context of human rights. Next we analyze human rights in Ciudad Juárez and present a case study of the binational Asociación de Familiares y Amigos de Personas "Desaparecidas"/ Association of Relatives and Friends of "Disappeared" Persons. This is an organization that attempts to create solidarity among family members whose loved ones have disappeared. In the material sense, they seek accountability of government institutions that appear to be unresponsive to their plight. A discussion of other NGOs will follow to provide examples of other groups that are working in the human rights arena: Casa Amiga, Casa del Migrante, and the American Friends Service Committee, and their Immigration Law Enforcement Monitoring Project. Lastly, to document the challenges faced by workers and low wages, La Mujer Obrera, will be highlighted.

Human Rights activists are highly motivated to do the work they do. They organize because they have material, purposive, and solidary motivations for promoting their causes. Human rights activists are global citizens, with a non-nationalistic vision of social conscience and social justice. They see an injustice against one person as an injustice against everyone, including themselves. Many of the human rights activists are religious and spiritually grounded in their work. To many of them, their work is a part of a personal quest for social justice. Personalism does not fuel these organizations either; rather, their solidary with the oppressed and the victimized of the world does. Consider these Biblical refrains.

Do this in remembrance of Me.

—Sacramental ritual

If then you have not been faithful with the dishonest wealth, who will entrust to you the true riches? ... You cannot serve God and wealth.

—Luke 16:1–3.

Human Rights in U.S.–Mexico Relations

Activists in the human rights arena are constantly struggling to promote their agenda on both sides of the border because human rights issues transcend the border. The issues presented will be immigration, the disappeared, and violence against women. Success in the human rights arena is difficult to measure. While success can be measured in a legal sense, for example, an individual wins a case that was presented with the help of a human rights organization against the INS, a better indication of success would be preventive: the elimination of such event. Yet few organizations have the adequate resources to monitor human rights abuses. Additionally, people who do not have legal papers are reluctant to report any abuse or ill-treatment lest they get deported.

Human rights groups on the border, as we will show, have few financial resources; they challenge governments and systems that view their cause in a way that is demeaning to their efforts. The critical rhetoric surrounding the defense of young women who have been victims of rape gravitates around the following queries: "Why was she out so late? What was she wearing? What did she do to provoke him?" Those defending the disappeared in Ciudad Juárez are questioned about the moral character of the victims. "Was he/she involved in drug dealing?" "Did he/she use drugs?" And those defending immigrants are barraged with statements such as "Why defend people who take our jobs away? Why help people who come here and take advantage of the welfare system, put their children in school, and not pay taxes?"

Clearly, the work of human rights advocates on both sides of the border is not an easy task. Nevertheless, there are bonds and connections between human rights organizations that transcend the border that we will highlight as examples of cooperation in this arena.

The Non-Existent Human Rights Institutional Shroud

On the bilateral agenda between the United States and Mexico, human rights is a priority but not at the highest level.[2] While Mexico has vehemently complained about the deaths on the border, on the broader bilateral agenda, human rights issues are discussed symbolically and seldom have they been as important as NAFTA or the La Paz Agreement. Critics of free trade perceive Mexico as being more concerned with trade issues rather than human rights concerns. Traditionally, Mexico is at a disadvantage in the bilateral relationship because it is not as powerful as the United States; it can only raise these issues to the point that it will not jeopardize the broader bilateral relationship. U.S. violations of the human rights of Mexicans in the United States are likely to receive much media attention in Mexico and damage the bilateral relationship.[3] Mexico's consular offices are tasked with the monitoring of human rights violations in the United States.

When Vicente Fox and George W. Bush had their first visit, Fox was seeking an open border policy and amnesty for the more than three million Mexicans now living illegally in the United States. President Bush promised to work with both Mexican officials and the U.S. Congress on a new program for migrant workers under which Mexicans would be given one-year work permits.

Human rights abuses are viewed differently in each country. In Mexico, patriotic sentiments arise when a *Mexicano/a* is abused by the

Border Patrol or dies in their attempt to cross the border. *Mexicanos/as* tend to view the illegal immigration as economic issue: people having to leave their country to seek employment opportunities to be able to provide for their families. Jobs have long been available in the United States, in permanent and temporary supplies, the latter enshrined in the Bracero program of 1942–1964. Many crossed for work, sent for families, and regularized their residency and later citizenship. Family unification principles have been embedded in immigration policies for much of the late twentieth century.

There are other human rights violations that do receive more media attention but differently in each country. Mexico has raised the issue of Mexican nationals who are sitting on death row in the United States and especially in the state of Texas. The death penalty is anathema to Mexico; it is not practiced there. Moreover, Mexicans raise certain concerns regarding the American judicial system given that the majority of death row inmates are minority and poor. In many instances, they cite language barriers that might have played a role in the judicial process, specifically police officers making arrests who do not speak Spanish, inmates, and public defenders that do not understand each other. Miguel Flores, a Mexican national, was put to death in the fall of 2000. The following excerpt describes the concerns and recourse that the Mexican government took on his behalf prior to his execution:

> The Mexican government had filed protests with Governor Bush and the U.S. State Department, calling for a stay of execution in Flores' case on the grounds that he was sentenced to death in violation of the Vienna Convention on Consular Relations. At the time of his arrest, Flores was not notified by Texas authorities of his right to contact the Mexican consulate. The Mexican government did not learn of his case until a year after his death sentence. The state of Texas contends that since the U.S. federal government, and not Texas, signed the treaty on consular relations, the state is not bound by it.[4]

Within the context of cross-border cooperation, the two governments have only superficially addressed this issue and it is clear that other issues are deemed more important by policy makers than human rights, such as NAFTA. Human rights have no "La Paz Agreement" or NAFTA agreements. Human rights per se are not addressed in a major binational agreement, treaty or accord. This is an area where the institutional shroud is virtually nonexistent. One can surmise that on the broader binational agenda, there is a tacit agreement between the two governments as to how far they are willing to push the envelope on the human rights issue. Mexico certainly does not want to alienate the United States and jeopardize other areas of bilateral cooperation—trade and the environment—to the human rights agenda. Why can Mexico and the United States strike up a free trade agreement but not address the issue of human rights at the same level?

Immigration

Border cities have their fair share and more of human rights and immigration organizations. Borders are gateway through which immigrants came to the United States. For many in the United States, Ellis Island symbolizes the gateway through which European immigrants came to the United States. Across the U.S.–Mexico border gateway, comparable numbers probably passed, but it is impossible to know precisely given the contrasts between a gateway island versus porous desert terrain which for many years had neither enforcement nor counts of crossers. Immigration is a global phenomenon. There are people on the move all over the world seeking employment opportunities, a better quality of life or even just adventure.[5] As we will discuss later in this chapter, migrants also find their way to Ciudad Juárez, where they have received a mixed reception.

In the United States the immigration issue is seen as a legal, not an economic issue. People who want to come to the United States can do so, but legally, there are quotas. The argument that employers seek labor and hire people without the benefit of documents, so as to increase profits, is seldom heard in the mainstream press.

Other immigrants, with or without the benefit of legal documents, enter the United States through El Paso, and some move on into the interior. This movement of people has led to violence, transgressions of human rights, and even deaths; there are people literally dying to come here. According to the American Friends Service Committee (AFSC), people die of exposure (extreme cold, sweltering heat), migrants are left inside trucks, or they are recklessly pursued by a Border Patrol car and accidents have occurred. There is a lot of violence and abuse. The AFSC in 1987 established the Immigration Law Enforcement Monitoring Project (ILEMP) to engage local communities along the Mexico–U.S. border, as well as national and international organizations, to challenge abuse and violence. In December 2000, ILEMP conducted the first Abuse of Authority Documentation Campaign.

Human Rights Abuses—El Paso

U.S. policy waxes and wanes in the degree to which borders are open or closed to migrants. The literature on immigration law is voluminous, and we do not intend to review it all. But the vantage point of borders provides us with great insight on the huge divide between immigration law or policy, and the enforcement of those laws and policies. We have lived through periods of limited and loose enforcement (1980s), coupled with extensive profiling and harassment of those who "looked like" immigrants in El Paso, and heavily policed and controlled borders (1990s). The context is a perfect set up for human rights problems and abuses.

In the early 1990s, Bowie High School students worked with the Border Rights Coalition to challenge Border Patrol harassment on and around school grounds. The harassment, ranging from verbal to physical and pointed loaded guns, entangled many citizens, including students, staff, and even the football coach. Fourteen students filed a lawsuit, and the Border Patrol settled out of court, leading to diminished harassment. The story is told and retold in the documentary, *The Time Has Come.* A year later, however, the Border Patrol set up its blockade along the border, moving heavy monitoring from El Paso's streets to the border itself.

Here on the border, human rights violations at the international point of entry do not receive attention by the Mexican or American governments. This is probably due to the fact the *fronterizos* (borderlanders) are so used to this kind of treatment, and conditioned that it is not something that they even think of as a violation of a human right. People who grow up on the border are socialized that the Border Patrol is part of one's reality. Border residents are conditioned that legally they are giving up their constitutional rights when they are at the port of entry, and subsequently they have become used to the occasional illtreatment that they receive upon reentry. However, there is an increased awareness among legal residents and citizens alike that they too have rights and can question the authorities as to why they are being stopped.

Violations of human rights occur at the hands of U.S. Border Patrol, Immigration and Naturalization Service (INS), and U.S. Customs officials. Students who come to University of Texas at El Paso report that upon entering the United States on a daily basis, they encounter a variety of abuses ranging from verbal abuse, to lines of questioning that are inappropriate by officials such as "is this really you in this picture?" and "are you sure that these documents are yours?" Female students report that they are asked (by male agents) to get out of their car and open the trunk especially if they have shorts or a short dress on. "Sometimes I know that they pick on women, and sometimes they flirt with you," reported a young female student. Other times, the agents just wave them by.

Mexican American and Mexican–Mexican

To be "Mexican" or "*Mexicano/Mexicana*" is to be different, even at the border. Schoolchildren know and act on the difference, even Mexican Americans from the first to *nth* generations. The virulent insult "wetback" (*mojado/a*) is as insulting as the n-word for African Americans. Of course, in Mexico, the permanently departed crossers also merit difference and insults: disloyal deserters who sold their souls for money and no longer speak proper Spanish. *Con el nopal en la frente* (with the cactus on the forehead) is another insult used against Mexicans who are brown skinned and physically "look" Mexican; the phrase refers to them as people who are denying their heritage, especially those who cannot speak Spanish. "You should have seen him/her, *con el nopal en la frente,* and he/she refused to speak Spanish to me" is a common statement made against Mexicans in the border region.

Mexican Americans are not a homogenous group of people. (We remove the hyphen, to avoid hyphenating "Americans"). There are Mexicans in El Paso who do not speak Spanish, who have never been to Ciudad Juárez, and who consider themselves to be Americans of Mexican descent. There are American citizens who have lived in Ciudad Juárez all of their lives, speak little English, and culturally are Mexican citizens. For example, their nationalistic fervor is awakened when they hear *Mexicanos al grito de Guerra* (Mexicans at the cry of war, [the beginning words of the Mexican national anthem]), as opposed to the first words of the U.S. national anthem. Mexican Americans who do go to Mexico at times are criticized for being *pochos* (not speaking Spanish well) and for being not Mexican enough. Likewise, Mexican–Mexicans criticize their compatriots who have left for the United States seeking a better life.

Population and Immigration on the Border

Mexico's population is less than half the size of its northern neighbor, but its natural growth rate far exceeds that of the United States. In the mid-1970s, Mexico began to pursue a vigorous family planning policy, complete with advertising campaigns and widespread contraceptive availability. This policy reduced the number of children from six to 3.5 per family in just two decades. The number of job seekers, however, still outpaces job creation and jobs that pay decent wages, as we noted in the previous chapter. Consequently, emigration has been a safety valve for inadequate numbers of jobs. Many migrants send money home, thereby creating transnational transfers far greater than foreign aid programs and without their costly bureaucracies. According to *Migration News,* a University of California publication, "It is estimated that remittances sent by *Mexicanos/as* to their families in Mexico is close to $6 billion dollars a year."[6]

Symbolic meetings and discussions regarding U.S.–Mexico relations have taken place in Mexico City and Washington, D.C. Efforts to address immigration issues can be seen in the following example. Mexican Senator Silvia Hernández, a member of the Partido Revolucionario Institucional (PRI) and chairwoman of the Mexican Congress' foreign affairs committee, headed a delegation of nine senators to the border region in August 2001. The group visited several federal agencies in the city including the Immigration and Naturalization Service (INS), the Drug Enforcement Administration (DEA), and the Federal Bureau of Investigations (FBI). Additionally, they met with Representative Silvestre Reyes, a Democrat, who previously served as the Border Patrol sector chief in the region, who stated "at the congressional level, it is also important to have that kind of (legislator-to-legislator) cooperation. This is the first opportunity for some of my colleagues to get a look at the border region. It's as misunderstood in Mexico City as it is in Washington, D.C."[7]

During the visit to El Paso, Senator Silvia Hernández expressed concern over undocumented immigrants working in the United States, paying taxes, contributing to the economy, and their rights. She emphasized that immigration policies can be destructive: "What we do not want is to have families destroyed."[8] Senator Hernández expressed that Mexico was interested in both an amnesty program and a guest worker program. Notwithstanding the complex issues that are on the bilateral agenda, such as drugs, crime, immigration, environmental concerns, and energy, it is important that politicians on both sides of the border come together for the common good. "Many facets of US– Mexican relations are ultimately at the mercy of elected officials, politicians, on both sides of the border. The better these politicians can relate to and with each other, the better the chance of cooperation and progress on any number of binational issues."[9]

While these efforts should be lauded, they too are used symbolically by politicians on both sides of the border. Mexicans who are critical of the government comment that if the Mexican Congress was that concerned about Mexican families, they would change their economic and social policies. Family separation, as a human rights issue, has not been adequately addressed by anyone in the government on either side of the border. However, market strategies make separation of families an issue for advertising purposes. In a television advertisement for telephone calling cards in Mexico, a girlfriend calls her boyfriend, a son calls his father, and a little girl calls her father who works in the United States with the calling card. While the United States does have a family reunification policy, it costs money and takes a long time to process through the INS bureaucracy.

Once inside borders, to be "undocumented" (or, an "illegal alien") was to live in potential fear of being asked for "papers," such as a birth certificate or a Resident Alien Card, on the streets, in workplaces, or even in the sacred sphere of the home, where the Border Patrol has more freedom to enter than local police. Every form one fills out about one's family can potentially expose members to the changing vagaries of immigration law. With a Mexican heritage population of three-fourths and more, many El Pasoans meet the Border Patrol's look-alike assumptions.[10] We occasionally hear horror stories about undocumented workers, who are no longer needed or for whom money is no longer available for wages, whose own employers call the INS. Workers' ability to organize and to voice public concerns is constrained in contexts like these. Employers rarely face interference when they pay perpetually minimum (or subminimum) wages to fearful employees.

The following ethnographic moment crystallizes the fear that some people live in because they do not have the proper legal documents to reside legally in the United States.

Ethnographic Moment 6.1: "Me la regalaron"
"They gave her to me as a present"

The setting was a colonia in southern New Mexico. Another professor, four students and I (Irasema) were still in the pilot phase of the interview process at this site. We were in the front yard of an interviewee's home; two students were conducting the interview; one was actually asking the questions while the other was taking copious notes. The rest of the research team was observing the process, also taking notes on occasion and gathering other data that anthropologists and some political scientists have a knack for. How many cars are parked in the vicinity of the house? Do they have license plates, current inspection stickers, and decorations? Who are the people in the pictures inside the home? What are some of the material things that the family owns? Is there a telephone, answering machine, heating, air conditioning, toys, etc.? What items are displayed in the curio? What are those boxes of Mexican candy doing next to the television?

The respondent spoke only Spanish and was engrossed in the interview. She was thoughtful about every question and never directly answered the question with a "yes" or "no"; she always prefaced her response. For example, when asked how many people lived in her home, she said, well it depends if you count my daughter and son-in-law who are staying with me for a while until their home is ready, and if you count my niece who is staying here until she makes up with her husband. Her response to her annual income was "well it depends on whether or not I work in the fields that year." Her interview crystallized how inaccurate official data gathering can be when people are not given a variety of options to list their own unique responses. We later learned through the use of ethnography that in addition to her "work," she sells Mexican candy, medicine, and other products, including gas cylinders from Ciudad Juárez to her neighbors who can't cross the border "porque no tienen sus papeles arreglados" [because they do not have their papers in order]. The respondent did not include this in her annual income figure.

During the whole interview process her relatives would come and go in and out of the house and the children played nearby with the household pets. One of the professors asked the little girl who was playing what her name was, how old she was, who the character was on her T-shirt, the names of the dogs and cats and what her favorite color was. "Azul" (blue) the little girl responded and then went on to explain how she was related to everyone in the household, "she is my cousin, she is my aunt, he is my uncle, she is my grandmother and my father Eduardo, well he is very lazy." At this point one of the aunts asked her to be quiet and to not be saying such things. The little girl repeated, "yes my father Eduardo is lazy, but by father Antonio is not. I have two fathers," she said.

An aunt said good-bye to the research team and stated that she was on her way to Ciudad Juárez "para hacer unos mandados" [run some errands]. Everyone responded "que le vaya bien" [have a good trip]. The interview process continued and the professor continued the conversation with the little girl. "Do you ever go to Ciudad Juárez?" The little girl responded "no porque no tengo sapaporte" [because I do not have a passport]; however, she did not pronounce "passport" in Spanish correctly. At that point one of the older cousins alerted the family that this little girl was "diciendo muchas cosas que no debería de decir" [saying too many things that she should not be saying].

When the interview ended the students thanked the interviewee, and as had been instructed by the professors, the student conducting the interview rhetorically stated "estamos a sus ordenes" [we are at your service]. "Que bueno" [good] the lady said in Spanish "because I have a big problem and maybe you can help me."

"A esta niña me la regalaron" [they gave me this little girl as a present], began the interviewee in Spanish: *"and she does not have papers to be here and she will be starting kindergarten and I do not know what to do because I am so afraid that they will take her away from me. I am the only mother that she has ever known. My son got involved with a 'cantinera' [barmaid] who works in Ciudad Juárez. She had several children with other men, this little one was the fifth child that she had delivered and she did not care for any of them. My husband and I made our son go get his little girl and we crossed her when she was just days old. Do you know someone at 'migración' (immigration) that can help me? I am afraid to go and ask because we may get in trouble and they may take her away from us. This is hard because many in the family 'estan arreglando' (in the process of legalizing with INS) and we do not want to jeopardize their applications because my husband is their sponsor. "*

The research team felt that so much had been given to them through the interview process and they could offer so little in return. The exchange between the interviewee and interviewers was definitely unbalanced. One of the professors suggested contacting the Archdiocese of Las Cruces where the Colonia Development Council was housed and request assistance there.

As we headed back we all thought aloud what other recommendations we could make to the family. We also thought about this little girl's mother: Did she ever wonder where her daughter was? We even thought that this little girl could have perhaps been taken away and crossed over the border without her mother's knowledge. What would INS do in this case? The fear in the grandmother's eyes and the tears that formed when she stated that *"me la pueden quitar"* [they can take her away from me] were very moving. However, we also remembered what the grandmother said as she gently pulled the little girl's loose hair into a ponytail held together with both her hands *" haber como me las arreglo porque ella va a empezar el kinder el mes que entra, verdad mija?"* (Let's see how I can fix this because she will start kindergarten next month, right mija? [contraction of mi hija, my daughter.]) To which the little one responded *"si ya voy a ir a la escuela!"* [yes, I will be going to school!]

The last dramatic U.S. immigration reforms occurred in 1986, with the Immigration Reform and Control Act (IRCA) and in 1996, with the Illegal Immigrant Reform and Immigrant Responsibility Act (IRAIRA). Until IRCA, employers who hired undocumented workers faced no penalty. IRCA was the first immigration law to extend liability from undocumented employees to include employers. While the staff to enforce employer sanctions has never been adequate to the task, the law has probably deterred some, but has most certainly increased the bureaucratization of employment and the market in false identification documents. The other important provision of IRCA was its amnesty provision for undocumented immigrants who could prove residence before 1982 (1986 for agricultural workers in deference to U.S. farmers' and ranchers' demand for labor). Three million people, through amnesty, applied to become naturalized citizens, and most of these people were born in Mexico. Amnesty acknowledged the continuing U.S. workforce needs, especially for workers willing to accept relatively low wages.

Whatever the "need" for migrant labor, Border Patrol agents worked with vigilance, in a bureaucratic system that rewarded "apprehension" and departures, to use the language of "catching" and "removing" the undocumented. Through the mid-1990s, El Pasoans were subjected daily to immigrant profiling. The Border Rights Coalition emerged to document abuse (with support from the American Friends Service Committee) and to advise immigrants of their rights.

Internationally, there is an awareness and commitment to address human rights issues in the U.S.–Mexico border region. In November, 1999, Mary Robinson, high commissioner for Human Rights at the United Nations, met with NGOs from the United States and Mexico in Tijuana, Baja California. Evidently, the meeting was held without the presence of government officials from Mexico at her request. She reported feeling "deeply moved" when she was given maps with crosses that represented the places where 456 deaths had occurred since 1994 at border crossings. NGOs emphasized the abuse that immigrants suffered at the hands of unscrupulous employers as well as by Mexican authorities.[11] According to other sources, the death toll at the U.S.–Mexico border has been rising by about 25 percent a year. In 2000, approximately 500 persons died.[12] There are many bodies that will never be found in the deserts and those that float down the Rio Grand/Río Bravo. Perhaps more awareness and pressure from the international community can assist the work of human rights groups in the region and demand that both governments address these problems. However, we are well aware that commitment and enforcement of international agreements and accords occur only at the volition of each individual country.

The anti-immigrant sentiment is not exclusively found in the United States. Within Mexico, there is an anti-immigrant sentiment as well.

Local officials in the Sonora border region stated that immigrants who entered the United States illegally and who were then abused by the Border Patrol deserved the ill-treatment. "It is like someone entering your home without your permission. They should get the necessary papers in order and *entrar como la gente decente* [enter like decent people]. Even within Mexico there are people who do not feel that immigrants that should have basic human rights. The former mayor of Nogales, Sonora, blamed many of the city's problems on the immigrants. "They come from poor *ranchos* [literally means ranches, but in this case referring to rural areas] and they are used to living without services." The mayor went on to add that the immigrants were a problem for the city because their children also overburdened the schools.[13] In the community of Columbus, New Mexico, the same complaint is echoed about the school children that cross the border daily from Palomas, Chihuahua, to attend school in the Deming School District. This same rhetoric and these arguments were made by former California Governor Pete Wilson in his defense of Proposition 187. Perhaps border politicians are more alike than they are ready to admit. In the following ethnographic moment, the divisive issue of education is presented. It is interesting to note how border residents differ in their opinions regarding access to education.

Ethnographic Moment 6.2: The Binational Meeting

The binational meeting, hosted by a major foundation, was truly inclusive and binational; one day was scheduled in Ciudad Juárez and the next in El Paso. The organizers were obviously very pleased with the large turn out. Television cameras, reporters, photographers, and high-level elected officials were all present. Participants were from both sides of the border—government officials, academics, activists—everyone could speak in the language that they were most comfortable with since simultaneous translation was provided. Important issues were discussed: education, immigration, trade, and human rights. The panels included federal, state, local government officials, and activists from both sides of the border. Doris Meissner, former INS commissioner, was the speaker and her counterpart who identified himself as the "Mexican Doris Meissner" also addressed the audience.

One of the panels dealt with education issues on the U.S.–Mexico border. A representative from the University of Texas at El Paso (UTEP) spoke of the Programa de Asistencia Estudiantil (PASE) program. The PASE program allows students coming from Mexico to pay in-state tuition rates;

therefore, many students take advantage of this program because otherwise they would have to pay out-of-state fees that are rather costly. UTEP has the largest contingency of Mexican students of any U.S. university. The PASE program has enabled many students from Mexico to get an education that they would not otherwise be able to obtain. The program is attractive to students from Ciudad Juárez because it provides them with a U.S. education that is perceived to be more prestigious than a Mexican education, and, at the same time, it is cheaper for them because they can continue to live at home.

Students who are enrolled through PASE state the following regarding the program. "If I were to go to Mexico City and study engineering it would cost my family a lot of money because of the housing and transportation costs"; "I am getting a degree in accounting and learning how people do that in the U.S.; that will help me when I apply for a job in Mexico"; "Special education is not readily available in Mexico, much less bilingual special education. I am glad that UTEP is here and that the PASE program is available; otherwise, I would have to go study someplace in the U.S. and that would cost a lot more money."

As the speaker went on to describe how the PASE program worked and how many students had benefited from it over time, people in the audience seemed eager to want to learn more about the program. During the question and answer session, people commented how wonderful the program was, how they had children attending UTEP because of this program, etc. Others in the audience wondered aloud if this program was specific to UTEP or if it was a border-wide program in the state of Texas, which it is. The presenter went on to provide brochures and gave names and numbers where people could learn more about the program. Clearly, everyone in the audience lauded the PASE program's success.

During a short break after the panel, a person from the United States, a Mexican American who worked for the federal government in a rather high position, commented to Irasema in a low voice, "Why do they have this kind of program for people from here? I wish that they had this kind of program for my kids. They go to UTEP and I have to pay lots of money for them to go there. Because of my income, my kids do not qualify for financial aid. Why don't do they something to help our kids on our side?

Clearly, the sentiment that this gentlemen conveyed regarding education is common throughout the border region. What is ironic is that this person was promoting and extolling the virtues of binational cooperation during his presentation. On the one hand, how can a person be speaking about the importance of binational cooperation and on the other hand begrudge the Mexican students who took advantage of the PASE program?

The northern border is a magnet for migrants from the central and south of Mexico. Newspapers in the interior of Mexico often run ads that recruit workers to the northern border. Workers are offered free transportation and a "well-paying" job in border cities. In Ciudad Juárez, community activists, journalists, and academics detect an anti-immigrant sentiment especially against migrants from other states in Mexico. For example, residents of the state of Veracruz, (known as both *Veracruzanos* and *Jarochos*) have migrated to the city with the hope of finding work. The term *Juarochos* has been coined to emphasize the link between *Veracruzanos* and Ciudad Juárez. Among *Juarenses* (residents from Ciudad Juárez) it is not uncommon to hear negative jokes about people Veracruz as well as from Torreon, Coahuila as well.

In the summer of 1999, Presidente Municipal Gustavo Elizondo wrote a letter to the governor of Veracruz, Miguel Aleman, stating that thousands of *Veracruzanos* had been lured to Ciudad Juárez by false promises of high paying jobs and homes. The *presidente municipal* asked the governor to inform people in Veracruz about the deceptive practices of ruthless people who should be punished. Elizondo also advised the governor on the inordinate number of people seeking assistance from the local government to return to their home state. He wrote "many women are exploited and turn to prostitution out of desperation."[14]

Others called for the creation of a "border patrol" that would be stationed in the outskirts of the city to stop emigration into Ciudad Juárez. The *Jarochos* have organized and have created an organization to help other *Veracruzanos* assimilate to life in this border city.

Immigrants everywhere face similar struggles adjusting to life in a new place, acceptance by the new community, economic hardships, and discrimination. It is not an easy feat to insert oneself into a new place especially when there is a perception and a reality that you are not really welcomed; in this case the *maquiladoras* like the new workers, but the community does not like the workers. The community of Ciudad Juárez has more things to worry about than the immigrants who arrive in the hopes of finding jobs. Crime and disappearances, rapes and other violence are rampant in Ciudad Juárez.

Crime, Disappearances, Rapes, and Other Violent Activity

The U.S. Department of State travel advisory page updated on October 19, 2001, included the following:

TRAVELING TO/THROUGH BORDER CITIES: Visitors to border cities such as Tijuana, Ciudad Juárez, and Nuevo Laredo should remain alert and be aware of their surroundings at all times. Visitors are very vulnerable when visiting the local "red light districts," particularly if they are departing alone in the early hours of the morning. Municipal and traffic police are aware of the danger and regularly check the area for persons carrying weapons or drugs and for drunk drivers. Nonetheless, Americans can still fall victim to crime in these districts.

U.S. citizens should be aware that innocent bystanders are at risk from the increase in drug related violence in the streets of border cities. In Ciudad Juárez, Nuevo Laredo, and Tijuana, shootings have taken place at busy intersections during daylight hours. The perpetrators of drug violence are not intimidated by local law enforcement because arrests in these shootings are extremely rare. In Ciudad Juárez, several U.S. citizens, including innocent bystanders, have been killed in drug-related shootings over the past three years. Some of these shootings have taken place on principal thoroughfares and outside popular restaurants and other public places, including convenience stores, a currency exchange, and a gas station."[15]

To borderlanders, this travel advisory is not something that they like to think about every day. Residents of Ciudad Juárez and other border communities that rely on American tourists for their livelihood resent these kinds of messages because it scares people away from the border. "People are murdered every day in the U.S. too," state owners and workers of local *curio* stores in the *mercado* (market) of Ciudad Juárez.

Over 5,000 people from El Paso work in Ciudad Juárez on a daily basis.[16] In this community, working in Ciudad Juárez is similar to someone living in a city like Los Angeles and commuting to work. Commuters in large urban centers in the United States like Los Angeles, or Chicago, probably commute longer distances to work than one would here, yet here people go to a foreign country. Ciudad Juárez has made headline news in other areas (both nationally and internationally) for reasons that portray the community in a negative light.

In Ciudad Juárez, the authorities have never adequately addressed the cases of the murdered and raped women, the executions and disappearances that have occurred. In November 2001, eight more women's bodies were found in Ciudad Juárez. A recent United Nations Children's Fund (UNICEF)-Desarollo Integral de la Familia (DIF) (The Holistic Development of the Family) report that indicated that children were being exploited in Ciudad Juárez for the sex industry hardly caused a stir in either side of the border. The report states:

> Part of those who are engaged in the sex trade are minors. On the one hand, there are street children, especially boys aged between 12 and 17 who occasionally prostitute themselves in order to be able to subsist and

pay for their addictions and this they do either in the town or crossing the border to offer their services. In this last case, the boys meet on Puente Negro to then cross to the other side."[17]

This example crystallizes that cross-border activity extends to the illicit sex market and exploitation of children. The report went on to depict the inordinate number of massage parlors where women (including girls) work as prostitutes. Additionally, the link between drug use and prostitution was well documented. Drug traffickers lure poor and young people into this illicit business; once they are addicted, they are forced to prostitute themselves to feed their habit. Why aren't people outraged that this is happening in their own community?

Successful Endeavors in the Human Rights Arena

In Ciudad Juárez/El Paso there are several organizations that address human rights issues. It is difficult to say that any one of these organizations is a "successful" organization because success in this arena would mean that these organizations would have no need to exist because, idealistically, government officials and law enforcement agents would respect human rights. One organization is binational, vocal, and has been able to survive amidst great adversity. It is the Asociación de Familiares y Amigos de Personas "Desaparecidas," also known as the Association of Relatives and Friends of "Disappeared" Persons. It is headed by a resident of El Paso, Texas, and was officially founded four years ago. The organization emerged with a couple's disappearance "from the face of the earth" in Ciudad Juárez. The disappeared man's father is a friend of one of the activist/founders of the organization, who is the present co-director of the association. "Well my friend's son was providing listening devices to the federal police, he was helping to catch criminals and it was top secret, but still it was leaked to the cartels and now they are missing." He said that this was the event that brought him into the business of advocating the investigation of the disappeared.

When newspapers and the media started publicizing the disappearance of this young couple, many other people started to come forward with their own stories of disappeared relatives and friends. Relatives and friends of disappeared people indicated that they had negative experiences with the authorities and that they were reluctant to continue pressing them for information. Under the guise of the war on drugs, authorities attributed disappearances and murders to the *ajuste de cuentas* (adjustment of an account involving a drug deal). "These people are afraid of the Mexican police and consider the American Drug Enforcement Agency (DEA) a dirty agency. The association has 'busted' the attorney general in Ciudad Juárez who didn't want to know about the 200 files of adults that have disappeared and over 164[18] women that have been raped, violated and murdered" according to the association informant.

Under the guise of the "War on Drugs," Mexican law enforcement agents tend to justify actions even if they are gross egressions of a basic human right. In Mexico, there is a growing concern that under the pretext of the war on drugs, people's human rights are being violated and people are afraid to go the authorities to report crimes or disappearances. In some instances, relatives of disappeared people report that police and law enforcement agents start interrogating them when they report a crime to the authorities. The power of the authorities to validate or invalidate a crime has strong psychological implications, especially when one attempts to report a crime committed against a son or a daughter and is humiliatingly asked, "what kind of person was your son or daughter?" Imagine the mixed emotions that people experience: on the one hand your loved one has disappeared and on the other hand people are questioning their moral character. People have reported that officials at times have demanded bribes to pursue a case.

The spokesperson for the Association of the relatives and friends of the disappeared claimed that:

> the government of Chihuahua stopped these investigations because they were leading to the young, middle management in the *maquila* industry that has money and power and the government does not want to do anything to scare the *maquiladoras* away. *Maquiladoras* are making families rich in Ciudad Juárez. If you investigated certain prominent families, you will see that they own much of the land in the city and probably all the way to Chihuahua City.

He went on to add that the government, in the case of the disappearances, does not move investigations forward. They claim that witnesses are afraid and that they do not have clues, so there is nothing that the government can do. According to the spokesperson of this organization, at the time (in the summer of 2001), there were 236 women dead and over 500 executions in Ciudad Juárez that were unresolved. However, public officials make statements such as "Ciudad Juárez is doing ok because Sinaloa has over 2,000 executions." According to the spokesperson for the association, "over 2,200 files have been reported missing from the new district attorney's office."

We are acutely aware of the discrepancies in the number of disappeared people, the number of murdered women, and the incidences of rape; there are various reasons for the discrepancy in the number of crimes. Human rights organizations claim that the authorities want to "keep the numbers" down because of the negative publicity that Ciudad Juárez received both nationally and internationally. Additionally, they believe that many young people come to the border because of the economic hardships in their families, or because they want to leave their homes and do not tell their families where they are going. This leads people to believe that when a young woman disappears in Ciudad Juárez, no one is looking for her because her family may not know her whereabouts. The authorities claim that human rights organizations inflate the figures of the disappeared and the murdered women to make them look bad.

With the discovery of the narco-cemeteries (in a ranch located outside of Ciudad Juárez), many bodies were found buried in a common grave. Initially, the media reported that there were hundreds of bodies, (but in the end nine bodies were found) in 1999; this led members of the association to launch a campaign about the deaths. Letters were faxed and sent to local, state, and federal officials in both countries. A local law enforcement officer from El Paso responded to the fax by saying "you know Mexico is another country, and we cannot tell Ciudad Juárez how to run their city. El Paso is ok." During the unearthing of nine bodies in a ranch outside of Ciudad Juárez in 1999, the Federal Bureau of Investigations (FBI) was asked to help with the investigation due to the fact that they had expertise and the technical wherewithal for the forensic studies that were needed. The U.S.–Mexican "mass graves" inves-tigation was halted when Mexican politicians and others complained (presumably nationalistic Mexicans) that the FBI presence was a violation of Mexico's sovereignty.[19]

Joint binational efforts are at times complicated and difficult to carry out because of the perception that someone is stepping on someone else's toes. Also, the fact that joint efforts are usually a north–south phenomenon, not the other way around, is seen as suspect. How would people in the United States feel if Mexican law enforcement officers were invited into the United States to assist with an investigation? Nevertheless, many *Mexicanos* welcomed the involvement of the Americans in the investigation because of the mistrust that they have of their own institutions and their ability to conduct investigations honestly and well. During this time, the head of the association sent a fax three times a day to the attorney general in Mexico City until he finally got a response. This activism has had a cost since members of the association have received various death threats. However, membership in the organization continues to grow as more people disappear or are found murdered. Again, an increased membership role is another indicator of success but is that really a good way to measure a successful human rights organization? Membership in this organization is growing because the association has started working with people in Tijuana, Baja California Norte and in Matamoros, Tamaulipas. This organization is organizing vertically along the border.

Membership in this organization is a source of moral support for family members who have lost loved ones. Being able to share one's plight with another person who is similarly situated must be helpful to anyone who experiences this kind of personal tragedy. The support network offered by the association as well as the growing membership allow for more people to work on this together and make demands of the authorities in unison rather than individually; after all, there is power in numbers. Membership and participation in this organization are very personal and in order to protect people's privacy they are reluctant to publicly publish a member directory.

In Ciudad Juárez, the *asociación* also has a co-director of this binational organization. She became involved in this struggle in the early 1990s when her brother-in-law, who went out one evening, disappeared. Her work focuses on asking the authorities in Mexico to "help them find" their loved ones, who are both Mexican and American citizens. She states that there are over 198 people who have disappeared in Ciudad Juárez, 22 of whom are U.S. citizens. She was interviewed in the early spring of 2001. According to a member of the *asociación,* this is an emotional struggle because it is difficult to live with the uncertainty of not knowing if your loved one is dead or alive. "A person cannot disappear from the face of the earth just because something had to happen to these people and logically there has to exist someone who is culpable" said a spokesperson for the *asociación.* At this point the group's strategy is to ensure that these disappearances, murders, and rapes are investigated. Allegations that the authorities are dragging their feet on the investigations are well documented.

Women's groups nationwide and internationally started to support the efforts of local women's organizations with the launching of the *Ni una más* (not one more) campaign in 1998.

Before the null response of the State of Chihuahua authorities to finish and resolve the deaths of women in Ciudad Juárez that now number 133, [this was the figure in 1998] the NGOs and feminist movement, ... have launched a national and international campaign: "*A parar la lista: Ni una más*" [Let's stop the list: Not one more].[20]

An anonymous source from an NGO hired by the government to help out with the investigation of the murdered women stated that she felt that either the investigators needed more experience and training in the investigation of sexually violent crimes or else they were dragging their feet. "When I was asked to come off board I started asking obvious questions regarding basic procedures. At first I thought that they were really naïve and inexperienced; it finally dawned on me that they were overlooking the obvious in some instances. At that point, I decided to depart gracefully from the investigation," lamented a highly respected psychologist whom we interviewed.

Activists and family members of victims blame the lack of progress made in the investigations of the disappeared and murdered women on the authorities. Family members of the victims have accused the police of being part of a cover up or protecting someone prominent and wealthy. A famous *Televisa* show, *Círculo Rojo,* aired in late November 2001, close to the site where eight women had been found, documented the concerns the victims' families had vis-à-vis the authorities. An aunt of one of the victims stated how she had sent six e-mails to Vicente Fox. "First I asked him to think of his daughters and then I mentioned our concerns and asked him to address the situation by providing more federal resources to the investigation. I have received an acknowledgement that my emails have been received," the woman said on the television show.

In Mexico human rights work is not an easy endeavor. In October 2001, Digna Ochoa y Placido, a human rights attorney in Mexico City, was shot to death at her office. The culprits left behind a message to other human rights defenders that they could meet similar fate.[21] Unfortunately, there have been other human rights workers and journalists who have been threatened or killed in the line of duty. Death threats, assassinations, and kidnappings are deterrents to people who work in the human rights arena in Mexico and preclude people from getting involved in similar work. In Ciudad Juárez, women's issues are of concern to many human rights organizations and have become a focal point for human rights organizations to rally around.

Diana Washington Valdez, a leading reporter on border issues, reported that she had been on the telephone with a member of a member of *Voces Sin Eco* (Voices Without Echo), a nongovernmental organization that advocates justice for the more than 300[22] women who have been killed in Juárez since 1993. (The number of disappeared was provided in 2001).

> The sound quality was unusually poor that day. There were strange and scratching noises in the background. We were on touchy ground. The call went dead immediately at the mention of a National Action Party member who was questioned by police about one of the victims. The line remained "blocked" for three straight days. I could not call that number, and the other party could not call me back.[23]

Various organizations have held rallies in Ciudad Juárez to raise awareness and bring attention to the issue of the disappeared women. Black crosses on pink backgrounds appear on walls, telephone and electricity posts to commemorate the deceased women. In downtown El Paso, there is mural on the side of a building where this black cross on pink stands out to remind everyone that the plight of these women is a binational concern.

Las Amigas—Los Amigos y las Casas de la Frontera

Casa Amiga

In Ciudad Juárez, there is an institution that is helping address the challenges that women face in the community—Casa Amiga (Friendly Home, fem.) has received, local, national, and international attention for its work in this arena. Casa Amiga has been able to establish many binational and international linkages throughout the course of its existence.

In 1992 women's raped and mutilated bodies were found in Ciudad Juárez. A group of women came together and formed Grupo 8 de Marzo, (the 8th of March Group) named after International Women's day in order to raise awareness of the crimes and to promote women's rights. In 1996 La Coordinadora de Organismos no Gubernamentales/ The Coordinating group of NGOs was founded to defend women's rights. The impetus for this organization emanated from a proposed change in article 219 of the Penal Code of the state of Chihuahua, which proposed outlawing abortion.[24]

Members of Grupo 8 de Marzo determined that there was great need for a shelter that would provide women who were victims of crime and sexual abuse that provide support, counseling and legal assistance to victims. Hence, Casa Amiga opened in 1999 with the help of a CNN reporter, the municipal government, institutions and people from El Paso, Texas, and a few *maquilas*. Women who have been raped, assaulted, or physically abused can avail themselves of medical assistance, counseling, social services and legal aid at Casa Amiga. There is more demand for their services than what they are able to provide. This help is for victims as well as for their families. Additionally, they give workshops at schools and places of work regarding sexual harassment.

Casa Amiga is only one of four rape crisis centers in Mexico, and the only one in Ciudad Juárez. It has numerous links to organizations in the United States. The Texas attorney general's office agreed to fund the training of rape crisis volunteers; a businesswoman's organization in El Paso donated $5,000 for the printing of needed educational materials. The El Paso Police Department's Crimes Against Persons Unit has provided training for police officers in Ciudad Juárez. The training involves police officers examining their own views about criminal sexual conduct, then work toward building a new trust between victims and police.[25] Private individuals from El Paso and other communities in the United States send donations to Casa Amiga. A fast-food chain from the United States has also donated money to Casa Amiga. Lots of organizations on both sides of the border support Casa Amiga.

Cross-border activity is common in the health care arena. Organizations that serve women in the United States report that they also have clients that come from Ciudad Juárez. Estimates indicate that one-third of all abortions reported in El Paso are performed on women who come from Mexico. American women also have been known to avail themselves of abortions in Mexico. American women had been traveling to Tijuana for abortions since at least the 1950s.[26]

The work of Casa Amiga and the success that it has had in raising awareness in the community is commendable because of the adversity it faces: hostility from the government, increasing public pressure to not air the community's "dirty laundry," sexist and patriarchical attitudes, limited funding, and an ever-increasing work load. It is important to note that the leadership of Casa Amiga has not gone unnoticed by other groups in the community who have expressed concern that they are monopolizing resources and using the organization.

The challenges that women face in the border region are many. The issues they encounter run the gamut from the legal, criminal, and medical to work-related concerns. Another *Casa* that is open to help migrants is the Casa del Migrante (House of the Immigrant).

Casa del Migrante

La Casa del Migrante in Ciudad Juárez is one of five homes dedicated to helping immigrants. The other homes are located in Tijuana and on the southern border with Guatemala. La Casa del Migrantes is part of a religious organization that was founded by Beato Juan Bautista Scalabrini in 1887 to provide services to immigrants and refugees. A Catholic priest runs La Casa del Migrante in Ciudad Juárez.

This home provides shelter, food, clothing, medical services, and spiritual guidance to people who have left their place of origin to seek a better life, either within Mexico or abroad. Many of those seeking services at the Casa del Migrante, deported from the United States, are victims of discrimination and abuse. The house has been in existence for 11 years in Ciudad Juárez and has never been closed "thanks in part to institutions and people of good will and heart."[27]

Casa del Migrante also has ties with a binational group "Solidaridad Fronteriza" (Border Solidarity), which is also a religious organization in El Paso and Ciudad Juárez. Casa del Migrante also works with other border communities to collaborate on information sharing, for example, in Nogales, Tucson, and Douglas, Arizona. Again, this is an example of linking border people.

The priest who runs Casa del Migrante never misses an opportunity to raise people's awareness to the plight of immigrants. Whether it is a public hearing or a meeting, he always welcomes the opportunity to share the Casa's mission with others and to elaborate on the root causes of migration. He feels that U.S. organizations have more technical where-withal, economic resources, and legal staff to work with immigrants. In Mexico, many of the human rights organizations rely on volunteers; in the United States, there are paid staff, attorneys, and other professionals who can help the cause of immigrants. In Mexico, that is not the case.

Casa del Migrante provides services to approximately 250–300 people a month. They are always seeking to collaborate with other organizations to bring about social justice on the border when dealing with issues of immigration, access to water and other environmental issues, and in raising wages in the *maquiladora* industry. According to the priest at Casa del Migrante "*la division fronteriza es teórica*" (the border exists only in theory). This organization is a friend to the immigrant, regardless of where they come from or where they are going. Other friends of immigrants also exist in the region.

American Friends

The American Friends Service Committee (AFSC), through their U.S.–Mexico Border Program (USMBP) works to end human and civil

rights abuses in the region. This is a purposive and religious organization that also works nationally and internationally. The American
Friends work to link border residents vertically as well. Throughout the
region, the American Friends have offices, staff, and programs from San
Diego/Tijuana to Brownsville/Matamoros. They monitor and document abuses and work together with a network of local human and civil
rights organizations on both sides of the border. Human rights violations occur on both sides of the border. In Mexico, *coyotes* (people who
smuggle people into the United States for a fee), drug dealers, law
enforcement officers, and *bandidos* (Mexicanos who prey on migrants in
Mexico, desperate to cross into the United States); all have been known
to violate people's rights. Reports of robbery, rape, and assault have been
documented in many areas. Unscrupulous *coyotes* offer their services to
help unsuspecting migrants enter the United States and then abandon
them either in the middle of the desert or in the back of a rented truck
without water or food. *Coyotes* and *bandidos* are some of the main
culprits in the human rights arena.[28]

The AFSC/USMBP has more resources available to them when
compared with organizations in Mexico. Their modus operandi is also
multifaceted; they work within the legal system, through educational
outreach efforts and in the development of policy. The AFSC/USMBP
files complaints on behalf of the migrants, secures legal representation,
and increases public awareness of human and civil rights violations.
Additionally, they monitor immigration law enforcement practices and
make recommendations on policy to representatives of both the United
States and Mexico. Their binational work is easily carried out because
many of their staff are bilingual and bicultural. A staff person of the
AFSC explained how she was able to work both sides of the fence so to
speak on this issue:

> I can work both sides on these issues. When I testify before the U.S.
> Congress I exclaim, "As an American citizen, I am deeply troubled by
> what we are witnessing in the border region in terms of senseless deaths."
> And when I testify in Mexico, I also exclaim *"Nosotros los Mexicanos,
> merecemos un trato digno ..."* (We Mexicans deserve to be treated with
> dignity).
>
> —Staff Member of AFSC

The work of this organization has had a profound effect in the human
rights arena throughout the border region in raising the human rights
issue in a binational context and in educating the public at large about
these issues. Irasema has witnessed how people in border communities

leave meetings where AFSC personnel have spoken: Participants leave with a new awareness and an increased sense of community self-esteem, a sense of empowerment just because their rights have been reaffirmed.

Women Workers

Mujeres Obreras: Working Women en Ambos Lados (on both sides)

Women work on both sides of the border in all kinds of jobs. At least two out of five women earn money, formally and informally, on both sides of the border. Low wages plague women on both sides of the border. In the United States in 1999, the Hispanic female median income was $11,314.[29] Maids from Ciudad Juárez who work in El Paso report making between $25 and $35 a day. This is obviously a lot more than a *maquila* worker who makes that same amount in a week, but, if they worked five-day weeks, salaries would total over half Hispanic women's income. Elsewhere, a study of informal incomes shows women earning comparable amounts on both sides of the border.[30]

Women in Ciudad Juárez

In Ciudad Juárez, women's work in factories has recently gotten a great deal of attention in research and action around the global economy. From the beginning a majority of assembly-line workers were women in the *maquiladoras* of Ciudad Juárez, as foreign (mostly U.S.) companies relocated assembly plants to places with reduced labor costs. Some of those "high-paid" workers got displaced from El Paso jobs. El Paso holds the dubious distinction of being a city with the largest number of NAFTA displaced workers (see Ethnographic Moment 2.1). These highly visible women workers, one group in Ciudad Juárez and the other in El Paso, have different profiles.

Younger women comprise the majority of these highly visible assembly-line workers in the export processing factories of Mexico's Border Industrialization Program. One of the first widely disseminated documentaries on globalized export processing, Lorraine W. Gray's *Global Assembly Line,* was filmed on Mexico's northern border and in the Bataan Export-Processing Zone of the Philippines.

In the first 15 years of Mexico's industrialization program, over three-fourths of the workforce was female, a proportion that shrunk to three-fifths, albeit a majority still of the approximately 200,000 *maquila* workers in Ciudad Juárez, the Mexican city with the largest concentration of northern border export-processing workers. The *maquiladora* industry has become more diversified over its third-of-a-century history, but some jobs are thought appropriate for women (electronics, garment, coupon sorting) and others for men (auto parts). Young women are recruited through newspaper advertisements that use pictures and the feminine and masculine linguistic forms (*operadoras, operadores*) to state their gender preference. At the downtown *plaza,* where people congregate across from the three-story market and next to the four-centuries old-cathedral, we have observed kiosk-based labor recruiters offering potential applicants bonuses to sign on employees in these high-turnover occupations: 700 pesos for first shift (approximately 10 pesos = $1) and 1,000 for second shift.

State government officials also help in the promotion of the talented labor pool: "We have it all," says Governor Patricio Martínez García. "We have excellent quality of labor, we possess important natural resources, and our men and women have the preparation and the ability to compete with their goods and services."[31] Of course, the governor does not mention the challenges that the workers face, such as lack of housing, transportation, or the notorious lack of water resources in the region.

In the *maquilas* generally, while some women have gradually moved into supervisory positions, celebrated in industry magazines like *Twin Plant News,* men control most operations at the lowest to highest levels and exercise surveillance equal to medieval panopticons.[32]

Other workers do not adapt so well. Teens seek employment at age 15 or even younger, if they are able to secure documents in the underground identification document cottage industry—industries that emerge with rule-laden immigrant and labor laws. One highly-visible murder case, associated with the women mutilation murders over the last ten years, involved a 14 year-old *operadora* (operator, worker) who was returning home after her second shift in a factory mini-bus. Last on the bus, she was raped and left for dead, but she managed to crawl to safety and identify the factory-subcontracted driver, who allegedly attacked her according to reports by border journalist Washington-Valdez in articles in the El Paso *Times.* While cases like these are news on both sides of the border, they are hardly news to the readers in the headquarter locations of the corporations with export-processing subsidiaries. When one of us contacted the *Milwaukee Journal-Sentinel* about the story, for the city of Milwaukee is home of corporate headquarters, it responded after two weeks with a blasé "you'll be contacted if a reporter wants to follow up."

Export-processing workers belong to unions at far higher rates than U.S. factory workers. However, most of these are "official" unions, affiliated with the formerly dominant ruling political party and are thus reluctant to negotiate for higher wages. Until her tragic death, in a plane crash, Guillermina Villalva led the active COMO, an organization that offered consciousness-raising and employment training courses for ex-*maquila* workers. It also organized a cooperative for scavengers who combed the Ciudad Juárez dumps for resale items.[33] While Villalva was critical of the industries, COMO did not organize export-processing workers, but rather ex-export-processing workers. COMO leaders interacted with researchers on both sides of the border, at local to national levels, yet it had no links to organizations with comparable constituencies of its own. Meanwhile, the cross-border organization FEMAP negotiates with *maquila* personnel departments, many of them staffed with social workers, to provide reproductive health outreach for workers, mainly contraceptive education and delivery. *Promotoras* (outreach workers) in El Paso are limited in numbers, and few if any do outreach in reproductive health.

Although Mexico has a very low official unemployment rate, people tend to be underemployed, or employed in the informal sector in order to be able to meet their basic needs. The "high" unemployment rate in Mexico also contributes to the lack of effective organizing because if workers start to unionize in a meaningful manner they are fired and black listed because they are so easily replaced. *Maquila* managers and human resources managers have indicated that they would like to pay *maquila* workers higher salaries, though they are precluded from doing so by government-set wage rates and by their own classification of workers. Managers have to find creative and alternative ways to remunerate their workers. This includes food baskets or food coupons at local stores, school supplies for children, English classes, parties, and other perks. "We would rather just pay more than have to organize these things, but we can't pay them more because the Mexican government won't let us" is a commonly heard justification by managers as to why *maquilas* pay so little.

According to a study conducted in 15 border cities by the Center for Reflection, Education and Action (CREA) for the Coalition for Justice in the *Maquiladoras*,[34] "the wages paid *maquiladora* workers for a full work week do not enable them to meet basic human needs of their family for nutrition, housing, clothing and non-consumables." There are over 3,500 *maquiladoras* on the northern Mexican border employing an estimated 1.2 million workers. Having to live in such dire conditions without running water, electricity, in makeshift houses and being at "nutritional risk" is a violation of human rights. The fact that full-time employment does not allow one to meet one's basic human needs much less those of one's family is a gross violation of human rights.

Women in El Paso

The high-profile women workers of El Paso are far older, on average, than Ciudad Juárez's working women. These women are middle-aged, monolingual Spanish speakers who worked in the most common light manufacturing industries—garment factories—These factories ranged from the widely known and large plants of Levi Strauss and Farah to medium-size, small, and informal sweatshops.

In the 1970s, still-legal but unethical practices existed among some of the small firms and sweatshops, operating on subcontracts with slim profit margins. Some firms would delay wage payments to workers and then go out of business several weeks thereafter, leaving their largely female workforce without recourse. Two decades ago, the organization La Mujer Obrera (LMO), the Working Woman, began organizing the unpaid women in high-visibility protest actions, covered by the media, that directed public attention to the scam. Indeed, some of these businesses would restart operations under new names. Without local success, LMO searched for legal tools to provide leverage for workers to be repaid. In the summer of 1990 they successfully lobbied for a new state law that would make these unscrupulous employers' practices a criminal offense.[35]

More recently, LMO has taken up the cause of NAFTA-displaced workers. Estimates for the number of displaced workers go as high as 25,000, but the official number is far less, based as it is on those who apply to and certify for trade adjustment assistance. Given the limited educational credentials in their backgrounds, most displaced workers cannot compete for new jobs that have been generated in El Paso, such as telemarketing, or the professional technical assistance that's linked to NAFTA-related jobs. The job boom in Ciudad Juárez, a boom associated with jobs that pay weekly wages equivalent to U.S. workers for a bit more than a half-day, is no alternative. Ex-workers prepared to enter a Byzantine bureaucratic application process can acquire training and benefits for approximately one and a half years. Most training programs are quite traditional, offering GED and English-language classes, and are not connected to job placement. Project Arriba, however, is an IAF-affiliated model, operating elsewhere in Texas, that is connected to job placement with a living wage. IAF's local affiliate, EPISO, helps leverage local and state money for the effort.

One of LMO's original organizers, Cecilia Rodríguez, left El Paso for New York and later San Francisco where she became involved in U.S. support for and solidarity with resistance in Chiapas, after the resistance that began January 1, 1994, a symbolic choice of date that coincided with the beginnings of NAFTA. LMO organizers in El Paso have finally realized successes in accomplishing their goals; they generate revenue for their small business development with their constituency in El Paso. Expansion to include constituencies in Ciudad Juárez would likely dilute efforts, given existing resource bases.

Over its 20 year history, LMO has moved from an outsider-protest organization to a complex variety of nonprofit organizations that still maintain a radical and collectivist edge. Each of the new organizations has its own mission and style. LMO's leader is María Flores, a former garment worker. Former LMO leader Cindy Arnold directs the El Puente Community Development Corporation, focused on economic development and connected to established, but change-oriented city leaders. Arnold served on high-profile boards, including the Empowerment Zone board. Yet another affiliated organization, the Asociación de Trabajadores Fronterizos (ATF), claims affiliation with 700 active members in factory and school committees. ATF promotes Spanish-speaking workers' involvement in the political process. Its leaders maintain a critical stance toward most publicly funded efforts.

LMO's origins, as the lone organization to defend unorganized, mostly women workers, continues to define its identity. On its own, through insider and outsider strategies, it has remodeled a huge warehouse space, established an income-generating child-care center and restaurant, and a *Mercado* that will provide *puestos* (stands or posts) that serve as incubators for small businesses. When LMO first started, unions and other advocacy groups ignored its constituency, and these memories inhibit coalition building.

Living in Ciudad Juárez—Working in El Paso

It is interesting to note that many Mexican women who come to work daily in El Paso work as maids and child care givers, taking care of other people's children. So on the one hand, the maids leave their children taking care of each other with relatives or friends, or on their own; on the other hand, they are helping to raise, nurture, and take care of someone else's children north of the border. This of course is a dilemma that many mothers face in the region: how does one balance work and family responsibilities in this cross-border environment?

Anecdotally in El Paso-Ciudad Juárez, maids who cross the border north to work at times report that they are not paid after a day's work, or that employers sexually harass them, or that they are treated badly and/or verbally abused by the people who hire them. Due to the illegal nature of their work situation, it is difficult for them to report such abuse to the authorities.[36] Unfortunately, this kind of exploitation is difficult to document and report; however, just because it cannot be quantified or verified other than through informal channels does not mean that it does not happen. These insidious human rights violations obviously are not part of the bigger bilateral agenda. The United States and Mexico are not engaged in negotiations regarding the plight of the maids on the border region. Violations of human rights have become so routine and ordinary that people do not even think of reporting these incidents.

It is important to note that maids and families across the border have also developed strong ties and bonds. Examples abound of families helping raise the children of maids, paying for their education, assisting them when they are ill, and becoming part of the family over time. Crossing the border to work can provide a better income than one earned in Mexico for the same kind of work. Additionally, families who hire maids provide financial loans, clothing, food, and other material goods that can help enhance the quality of life of the maid's family across the border.

Concluding Thoughts

In this chapter, we addressed the human wrongs that emerge in border-lands with little respect for and enforcement of human rights laws. International agreements, guidelines, and laws that cover transnational human rights are few and weak. No institutional shroud exists to protect or even symbolize attention to human rights abuses; only national agencies and the national cultural interpretations of specific events are brought to the human rights agendas. For example, when a Mexican national is executed in the state of Texas, all Mexicans are up in arms, but when a migrant is raped by a Border Patrol agent the outrage is not as loud.

Poverty on both sides of the border aggravates human rights abuses. The exploitation of women workers is symptomatic of the common undervaluation of work at the border. Although women workers on each side have distinctive characteristics, from the displaced workers in El Paso to the global assembly line workers in Ciudad Juárez, neither group earns living wages with benefits.

We highlighted several organizations with courageous human rights and human protection agendas. They work valiantly and at some personal risk to pursue their agendas. These organizations are built around personal tragedies and personal trust relationships. The organizations could use more strong allies, both locally and globally. The AFSC and CJM are beginning to create the weak ties that will strengthen local and personal ties but more linkages are necessary under a human rights legal shroud.

CHAPTER 7

CONCLUSIONS: TOWARD SOCIAL JUSTICE IN THE NORTH AMERICAN COMMUNITY

> The North American ... is not interested in knowing us and does not have the patience to understand.
>
> —Borderland activist

This activist, after decades of devoting his life to organizing at the northern Mexico border, is getting impatient with outsiders. An activist in the southwestern United States could echo the same dismay. We are pleased that readers had the motivation and patience to reach this point in our book. However, we worry about the many outsiders who have no interest in knowing the border and are impatient about understanding it.

Those who are distant from the borders—we call them outsiders—absorb and construct images and stereotypes about their own and neighboring countries. In their decisions and actions, they use these constructs about the border. When policy makers from the United States see the border, they see Mexico and when policy makers from Mexico see the border, they see the United States. They see immigrants, drug traffic, and disease. What they do not see is what is really there: a mish mash of languages, cultures, ways of life, and values—real energy, creativity, and vitality among the residents.

Outsiders in the interior rarely see the connection between their quality of life and the border region. On a daily basis, residents in the mainstream United States may be wearing clothes assembled in a *maquiladora*, driving a car partly assembled in a *maquiladora*, opening garage doors, turning on electronic equipment, and consuming medical supplies all assembled in *maquiladoras*. The border is important to their lives and economic well being. That well being is based on a border through which tremendous amounts of goods are transported. That traffic contributes to poor air quality and environmental health problems at the border.

The El Paso–Ciudad Juárez region, the largest of the U.S.–Mexico border metropolitan areas, is a zone of a commonality and difference. Its economy and people are tied together, but its official institutional shroud of governments and their bureaucratic agencies evoke not just difference, but division and the kind of decision that impoverishes the many and makes collaboration difficult. Nongovernmental organizations have begun to bridge the border, but face obstacles to their collaboration far greater than those that facilitate collaboration.

This chapter summarizes our analyses of cross-border collaboration. It highlights collaboration both within and across national territorial lines. While the chapter draws on conceptual frameworks that help make sense of border realities, we also aim to launch the borderlands toward a future that makes our nuanced title—*Fronteras no Más*—(No More Borders and just/only borders) the vision and reality. It behooves all of us who question borderlines to move from analysis to action to make those futures real.

Summary

Personal and Purposive Ties, Institutional Binds

Ciudad Juárez and El Paso are two large cities with a growing array of nongovernmental organizations. They share a cultural and linguistic veneer some writers glowingly refer to as *Mexicanidad*. In this region, personal and friendship ties are strong enough to imagine the day when the border is an integrated region, rather than just an interdependent region with wage and economic inequalities. But even with the region's overarching Mexicanness, there are differences of class, of immigration status, of immigration era, of Spanish-language capacity, of purposive commitments, and/or personal loyalty and enmity. These differences mean that coalitions and collaborations must be built, not merely assumed. And the opportunity to build collaborations is enormous in an area of common ground, where bilingualism is increasingly the norm.

The overarching political infrastructure makes collaboration difficult, for the infrastructure is not just one but many in two lands of complicated federalism. Mexican and U.S. governmental institutions, nominally democratic, are not mirror images of one another. These governmental differences are difficult for residents (much less distant outsiders and policy makers) to comprehend and utilize as opportune spaces for action. If someone had designed a complex system to "divide and rule," they couldn't have done a better job than the border. Moreover, U.S. federalism creates numerous borders and jurisdictions within the geographic space of what Mexico calls a municipality and in Texas, the United States, a county with city council, county commissioner, school trustee, and other district borders. These divisions complicate collaborative action even further.

On top of this infrastructure rests transnational institutions that we have called an institutional shroud. These transnational institutions are the product of national and transnational NGO actions to temper the excesses of free trade amid unequal relations, not the least of which between labor and commerce. Transnational institutions are plentiful in the environmental area, building on a century of narrow binational work through CILA/IBWC. They offer weak labor standards and a mechanism to which complaints are filed. The shroud occasionally supports democratic space and channels resources to the borderlands, but it often operates in ways that mystify and confuse real, rather than symbolic action. It creates the appearance of action. Borderlanders are hungry for action. The environmental shrouds offer models for NGO voices in the policymaking process; they set precedents for bureaucratic agencies long accustomed to doing their business behind closed doors. The existence of these mechanisms provides continued incentives for civil society to grow and collaborate across borders.

Most NGO actions are focused within a border rather than across borders. NGO activists are hard pressed to accomplish their goals on one side of the border, much less dream of managing the complexity of both sides. Few have cross-border operations and board members, two components complicated by extensive travel time, linguistic, and cultural complexities. The obstacles are daunting, given the resource scarcity and historic dearth of civic capacity. This leads to the constant chase: for money; for people to mobilize, hire and institutionalize their missions. Coupled with the chase is the insular quality to the region, isolated as it is geographically and even spiritually and ideologically from the "loose ties" that would give its "strong ties" of personalism and local knowledge more regional, national, and global leverage toward social justice. The insular quality is aggravated by national mainstreams in both countries—Mexico and the United States—that marginalize borderlanders through invisibility and budgetary starvation. Some global NGOs have not yet recognized that there is more to global mobilization than awareness campaigns, annual protests, and listservs. They need grounding, and borderlands are perfect places to begin.

Poor cousins in peculiar federal systems, El Paso politicians push for "fair share" funding, and politicians in Ciudad Juárez push for real municipal autonomy that would enable local government to generate more revenue. NGOs in both places are virtually invisible to national and global organizations. NGOs chase funds, but are far from obtaining "fair shares." Indeed, funding sources often restrict spending to one side rather than permit spending on both sides of the border. Accolades go to those rare foundations, agencies, and boards that conceptualize and fund a border region and not just places within nations: their boards reflect regional diversity and their staff members can communicate across cultural, linguistic and institutional complexities that make cross-border organizing a pioneering endeavor. Despite advances, many organizations continue to wear blinders to cross-border collaborations, nevertheless.

Despite daunting obstacles, we identified cases of cross-border collaboration and coalition building. These success stories connect local people and organizations to regional, national, and international organizations. Among these cases, we discussed environmental activists, labor unions, and human rights activists. Their motivation is either ideological, religious, personal, and materialist. Philanthropic organizations like FEMAP have also been able to negotiate the border terrain successfully, although they challenge power relations in households more than society. Compared to business and commerce, however, social justice advocates do not enjoy the obviously high profit stakes, earnings, and official incentives to cross-border organizing.

Although we identified effective cases, we are dismayed with human rights abuses that persist in the region with little resolution. Instead, human wrongs are perpetuated in everyday routine harassment and violence. Immigration lawyers and activists are barely able to meet the demand for legal and refugee assistance with the ever-tightening immigration laws. And violence persists, including unresolved murders of girls and women. The border is a gendered terrain in which women's voices and lives are less valued. Coupled with non-citizens and the working poor, a sizeable majority seeks and deserves social justice.

Social justice organizations work on either side of the border, but some of the largest and most visible have no cross-border agenda. Some would label the absence of a cross-border agenda as focus and strategic action, but we lament the missed opportunities to collaborate, coalesce with strength, and exercise enough collective power to begin to change power relations that have long been stuck in ways that reinforce the privileged, Americans all—Mexican and U.S. alike. Moreover, some of these organizations are reluctant to join forces, to collaborate given historical enmities rooted in different organizing tools, constituencies, and personalism. Organizations "take on" their potential social justice allies with conflictual models as much or more than they would with their foes. In a cultural communication context where personal factors make a big difference, such organizations do disservice to the overarching social justice agenda.

What, Then, Is to Be Done?

Cross-border organizing is a daunting prospect. We celebrate its emergence and sustenance, for more factors block it than facilitate it. As the book and our brief summary show, cross-border organizing is possible and concrete outcomes are achievable. It can grow, strengthen, and deepen through collaborative work. But these collaborations need to occur across borders: institutional, territorial, and cultural; they need to span the local and the global to combine strong and weak ties, including the resources and networks that come with weak ties. Without growth in cross-border organizing, the power and authority of business and commerce in the officially sanctioned regional and globalized economy will overwhelm civic capacity. If global NGOs are to have real legitimacy beyond consciousness-raising, electronic listservs, and protests, they must be grounded in real people and personal ties.

We extract kernels of wisdom from the analysis and list them below as strategies for change. These strategies contain equally profound implications at the national, regional, and international levels at the levels of policy and law.

- Relevant both to NGOs and official institutions, we urge people to conceptualize interdependent and integrated regions and communities while acknowledging still-existent territorial lines. States in federal systems govern with "difference" in their nations. Nations within the European Union govern with difference within their fifteen-country community. Canada, Mexico, and the United States should begin thinking and acting along these lines.
- Border regions should be as open to civic activists and their movements as border regions are open to business, commerce and trade. With civic activists encompassing potentially large numbers, we necessarily imply movement toward more open borders for work and civic action.
- Schools should open up civic education, both to transnational common interests and to connecting ideas to action, in the communities. Civic and social studies curricula are focused on the nation and nationalist interpretations of national histories. Students should get wider and comparative exposure to other cultures and institutions.

Student learning should be connected to community action, including the binational community in borderlands contexts. At least bilingual capacity should be prized valued, and taught at all educational levels. Optimally, multilingual capacity should prevail in the North American multilingual community. Residents of the European community live in this complex, but rich reality and learn languages from childhood on into adulthood.

- Just as business gets cues, incentives, and subsidies for transnational activities, so also should NGOs and civic organizations. Democracy should be elevated to the level of free trade in policy and budgets.

- Funders should acknowledge borderlands and remove budgetary restrictions that hinder spending beyond national borders. A North American transnational service, beyond *Servicio Social* and AmeriCorps/Vista, would develop a leadership corps for the future.

- Borderland NGOs should make it common practice to include members and leaders from both sides in their ranks. Much is to be learned about common agendas and creative strategies to use spaces in the democratic openings that prevail on both sides of the border.

- People in borderland NGOs and public agencies should engage with one another in relationships characterized by civility. They should engage with respect. They should listen to and observe cultural subtleties and nuances. They should be open and think outside historic memories and nationalist boxes.

- People should acknowledge the personal and build relationships of trust as they proceed to work on reasoned, ideological, principled, and purposive agendas. Once the purpose of organizing has taken hold, they should be able to agree to disagree and to move beyond friendships and "enemyships" in pursuit of common agendas. They should avoid gossip and use new democratic spaces for open and transparent dialogues.

- Institutional shrouds must change in ways that open access to NGOs and democratic voice. Rule of law should prevail, and when political strategies are exhausted, lawsuit mechanisms should be available to provoke accountability.

- Minimum wages must increase on both sides of the border, but especially in Mexico. Border wages seem to be centuries away from social justice in wage terms, but employers can begin by acknowledging the reality that four times Mexico's current minimum wage is a minimal standard.

- NGOs and businesses should work together to encourage employment standards, as did some employers under apartheid in South Africa with Sullivan guidelines. Transnational standards should be adopted and enforced within governments as well.
- Global NGOs should ground their loose networking with strong personal ties at borderlands. Listservs that claim a global reach should sort names and contacts by geographic region to facilitate local contacts and personal relationship building.
- Portable insurance should be available to citizens and noncitizens with preferred provider lists to ensure quality and accountability of healthcare.
- Human rights agreements should be developed and elevated to the levels of La Paz (environmental) and NAFTA (trade) agreements in terms of their enforcement authority.
- Immigration law enforcement should take family unification seriously, including people without the wherewithal and resources for expensive lawyers.
- Crimes against people should be elevated to the level of drug crimes. The murdered girls and women deserve cross-national attention from local police and national investigation agencies.
- National agencies would do well to utilize one office or department to deal with border issues rather than fragment efforts within a single organization.
- Borderlanders deserve "living wages" with health benefits. Poverty and its special bordered dimensions also need attention. Living wages would go along way in reducing poverty at the border.

The U.S.–Mexico borderlands are now visible to the national heartlands and to North America as a whole. Power relations between the border and the interior, and between the more and less privileged, must change with the move toward social justice. North American institutional shrouds, coupled with strong, cross-border NGOs, provide the framework in which to address problems with the environment, living wages, and human rights. The North American Union (NAU) is an imagined future, but we can seize the structures of opportunity to begin building the bridges and transcending the divisions to act on common interests now.

Epilogue

As we are finalizing this book, September 11, 2001 came and went, leaving a legacy for the world and its borders. We were horrified with the many kinds of losses that people experienced in the aftermath, regardless of their citizenships. Borderlanders also lost much after September 11. The borders closed down and slowed down, disrupting normal movements, education, and work. Out of respect for tragedy in the United States, Mexico's September 16 celebrations did not occur on U.S. soil. Lines at the border were long, and people waited hours to cross. Some of our students called frantically from their cells phones: "they're asking for my birth certificate." As people in the United States worried about anthrax, two children were asphyxiated in back of their parents' truck while waiting hours to cross the border as carbon monoxide silently crept into the vehicle. Few in the mainstream United States would know of or add those children's deaths to the victim count.

People avoided attending meetings on both sides of the border, from governors to researchers to community activists. Now as the December holidays approach, the *posadas* (the twelve days of Christmas celebrations) begin and people prepare for quiet time with families. The lines at the border have gotten shorter. Applications for the Dedicated Commuter Lane permits have shot up, for those who can afford the fees, but even they have to wait for the FBI checks and ever-hungry bureaucracy to do its work, a process now lengthened with the increased demand for permits and heightened scrutiny.

The dream for more open borders, always waxing and waning, seems dim for now. But we are optimistic over the long haul for an integrated border with respect for rights, decent wages, and environmental stewardship.

Despite the post-9/11 doldrums over border crossing, we are heartened with the growing strength of the Coalition Against Violence Toward Women and Families. With participants from Ciudad Juárez, El Paso, and Las Cruces (NM), participants are using their strategic positions and organizational strengths to heighten visibility on the mutilation-murders of girls and women (especially in Ciudad Juárez), to maintain the pressure, to fund-raise for the victims' families, and to demand concrete solutions. A huge rally was held the day after International Women's Day, March 9, in El Paso's downtown plaza; participants marched just blocks to the border and were met with a group of protestors from Mexico in a show of joint solidarity. The Mexican press exercised censorship (bad publicity), but people found out anyway. Several politicians have belatedly, but finally joined the bandwagon in pressing for binational cooperation between the state attorney generals' offices and local police forces. If the police can cooperate over auto theft, why can't they cooperate over female mutilation-murders? Lourdes Portillo's striking film, *Señorita Extraviada*, has been shown several times at UTEP. Mexican and U.S. students alike engaged in a silent protest on the UTEP free-speech lawn, dressed in mourning and carrying the bright pink signs with crosses. Ni una más! Not one more death!

ENDNOTES

Chapter 1   Introduction: Toward Social Justice at the U.S.–Mexico Border

1. Timothy Dunn, *The Militarization of the U.S.–Mexico Border, 1978–1992: Low-Intensity Conflict Doctrine Comes Home* (Austin: Center for Mexican American Studies, University of Texas, 1996); selections from David Spener and Kathleen Staudt, eds., *The U.S.–Mexico Border: Transcending Divisions, Contesting Identities* (Boulder: Lynne Rienner Press, 1998), esp. the concluding chapter. Irasema Coronado and Edward J. Williams, "The Hardening of the U.S.–Mexico Borderlands: Causes and Consequences," *Boundary Security Bulletin* vol. 1, no. 4. University of Durham, England, 1994.
2. David Spener and Bryan Roberts, "Small Business, Social Capital, and Economic Integration on the Texas–Mexico Border," in Spener and Staudt, 1998, pp. 83–104; Kathleen Staudt, *Free Trade? Informal Economies at the U.S.–Mexico Border* (Philadelphia: Temple University Press, 1998).
3. On numbers for displaced laborers, see Kathleen Staudt and Randy Capps, "Con La Ayuda de Dios? El Pasoans Manage the 1996 Welfare and Immigration Law Reforms," forthcoming in *Living in the Interim: Immigrant Communities and Welfare "Reform" in North America*, Ana Aparicio, Phil Kretsedemas, and Kalyani Rhai, eds, (NY: Praeger-Greenwood). Also see La Mujer Obrera, *Exploring and Promoting Adequate Health Care Coverage Among Displaced Workers*, presented by Suzanna and Abel Fernández, El Paso, 1999.
4. Sidney Tarrow, *Power in Movement: Social Movements and Contentious Politics* (NY: Cambridge University Press, 1998), pp. 19–20.
5. Benjamin Márquez, *Power and Politics in a Chicano Barrio: A Study of Mobilization Efforts and Community Power in El Paso* (Lanham, MD: University Press of America), 1985; Staudt; U.S. Commission on Civil Rights, *Mexican American Education Study, 1971–74* (six volumes) (Washington, D.C.: U.S. Commission on Civil Rights).
6. Ellwyn Stoddard, "Patterns of Poverty Along the U.S.–Mexico Border," El Paso: Center for Inter-American and Border Studies, University of Texas at El Paso, 1978.
7. On poverty figures in Mexico, see Sarah Anderson, "Seven Years Under NAFTA," Institute for Policy Studies, Washington, D.C., August 2001, based on World Bank figures.
8. Gloria Anzaldúa, *Borderlands/La Frontera: The New Mestiza* (San Francisco: Spinsters/Aunt Lute Press), 1987; Spener and Staudt, 1998, selections.

9. Oscar Martínez, *Border People: Life and Society in the U.S.–Mexico Borderlands* (Tucson: University of Arizona Press, 1994), 60; then pp. 6–9 on categories.
10. Oscar Martínez, "The Dynamics of Border Interaction: New Approaches to Border Analysis," in *Global Boundaries*, ed. Clive H. Schofield (London: Routledge, 1994), 4.
11. David M. Fetterman, *Ethnography: Step by Step* (Newbury Park: Sage Applied Social Research Methods Series), Volume 17.
12. Robert K. Yin, *Case Study Research: Design and Methods* (Newbury Park: Sage Applied Social Research Methods Series), Volume 5.
13. Clifford Geertz, *The Interpretation of Cultures: Selected Essays* (NY: Basic Books, 2000 [1973, originally]).
14. See Deborah Stone, *Policy Paradox: The Art of Political Decision-Making* (NY: W. W. Norton, 1997), on numeric metaphors.
15. Robert Alvarez, ed. *Human Organization* 60, 2 (special issue on the U.S.–Mexico border), 2001.
16. In Spener and Staudt, introductory chapter, "Aspiring Global Cities," is used in Staudt 1998, ch. 3.
17. Carnegie Endowment for International Peace and Instituto Tecnológico Autónomo de México, *Mexico–U.S. Migration: A Shared Responsibility* (Washington, D.C., CEIP, 2000), Karl Eschbach et al., "Death at the Border," *International Migration Review* 33, pp. 430–54.
18. Tanis Slant et al., *Illegal Immigrants in U.S.–Mexico Border Counties: Costs of Law Enforcement, Criminal Justice and Emergency Medical Services*. Commissioned by the U.S./Mexico Border Counties Coalition. (Tucson: University of Arizona Institute for Local Government, 2001).
19. John Sharp, *Bordering the Future* (Austin: Texas State Comptroller's Office, 1998). Also on the texas.gov website.
20. Edmé Domínguez, "Regionalism from the People's Perspective: A View of Mexican Women Reactions to Integration," paper presented at the International Studies Association Annual Meeting, February 1999, Washington D.C.. Forthcoming in the *International Feminist Journal of Politics*, 4, 2, 2002.
21. Murray Edelman, *The Symbolic Uses of Politics* (Champaign-Urbana: University of Illinois Press) 1964.

Chapter 2   Collaboration at Borders: The Two Faces of Personalism

1. Harold Laswell is the classic political scientist writing in *Politics: Who Gets What, When and How?* (NY: McGraw Hill, 1936).
2. Margaret Keck and Kathryn Sikkink, *Activists Beyond Borders: Advocacy Networks in International Politics* (Ithaca: Cornell University Press, 1995), 1, 12.
3. Christina Gabriela and Laura Macdonald, "NAFTA, Women and Organizing in Canada and Mexico: Forging a 'Feminist Internationality'," *Millennium: Journal of International Studies* 23, 3, 1994, pp. 535–562; Heather Williams, "Mobile Capital and Transborder Labor Rights Mobilization," *Politics and Society* 27, 1, 1995, pp. 139–66; Debra Liebowitz,

Gender and Identity in an Era of Globalization: Transnational Organizing in North America. Ph.D. Dissertation, Rutgers University, 2000; Mary K. Meyers and Elisabeth Prügl, eds. *Gender Politics in Global Governance* (Lanham, MD: Rowman and Littlefield, 1999).

4. Catherine Hoskyns, "Gender and Transnational Democracy: The Case of the European Union," in Meyer and Prügl 1999, pp. 72–87.

5. Robert Chaskin et al., offers a good summary and literature review in *Building Community Capacity* (NY: Aldine de Gruyter, 2001). Also see an old, but contemporary U.S. civic organization, the National Civic League and its website www.ncl.org.

6. The sociological concept of social capital has been revived in Robert Putnam, *Bowling Alone: The Collapse and Revival of American Community* (Cambridge: Harvard University Press, 2000). On its use at the border, see Staudt 1998, and Peter Ward, *Colonias and Public Policy in Texas and Mexico* (Austin: University of Texas Press, 1999).

7. Steffen Schmidt et al., *Friends, Followers, and Factions: A Reader in Political Clientelism* (Berkeley: University of California Press, 1977); Peter Smith, *Labyrinths of Power: Political Recruitment in Twentieth-Century Mexico* (Princeton: Princeton University Press, 1970).

8. James Q. Wilson, *Political Organizations* (NY: Basic Books, 2nd edition, 1993).

9. Notable exceptions include Antonio Ugalde, *Power and Conflict in a Mexican Neighborhood* (Albuquerque: University of New Mexico Press, 1970); Wayne Cornelius, *Politics and the Migrant Poor in Mexico City* (Stanford University Press, 1974).

10. William Domhoff, *Who Rules America?* (NY: Mayfield, 3rd edition, 1998).

11. Those who locate personalism and patrimony in "modern" bureaucracy include Rosabeth Kanter, *Men and Women of the Corporation* (NY: Basic, 1992, 2nd edition), and Kathleen Staudt, *Women, Foreign Assistance and Advocacy Administration* (NY: Praeger, 1985).

12. James Scott, *Domination and the Arts of Resistance* (New Haven, CT: Yale University Press, 1990), pp. 142–3.

13. Carlos Vélez-Ibañez, *Border Visions* (Tucson: University of Arizona Press, 1996); Saguaro Foundation.

14. Gabriel Almond and Sidney Verba, *The Civic Culture* (Boston: Little Brown, 1963), 16.

15. Geerte Hofstede, *Culture's Consequences* (Beverly Hills: Sage, 1985).

16. Irasema Coronado and Duncan Earle, "American Community Survey: Perceptions of Colonia Residents," Washington, D.C.: U.S. Census Technical Report, 2001; Staudt 1998.

17. Márquez 1985.

18. U.S. Commission on Civil Rights, *Mexican American Education Study*, 1971–74. Washington, D.C.: U.S. Commission on Civil Rights.

19. Wendy White Polk, "Ann Schaechner (Interview): Nonprofit Professionalism," *El Paso, Inc.,* March 5–9, 2000.

20. Mark Granovetter, "The Strength of Weak Ties," *American Journal of Sociology* 78, 6, 1974, 1, 371. His work has spawned many replications in specific context, as well as the journal *Social Networks*.

21. Keck and Sikkink, 206.
22. This communication chart draws from Raymond Cohen, *Negotiating Across Cultures: Communication Obstacles in International Diplomacy* (Washington, D.C.: U.S. Institute of Peace Press, 1991).
23. Carol Gilligan, *In a Different Voice* (Cambridge: Harvard University Press, 1982); Debra Tannen, *Gender and Discourse* (NY: Oxford University Press, 1996).
24. Renne Labloire and David Palmer, *Perspectives on NGO Capacity-Building in Mexico.* Presented to the David and Lucile Packard Foundation, 1999.
25. Robert Chaskin et al., *Building Community Capacity*, (NY: Aldine de Gruyter, 2001) provides a good review.

Chapter 3   Political Institutions, NGOs, and Accountability
in the Borderlands

1. Gregory Kelson, "International Labor Policies and the North American Free Trade Agreement: Are Women Getting Their Fair Share?" *Journal of International Women's Studies* (http://www.bridgew.edu/DEPTS/ARTSCNCE/JIWS/may00/kelson.htm).
2. Stephen Mumme, "Managing Acute Water Scarcity on the U.S.–Mexico Border," *Natural Resources Journal* 39, 1, Winter 1999, pp. 149–67, for example.
3. Robert A. Hackenberg and Robert R. Alvarez, "Close-ups of Post-Nationalism: Reports from the U.S.–Mexico Borderlands," *Human Organization* 6, 2, pp. 97–103.
4. Marshall Carter, "Agency Fragmentation and its Effects on Impact: A Borderlands Case," *Policy Studies Journal*, 1978, 7, pp. 862–3; John Sloan and Jonathan West, "The Role of Informal Policy-Making in U.S.–Mexico Border Cities," *Social Science Quarterly*, 58, 2, 1977, pp. 277–82; William D'Antonio and William Form, *Influentials in Two Border Cities: A Study in Community Decision-Making* (Notre Dame: University of Notre Dame Press, 1965).
5. Mary Walshok, "A Research University Perspective," in *Civic Responsibility and Higher Education*, Thomas Ehrlich, ed (Phoenix: American Council on Education and Oryx Press), 2000, pp. 295–305. Also see the San Diego Dialogue website: http://www.sddialogue.org.
6. Staudt has been on the FEMAP (honorary) board for ten years. Analysis of its cross-border micro-enterprise projects is found in Staudt 1998, ch. 7. The 10 percent figure comes from internal FEMAP documents, based on research from its Executive Director, Dr. Enrique Suárez.
7. Community Scholars has a web site: http://www.comunityscholars.org. For two years, Staudt served on its board and help recruit more Ciudad Juárez board members.
8. Staudt and Capps 1998.
9. David Korten, *Getting to the 21st Century: Voluntary Action and the Global Agenda* (West Harford, CT: Kumarian Press, 1990).

10. Jutta Blauert and Simon Zadek, *Mediating Sustainablility: Growing Policy from the Grassroots* (West Hartford, CT: Kumarian Press 1998), p. 61.
11. Elizabeth Mueller, *Building Community Development Capacity in El Paso*. (New Brunswick, NJ: Rutgers University Center for Urban Policy Research, Report No. 4, 1998, p. 78. available at http://policy.rutgers.edu/cupr.indexleg.htm.
12. Mueller 1998, 26.
13. Dennis Shirley, *Community Organization and Urban School Reform* (Austin: University of Texas Press, 1997). Staudt has worked with EPISO since 1999, accompanying participants to large Austin rally in March 1999 and serving as a mentor professor for an Alliance School, Ysleta Middle School, since 1998.
14. The numbers for Ciudad Juárez are difficult to acquire. Our estimate is based on reports to us from informed leaders, plus FECHAC (Fundación del Empresariado Chihuahuense and State of Chihuahua (http://www.chihuahua.gob.mx) counts of 545 and 84 respectively, some of the former numeric counts of which are registered in Chihuahua City, but operate in Ciudad Juárez, one of Mexico's five largest cities. Thanks to Héctor Padilla of the Universidad Autónoma de Ciudad Juárez (UACJ) and Angel Gómez. Also Cynthia Zúñiga, "Organizaciones No Gubernamentales en Perspectiva Comparativa Ciudad Juárez/El Paso," unpublished research paper, 2001.
15. This comes from the bowels of the U.S. government Internal Revenue's website, and thanks to nonprofit legal expert Steven Meador for locating it.
16. Stone 1997.
17. Victoria Rodríguez, *Decentralization in Mexico* (Boulder: Westview, 1997); Victoria Rodríguez and Peter Ward, eds., *Opposition Government in Mexico* (Albuquerque: University of New Mexico Press, 1995).
18. Judith Torney-Purta et al., on "citizenship canons" in *Civic Education Across Countries: Twenty-Four National Case Studies from the IEA Civic Education Project* (Amsterdam: International Association for the Evaluation of Education Achievement, 1999 (mostly northern countries, Mexico not included). Also see Susan Rippberger and Kathleen Staudt, *Pledging Allegiance: Learning Nationalism in School at the U.S.–Mexico Border* (NY: Routledge/Falmer 2002 Forthcoming).
19. Keck and Sikkink, 16.

Chapter 4   Institutional Shrouds: National Sovereignty and Environmental NGOs

1. Vicente Fox, "More Trust Needed on Both Sides of the Border: Vicente Fox" *New York Times*, September 4, 2001.
2. United States Environmental Protection Agency, Fourth Report of the Good Neighbor Environmental Board. Washington, D.C., 2000.
3. David Pérez López, "Flor y Fauna en la Antigua Cuenca del Bravo" *El Diario de Juárez* July 8, 2001: Especial 3B.

4. Paul Ganster, Border Environment Research Reports, Number 1, June 1996, Environmental Issues of the California–Baja California Border also available at http://www.scerp/org/scerp.docs/berrl.html.

5. Eliot Shapleigh, "Texas Borderlands: Frontier of the Americas," Senate District 29 District www2.elpasonet.net/~borderlands/TBOverview.htm Shapleigh.

6. Héctor Padilla, "Medio Ambiente y Acción Pública," *Medio Ambiente, Ciudad y Orden Jurídico*, ed. Mario Bassols and Patrice Melé (Mexico City: Miguel Angel Porrúa Grupo Editorial and Universidad Autónoma Metropolitana).

7. Saul Landau and Sonia Angulo, *Maquila: A Tale of Two Mexico's* (video) Pomona, CA: College of Letters, Arts and Social Sciences Mediavision, California State Polytechnic University, 2000.

8. Allen Blackman and Jeffrey Bannister, "Cross-Border Environmental Management and the Informal Sector: Ciudad Juárez Brickmakers Project," eds. Richard Kiy and John Wirth *Environmental Management on North America's Borders* (College Station: Texas A & M University Press, 1998).

9. Irasema Coronado has visited numerous *colonias* in El Paso County in 2000 during a research project with the U.S. Census Bureau. Several of the *colonias* did not have paved streets.

10. Irasema Coronado and Duncan Earle, "Barriers to Enumeration in *Colonias* on the U.S. Mexico Border" Technical Report, U.S. Census Publication, 2001.

11. John Sharp, *Bordering the Future: Challenge and Opportunity in the Texas Border Region* (Austin, Texas: Comptroller of Public Accounts, 1998).

12. Local officials from Matamoros, Tamaulipas and Brownsville, Texas discussed the problems with tires at great length before the Good Neighbor Environmental Board Meeting, Brownsville, Texas, Nov. 2–3, 2000.

13. Implementation by the IBWC of the broad provisions of the treaties and other international agreements requires specific agreements by the IBWC for planning construction, operation and maintenance of joint works and the manner of sharing the costs and other joint activities. Such agreements constituting decisions or recommendations, subject to the approval of the two governments, are recorded in the form of minutes recorded in English and Spanish, signed by each commissioner and attested to by the secretaries. Copies thereof are forwarded to each government within three days after being signed. Once approved by both Governments, the minutes are binding obligations upon the two governments. More information is available at: http://www.ibwc.state.gov/ORGANIZA/about_us.htm.

14. Helen Ingram et al., *Divided Waters* (Tucson, Arizona: University of Arizona Press, 1995), 215.

15. The All-American Canal located in southeastern California is 80 miles long and is part of the federal irrigation system of the Hoover Dam. Water from the Colorado River is diverted into this canal and subsequently affects Mexico's water supply.

16. An environmental activist shared this anecdote and information with us at a meeting.

17. Helen Ingram et al., 1995.
18. *El Paso Times,* Nov. 12, 2001, Section 2B.
19. The official title of the La Paz Agreement is the United States Department of State. 1983. Environmental Cooperation: Agreement between the United States of America and Mexico. August 14. TIAS no. 10827. United States and treaties and other international agreements. Washington, D.C.: GPO.
20. Irasema Coronado was an intern at the USEPA at the time this document was being drafted. A staffer working on the IBEP shared this observation.
21. United States Environmental Protection Agency, Washington, D.C., Good Neighbor Environmental Board n.d. pamphlet.
22. United States Department of State, Dispatch 623, September 14, 1993.
23. Ken Ellingwood, "U.S.–Mexico Bank Fizzling" *Los Angeles Times,* July 15, 2001.
24. Irasema Coronado attended the hearings.
25. Border XXI Program Overview, Spring 1999 Fact Sheet U.S.–Mexico Border XXI Program Framework Document 1996 United States Environmental Protection Agency, Washington, D.C.
26. Padilla, "Medio Ambiente."
27. Ibid.
28. More comprehensive information can be found at http://www.epa.gov/usmexicoborder.
29. "The little *priista* that we all carry inside of us" is a diminuative reference to a member of the former ruling party, Partido Revolucionario Institucional (PRI). This term was originally coined by Felipe Calderon, a member of the Partido Acción Nacional (PAN). Presently, he is a federal deputy.
30. Steven Barracca, "Reforming Mexico's Municipal Reform: The Politics of Devolution in Chihuahua and Yucatan," *Journal of Law and Border Studies,* 2001, vol.1, no. 1, pp. 31–74.

Chapter 5   Cross-Border Trade: An Institutional Model for
Labor Unions and NGOs?

1. David Diamon, "Executive Pay-Chart." Electronic Business, 1998 Highest-Paid Executives more information available at www.e-insite.net/eb.
2. Robert Reich, *The Work of Nations* (NY: Vintage, 1992).
3. Hoskyns 1999.
4. Tim Bissel and Daisy Pitkin, "A Complete Guide to FTAA Resistance," Posted by Campaign for Labor Rights, April 10, 2001. More information can be found at www.summersault.com/agi/clr.
5. From El Paso's electronic weekly news: www.stantonstreet.com. In March 2001, journalist Sito Negron conducted extensive interviews with the candidates and comparisons of their positions and responses to his queries.

6. Dale Story, *Industry, the State, and Public Policy in Mexico* (Austin: University of Texas Press, 1986).
7. Staudt 1998, chapter 3, especially. Also see selections in Ward and Rodríguez, eds. on the PAN. Peter Ward and Victoria Rodríguez, co-eds, *Opposition Government in Mexico* (Albuquerque: University of New Mexico Press, 1995).
8. Saul Landau and Sonia Angulo, *Maquila: A Tale of Two Mexicos* (video). (Pomona, CA: College of Letters, Arts and Social Sciences Mediavision, California State Polytechnic University, 2000).
9. Landau and Angulo, 2000. For Texas–Mexico figures see Victoria Rodríguez and Peter Ward *Reaching Across the Border: Intergovernmental Relations between Texas and Mexico* (Austin, Texas: LBJ School of Public Affairs: University of Texas, 1999), 6.
10. Louis Uchitelle, "America's Newest Industrial Belt," *New York Times*, March 21, 1993. Business.
11. World Bank, *World Development Report: Knowledge for Development.* (Washington, D.C./NY: World Bank/Oxford University Press, 1999). *The World Development Report* (Washington, D.C.: World Bank 1983) was the major initial document to cogently argue and develop this theme.
12. Staudt served on a city planning board wherein such standards were part of the dialogue. One sees billboards in the region advertising these standards. Also see World Bank, 1999, p. 28.
13. David Moberg, "Union Cities," *The American Prospect*, September 11, 2000, pp. 35–7.
14. Nathan 1987.
15. Based on Staudt's conversations with strategic actors who are involved and observant of the organizations. Even the loosely tied activists from afar recognize this local divide. By the late 1990s, activists moved away from garment protectionist strategies toward worker-owned small restaurant and child care businesses via La Puente Development Corporation.
16. See www.epfta.org for El Paso's Foreign Trade Association. Silvestre Reyes 2001 News Releases, 16th Congressional District (various).
17. Spener and Roberts 1998, 87.
18. Hathaway 2000, 60. His opening epigraph is found on p. 23.
19. Hathaway 2000, 76, pp. 104–5.
20. Hathaway 2000, pp. 12–13.
21. Hathaway 2000, pp. 16–20, 233. Also see Kelson 2000.
22. Coalition for Justice in the Maquiladoras (CJM) Summer/Fall 2000, *Annual Report* 10, 2.
23. CJM. The standards are represented in Kamel and Hoffman 1999.
24. *Mexico Labor News & Analysis*, April 2001, 8–11.
25. Francisco Lara, "Transboundary Networks for Environmental Management in the San Diego-Tijuana Border Region," in L.A. Herzog, ed., *Shared Space: Rethinking the U.S. Mexico Border Environment* (La Jolla, Center for U.S.–Mexican Studies, University of California, San Diego, 2000), pp. 155–81.

26. Mexico's Social Security website is www.imss.gob.mx. Coupled with its Census website noting Chihuahua's population of 3,052,907 (www.inegi.gob.mx), we came up with gaps, though workers' families are covered.

27. We have seen wild fluctuations of the percentage of the medically uninsured population, from a third to 60 percent, but these 1997 figures come from a UCLA study cited in local health reports. The 10 percent indigent population is commonly used by a collaborative organization called Community Voices, though it is probably an underestimated, informed guess. Staudt's *Free Trade?* study collected data on cross-border movement to access medical services (1998, ch. 4) and provided figures on cost differences. A FEMAP internal study by Dr. Enrique Suárez notes a 10 percent El Paso user figure for its Ciudad Juárez hospital facility. For four years, Staudt has participated in evaluation and planning processes with Community Voices, and she thanks Núria Homedes for many conversations on this and other health topics. Both have interviewed health providers in connection with that work. See Homedes and Ugalde, forthcoming.

28. Staudt and Capps 1998 did an extensive study on immigration and welfare reform, drawing on interviews with officials, community leaders, and 100 residents of the 79905 zip code area. Local media covered divergent local and state sentiments.

29. David Warner has long promoted the idea of portable health insurance (see Warner 1999), and selected examples of private employers utilizing this idea in Arizona and California are available. Staudt interacted with medical providers and visited the official Texas government website for the changing fate of this legislative initiative, www.texas.gov.

30. John Sharp, *Bordering the Future: Challenge and Opportunity in the Texas Border Region* (Austin: Texas Comptroller of Public Accounts, 1998).

Chapter 6   Human Rights and Human Wrongs

1. Jesse Arrieta, "Poder de la Mujer," McNair Scholar's Research Presentation, November 10, 2001, University of Texas at El Paso.

2. Sydney Weintraub et al., *Migration Between Mexico and the United States Binational Study 1998*, Mexican Ministry of Foreign Affairs, Mexico City and U.S. Commission on Immigration Reform, Washington, D.C.

3. Ibid, 504.

4. Paul Scherrer and Kate Randall, "Texas Executes Mexican National," www.wsws.org/articles/2000/nov2000/exec-n11.shtml.

5. Myron Weiner, *International Migration and Security* (Boulder, Colorado: Westview Press, 1993); Douglas Massey, *Economic Development and International Migration in Comparative Perspective* (Washington, D.C.: Commission for the Study of International Migration and Cooperative Economic Development, 1989).

6. Mexico: Fox, Remittances. 2000. *Migration News* Dec. 2000, vol. 7, no. 12 http://migration.ucdavis.edu/

7. Jodi Garber, "Mexico Officials Urge Opening U.S. to Trucks," *El Paso Times,* August 13, 2001: B1.

8. "Binational Cooperation Reyes Hosts Five Senators from Mexico."

9. *El Paso Times* Op. Ed. August 13, 2001: 6A.

10. Debbie Nathan, *Women and Other Aliens: Essays from the U.S.–Mexico Border* (El Paso: Cinco Puntos Press, 1991).

11. Dora Elena Cortes et al., "Celebro Robinson reunion a puerta cerrada con ONG *El Universal* A 13, November 26, 1999: A:13.

12. "Mexico–U.S. Migration: A Shared Responsbility," Carnegie Endowment for International Peace and Instituto Tecnológico Autónomo de Mexico, 2001.

13. Irasema Coronado, "Who Governs in a Binational Context? The Role of Transnational Political Elites," Unpublished dissertation, University of Arizona, 1998.

14. Luis Carlos Cano, "Llegan Miles de Veracruzanos a Ciudad Juárez" *El Universal* July 19, 1999.

15. Department of State Web site, www.travel.state.gov/mexico.html.

16. This figure was reported by an official at the Chamber of Commerce and could not be confirmed anywhere else.

17. UNICEF-DIF, "Boy and Girl Victims of Sexual Exploitation in Mexico," www.ssw.upenn.edu/restes/Mexico_Final_Report_001015.pdf, 2000.

18. The number of disappeared women varies depending on the source and the time frame that we conducted interviews. Hence, the discrepancy in the figures.

19. Diana Washington Valdez, "Bodies Everywhere," *El Paso Times,* June 25, 2000, B1.

20. Sonia Del Valle, "A parar la lista: Ni una más," www.nodo50.org/mujeresred/mexico-juarez-htm, May 18, 1998.

21. Amnesty International, www.amnesty-volunteer.org/usa/group137/digna.html.

22. Again, the inconsistency in reported number of disappeared women from another source.

23. Diana Washington Valdez, "Phone Taps in Mexico Uncovered," *El Paso Times,* July 9, 2001: B1.

24. Carlton Stowers, "The Angel of Juárez," *Dallas Observer,* January 4, 2001.

25. Ibid.

26. Leslie Reagan, "Crossing the Border for Abortion: California Activists, Mexican Clinics and the Creation of a Feminist Health Agency in the 1960s," *Feminist Studies* 26: 2, Summer 2000, pp. 323–48.

27. Red Casa del Migrante www.migrante.com.mx/ciudadjuarez.html.

28. Irasema Coronado, "Who Governs in a Binational Context? The Role of Transnational Political Elites," Unpublished dissertation, University of Arizona, 1998.

29. Christine Thurlow Brenner, "Educational Trends and Income in El Paso: A Longitudinal Perspective" University of Texas at El Paso: Institute for Policy and Economic Development Technical Report, 2001: 2001–07.

30. Staudt 1998.
31. "Chihuahua: The State With it All." *Twin Plant News*, November 30, 2001, vol. 17, no. 4.
32. Leslie Salzinger, "Making Fantasies Real: Producing Women and Men on the *Maquila* Floor," *NACLA Report on The Americas* 34.5 (2001), 13–19.
33. Devon Peña. *The Terror of the Machine Technology, Work, Gender, and Ecology on the U.S.–Mexico Border* (Austin, TX: Center for Mexican–American Studies, University of Texas) 1997.
34. Coalition for Justice in the *Maquiladoras, Making the Invisible Visible: A Study of Maquila Workers in Mexico* (Hartford, CT: CREA), 2000.
35. For more information see *La Mujer Obrera* website, www.grass-roots.org/usa/mujer.shtml.
36. Debbie Nathan, *Women and Other Aliens: Essays from the U.S.–Mexico Border* (El Paso: Cinco Puntos Press, 1991).

BIBLIOGRAPHY

Agreement between the Government of the United States of America and the Government of the United Mexican States Concerning the Establishment of a Border Environment Cooperation Commission and a North American Development Bank.

Alinsky, Saul. 1971. *Rules for Radicals*. NY: Random House.

Almond, Gabriel and Sidney Verba. 1963. *The Civic Culture*. Boston: Little Brown.

Alvarez, Robert R. (guest editor) 2001. *Human Organization*. 60, 2 (special issue on the U.S.–Mexico border).

American Friends Service Committee. www.afsc.org./border.

Americas Refugee Asylum Project Newsletters, Las. 1998.

Amnesty International. http://amnesty-volunteeer.org/usa/group137/digna. html.

Arthur Andersen North American Business Sourcebook. 1994. Chicago, Illinois: Triumph Books.

Anderson, Benedict. 1991. *Imagined Communities: Reflections on the Origins and Spread of Nationalism*. London: Verso.

Anderson, Sarah. 2001. "Seven Years Under NAFTA." Institute for Policy Studies. Washington, D.C.

Anzaldúa, Gloria. 1987. *Borderlands/La Frontera: The New Mestiza*. San Francisco: Spinsters/Aunt Lute Press.

Aqua Link Water Systems Newsletter. Summer 2001.

Arrieta, Jesse. 2001. "Poder de la Mujer." McNair Scholar's Research Presentation, November 10. University of Texas at El Paso.

Barracca, Steven. 2001. "Reforming Mexico's Municipal Reform: The Politics of Devolution in Chihuahua and Yucatan," *Journal of Law and Border Studies*, vol. 1, no. 1, 31–74.

Bénitez, Rohry et al., 1999. *El Silencio que la Voz de Todas Quiebra: Mujeres y Victimas de Ciudad Juárez*. Chihuahua, Chihuahua: Azar.

"Binational Cooperation: Reyes Hosts Five Senators from Mexico." Editorial. El Paso Times August 13, 2001: 6A.

Bissel, Tim and Daisy Pitkin. 2001. "A Complete Guide to FTAA Resistance." Posted by Campaign for Labor Right. April 10. www.summersault.com/agi/clr.

Blackman, Allen and Jeffrey Bannister. 1998. "Cross-Border Environmental Management and the Informal Sector: Ciudad Juárez Brickmakers Project," in *Environmental Management on North America's Borders*, Richard Kiy and John Wirth, eds. College Station: Texas A & M University Press.

Blauert, Jutta and Simon Zadek. 1998. *Mediating Sustainability: Growing Policy from The Grassroots*. West Hartford: Kumarian Press.

Border Eco Web (Guide to finding Environmental Information about the U.S.– Mexican Border Region through the Internet). www.borderecoweb.sdsu.edu.

Border Environmental Cooperation Commission (BECC) Comisión de Cooperación Ecológica Fronteriza (COCEF) www.cocef.org.

Border Rights Coalition/Coalición de Derechos Fronterizos, 1996–8. Newsletter-like mailings/packets.

Brenner, Christine Thurlow. 2001. "Educational Trends and Income in El Paso: A Longitudinal Perspective" University of Texas at El Paso: Institute for Policy and Economic Development Technical Report: 2001-7.

Brofenbrenner, Kate, ed. et al., 1998. *Organizing to Win: New Research on Union Strategies*. Ithaca, NY: Cornell University Press.

Callsen, Paul. 1985. *Informal Transborder Relationships Among Municipal Officials: El Paso, Tx; Ciudad Juárez, Chihuahua*, University of Texas El Paso, MPA Thesis.

Cano, Luis Carlos. "Llegan Miles de Veracruzanos a Ciudad Juárez," *El Universal* July 19, 1999 serpiente.dgsca.unam./mx/universal/net

Carnegie Endowment for International Peace and Instituto Tecnológico Autónomo de México, 2000. *México–U.S. Migration: A Shared Responsibility.* Washington, D.C.: CEIP.

Carter, Marshall. 1978. "Agency Fragmentation and its Effects on Impact: A Borderlands Case." *Policy Studies Journal, 7* (special issue), 862–3.

Chambers, Robert. 1996. " The Primary of the Personal," *Beyond the Magic Bullet: NGO Performance and Accountability in the Post-Cold War World,* Co-editors Michael Edwards and David Hulme. West Hartford, CT: Kumarian, 241–53.

Chaskin, Robert et al., 2001. *Building Community Capacity,* NY: Aldine de Gruyter.

"Chihuahua: The State With it All." 2001. *Twin Plant News,* November 30, 17, 4.

Clark, John. 1991. *Democratizing Development: The Role of Voluntary Organizations.* Hartford, CT: Kumarian Press.

Coalition for Justice in the Maquiladoras. 2000. *Making the Invisible Visible: A Study of Maquila Workers in Mexico.* Hartford, CT: CREA.

Cohen, Raymond. 1991. *Negotiating Across Cultures: Communication Obstacles in International Diplomacy.* United States Institute of Peace Press, Washington, D.C.

The Complete Twin Plant Handbook. Annually updated. Solunet, El Paso. www.solunet.com

"Cooperate to Clean Up: Shared Problems Require Binational Solutions." Editorial. El Paso *Times.* October 7, 2001: 6A.

Cornelius, Wayne. 1974. *Politics and the Migrant Poor in Mexico City.* Stanford: Stanford University Press.

Coronado, Irasema. 1998. "Who Governs in Binational Context? The Role of Transnational Political Elites." Unpublished dissertation, University of Arizona.

————. 1996. "Conflictos Ambientales Internacionales e Intranacionales" II *Simposium de Estudios Fronterizos.* El Colegio de la Frontera Norte: Piedras Negras, Coahuila, December.

————. 1995. "Legal Solutions vs. Environmental Realities: The Case of the United States–Mexico Border Region," *University of Connecticut Journal of International Law,* 10, 2, Spring 281–300.

———— and Duncan Earle. 2001. "American Community Survey: Perceptions of *Colonia* Residents," Technical Report, U.S. Census.

———— and Duncan Earle. 2000. "Barriers to Enumeration in *Colonias* on the U.S.–Mexico Border," Technical Report, U.S. Census.

———— and George Kourous. 1999. "Water Conflict in the Borderlands," *Borderlines,* 7, 6, Albuquerque, New Mexico, July, 1–4.

———— and Francisco Lara. 1995a. "Sustainability of Development in Border Context: The Case of Ambos Nogales" in *Sustainable Development in the 21st Century Americas: Alternative Visions of Progress,* Conference Proceedings, B. A. Suderman, J. C. Jacob, and M. Brinkerhoff, eds. Division of International Development, University of Calgary, Alberta, Canada, 104–15.

———— and Francisco Lara. 1995b. "Relaciones Sociales y Cooperación Transfronteriza en la Region Sonora-Arizona," *Estudios Sociales,* V, 10, December 1995, 171–196.

———— and Edward J. Williams. 1994. "The Hardening of the United States–Mexico Borderlands: Causes and Consequences," *Boundary and Security Bulletin,* vol. 1, no. 4, University of Durham, England.

Cortes, Dora Elena et al., 1999. "Celebro Robison reunion a puerta cerrada con ONG," *Diario de Juárez.* November 26: A13.

Council of State Governments-West. 1998. Mexican Border Northern States Directory of Elected Officials.

D'Antonio, William and William Form. 1965. *Influentials in Two Border Cities: A Study in Community Decision-Making.* Notre Dame: University of Notre Dame Press.

Davidson, Miriam. 2000. *Lives on the Line: Dispatches from the U.S.–Mexico Border.* Tucson: University of Arizona Press.

Del Valle, Sonia. "A parar la lista: Ni una más." www.nodo50.org/mujeresred/mexico-juarez-htm, May 18, 1998.

Diamon, David. 1998. "Executive Pay-Chart." Electronic Business 1998 Highest-Paid Executives, www.e-insite.net/eb.

Domhoff, William. 1998. *Who Rules America?* NY: Mayfield, 3rd edition.

Domínguez, Edmé. 1999. "Regionalism from the People's Perspective: A View of Mexican Women Reactions to Integration." Paper presented at the International Studies Association Annual Meeting, February, Washington, D.C. Forthcoming *International Feminist Journal of Politics,* vol. 4, no. 2, 2002.

Dunn, Timothy. 1996. *The Militarization of the U.S.–Mexico Border, 1978–1992: Low- Intensity Conflict Doctrine Comes Home.* Austin: Center for Mexican American Studies, University of Texas.

Eber, Christine. 1995. *Women and Alcohol in a Highland Maya Town.* Austin, Texas: University of Texas at Austin Press.

Edelman, Murray. 1964. *The Symbolic Uses of Politics.* Champaign-Urbana: University of Illinois Press.

El Paso Free Trade Association. www.epfta.org

Ellingwood, Ken. 2001. "Migrants: Report Says Crossings Have Become Riskier but Finds No Evidence of a Decline." *San Diego Times* retrieved on August 22, 2001 through www.fundacionmexico@yahoogroups.com.

Ellingwood, Ken. "U.S.–Mexico Bank Fizzling." *Los Angeles Times* July 15, 2001.

Emerson, Peter et al., 1998. "The South Mexico-United States Case Studies Managing Air Quality in the Paso del Norte Region," in Richard Kiy and John Wirth, eds. *Environmental Management on North America's Borders,* College Station, Texas A & M University Press.

Eschbach, Karl, Jacqueline Hagan and Néstor Rodríguez. 1999. "Death at the Border," *International Migration Review,* 33, 430–54.

Esperanza Peace and Justice Center. May 2001. La Voz de la Esperanza newsletter, 14, 4.

Federación Mexicana de Asociaciones Privadas, A. C. (FEMAP). 1995+ Newsletters, Annual Reports (various).

Federal Reserve Bank of Dallas. June 2001. *The Border Economy.*

Fetterman, David M. 1989. *Ethnography: Step by Step.* Newbury Park: Sage Applied Social Research Methods Series, Vol. 17.

Figueroa, Lorena. "Agua, Desafío en la Frontera: Autoridades analizan los recursos, conservación y preservación del liquado, en reunión cumbre binacional," *Diario de Juárez,* May 13, 2001.

Forgotten River Advisory Committee Newsletter 2001. *Going, Going Gone?* Austin: Texas Center for Policy Studies.

Fox, Vicente. "More Trust on Both Sides of the Border: Vicente Fox," *New York Times,* September 4, 2001.

Gabriela, Christina and Laura MacDonald, 1994. "NAFTA, Women and Organising in Canada and Mexico: Forging a "Feminist Internationally," *Millenium: Journal of International Studies,* 23, 3, 535–62.

Ganster, Paul. 1996. Border Environment Research Reports, Number 1. "Environmental Issues of the California Border." www.scerp/org/scerp/docs.berrl.html.

Garber, J. "Mexico Officials Urge Opening U.S. to Trucks," *El Paso Times,* August 13, 2001: A1.

Garber, J. "Mexican Senators Come to Study Border Issues," *El Paso Times,* August 10, 2001. B1.

Geertz, Clifford. 2000 (1973). *The Interpretation of Cultures: Selected Essays.* NY: Basic Books.

Gilligan, Carol. 1982. *In a Different Voice.* Cambridge, MA: Harvard University Press.

Grannovetter, Mark S. 1974. "The Strength of Weak Ties," *American Journal of Sociology* 78, 6: 1360–80.

Hackenberg, Robert A. and Robert R. Alvarez. 2001. "Close-ups of Post-Nationalism: Reports from the U.S.–Mexico Borderlands." *Human Organization,* 6, 2, 97–103.

Hathaway, Dale. 2000. *Allies Across the Border: Mexico's Authentic Labor Front and Global Solidarity.* Cambridge, MA: South End Press.

Herzog, Lawrence A. 2000. *Shared Space: Rethinking the U.S.–Mexico Border Environment.* LaJolla, CA: Center for U.S.–Mexican Studies University of California, San Diego.

Hofstede, Geert. 1985. *Culture's Consequences.* Beverly Hills, CA: Sage.

Homedes, Núria and Antonio Ugalde. 2001. "Fostering Binational Cooperation: Barriers and Opportunities." Unpublished manuscript under review.

Hoskyns, Catherine. 1999. "Gender and Transnational Democracy: The Case of the European Union, "*in Gender Political and Global Governance.* Mary K. Meyer and Elisabeth Prugl. Eds. Lanham, MD: Rowman and Littlefield, 72–87.

Howard, Cheryl and Zulma Méndez. 1999. "Violence, Women and Work." Workshop #II. *Families and their Insertion into Labor Markets,* University of Texas-Brownsville/DIF, Matamoros, March 5–6, 48–51.

Human Rights Watch. 2001. *Trading Away Rights: The Unfullfilled Promise of NAFTA's Labor Side Agreement* 13, 2 www.hrw.org/reports/2001/nafta/ (consulted 7/15/01).

Human Rights Watch. 1996 (1999). "No Guarantees: Sex Discrimination in Mexico's Maquiladora Sector." In Kamel and Hoffman, 31–35.

Immigration Law Enforcement Monitoring Project (ILEMP) of the American Friends Service Committee. 2001. "Human Rights Abuses in the El Paso/ Ciudad Juárez Border Region: "'Behind Every Abuse is a Community'." Report for Press Conference and UN Conference on Racism, Racial Discrimination, Xenophobia, and Related Intolerance.

Ingram, Helen et al., 1995. *Divided Water: Bridging the U.S.–Mexico Border* Tucson: University of Arizona Press.

Ingram, Helen and Anne Schneider. 1997. *Policy Design for Democracy.* Lawrence: University Press of Kansas.

Instituto Mexicano de Seguro Social. www.imss.gob.mx.

Instituto Nacional de Estadística, Geografía e Informática, www.inegi.gob.mx.

International Boundary and Water Commission. 1999. Annual Report, El Paso, Texas.

International Boundary and Water Commission. 2000. Annual Report, El Paso, Texas.

International Boundary and Water Commission. www.ibwc.state.gov/ ORGANIZA/about_us.htm

International Community Foundation, Annual Report 1999–2000, San Diego, California.

Kamel, Rachael and Anya Hoffman. 1999. *The Maquiladora Reader: Cross-Border Organizing Since NAFTA.* Philadelphia: American Friends Service Committee.

Kanter, Rosabeth. 1992. *Men and Women of the Corporation.* NY: Basic 2nd edition.

Keck, Margaret and Kathryn Sikkink. 1995. *Activists Beyond Borders: Advocacy Networks in International Politics.* Ithaca, NY: Cornell University Press.

Kelly, Mary and Cyrus Reed. 2001. *A Call for the NAFTA-Created Environmental Institutions to Be Strengthened—Not Weakened—by the U.S. and Mexican Governments.* Austin: Texas Center for Policy Studies.

Kelly, Mary, Cyrus Reed, and Linda Taylor. 2001. "The Border Environment Cooperation Commission (BECC) and North American Development Bank (NADB): Achieving their Environmental Mandate." Austin: Texas Center for Policy Studies.

Kelson, Gregory. 2000. "International Labor Policies and the North American Free Trade Agreement: Are Women Getting their Fair Share?" *Journal of International Women's Studies.* www.bridgew.edu/DEPTS/ARTSCNCE/JIWS/may00/kelson.htm (22 pages).

Kidder, Thalia and Mary McGinn. 1995. "In the Wake of NAFTA: Transnational Workers' Networks." *Social Policy* 25, 4, 14–21.

Kolenc, Vic. 2000. "Protest Group Now Works Within System." *El Paso Times* May 28, section 1.

Korten, David. 1990. *Getting to the 21st Century: Voluntary Action and the Global Agenda.* West Hartford, CT: Kumarian Press.

Kraus, J. L. 2001. "Private Sector: An Opportunity for Sustainability." *Twin Plant News,* May, 38–40.

La Mujer Obrera, www.grass-roots.org/usa/mujer.shtml.

La Mujer Obrera. 1999. *Exploring and Promoting Adequate Health Care Coverage Among Displaced Workers.* Presented by Suzanna and Abel Fernández. El Paso.

Labloire, Renne and David Palmer. 1999. *Perspectives on NGO Capacity-Building in Mexico.* Presented to the David and Lucile Packard Foundation.

Landau, Saul and Sonia Angulo. 2000. *Maquila: A Tale of Two Mexicos.* (video). Pomona, California: College of Letters, Arts and Social Sciences Mediavision, California State Polytechnic University.

"Landmark study shows Mexican maquiladora workers not able to meet basic needs on sweatshop wages," Press Release. 2000. Coalition for Justice in the Maquiladoras Annual Report. (Summer/Fall) vol. 10, no. 2.

Lara, F. 2000. "Transboundary Networks for Environmental Management in the San Diego-Tijuana Border Region," *Shared Space: Rethinking the U.S. Mexico Border Environment,* L.A. Herzog, ed. La Jolla: Center for U.S. Mexican Studies, University of California, San Diego, 155–81.

Laswell, Harold. 1936. *Politics: Who Gets What, When, How?* NY: McGraw Hill.

Liebowitz, Debra. 2000. *Gender and Identity in an Era of Globalization: Transnational Organizing in North America.* Ph.D. Dissertation. New Brunswick: Rutgers University.

Márquez, Benjamin. 1995. "Organizing Mexican–American Women in the Garment Industry: La Mujer Obrera," *Women and Politics* 15, 65–87.

Márquez, Benjamin. 1985. *Power and Politics in a Chicano Barrio: A Study of Mobilization Efforts and Community Power in El Paso.* Lanham, MD: University Press of America.

Martínez, Oscar J. 1994a. *Border People: Life and Society in the U.S.–Mexico Borderlands.* Tucson: University of Arizona Press.

Martínez, Oscar J. 1994b. "The Dynamics of Border Interaction: New Approaches to Border Analysis." in *Global Boundaries,* ed. Clive H. Schofield. London: Routledge.

Massey, Douglas S. 1989. *Economic Development and International Migration in Comparative Perspective.* Commission for the Study of International Migration and Cooperative Economic Development. Washington, D.C.

Mexican Labor News and Analysis (various issues). A United Electrical, Radio and Machine Workers of America (UE)-Authentic Labor Front (FAT) collaboration. Dan La Botz, ed.

Mexico: Fox, Remittances. 2000. *Migration News,* December, 7, 12, www.migration.ucdavis.edu/.

Mexico Labor News & Analysis, April, 2001, 8–11.

Mexico Solidarity Network. August 25–September 3, 2001. "Mexican Immigrants," msn@mexicosolidarity.org.

Meyer, Mary K. and Elisabeth Prugl, co-eds. 1999. *Gender Politics in Global Governance.* Lanham, MD: Rowman & Littlefield.

Migration Between Mexico and the United States, A Binational Study. 1998. Mexico City and Washington, D.C.: Mexican Ministry of Foreign Affairs and the U.S. Commission on Immigration Reform.

Milloy, R. E. "A Rift over Rio Grande Water Rights," *The New York Times,* September 18, 2001: A14.

Moberg, David. 2000 "Union Cities," *The American Prospect.* September 11, 35–7.

Mueller, Elizabeth J. 1998. *Building Community Development Capacity in El Paso.* New Brunswick, NJ: Rutgers University Center for Urban Policy Research, Report No. 4. www.policy.rutgers.edu/cupr.indexleg.htm.

Mumme, Stephen. 1999. "Managing Acute Water Scarcity on the U.S.–Mexico Border," *Natural Resources Journal,* Winter, 39, 1, 149–67.

NACLA *Report on the Americas.* 2000. Special Issue on Borders 33, 3.

NADB Water Projects (Financing Approved) as of July 2001 mimeo.

NAFTA Works. 1996+ Monthly Newsletter. SECOFI–NAFTA Office, Mexican Embassy, Washington, D.C. (English version).

Nalven, Joseph. 1984. "A Cooperation Paradox and an Airy Tale along the Border," *New Scholar,* 9, 1–2, 171–200.

Nathan, Debbie. 1997. "Double Standards: Notes for a Border Screenplay," *The Nation,* June 6, Reprinted in Kamel and Hoffman, 79–81.

Nathan, Debbie. 1987. *Women and other Aliens: Essays from the U.S.–Mexico Border.* El Paso: Cinco Puntos Press.

National Civic League. www.ncl.org

National Network for Immigrant and Refugee Rights. 2001. *From the Borderline to the Colorline: A Report on Anti-Immigrant Racism in the United States.* Oakland, CA: NNIRR.

Negron, S. 2001. Series on El Paso's Mayoral Race. Stantonstreet Online Guide. www.statonstreet.com.

North American Development Bank, Community Adjustment and Investment Program (CAIP). www.nadbank-caip.org.

Oehmke Loustaunau, Martha and Mary Sánchez-Bane, co-eds. 1999. *Life, Death, and In-Between on the U.S.–Mexico Border: Asi es la Vida.* Westport, CT.: Bergin and Garvey.

Ortiz, Victor. 1999. "Latinas on the Border and La Vista Grande: The Common Ground of Displacements and Breakthroughs." Working paper No. 45. East Lansing: Michigan State University, Julian Samora Research Institute.

Padilla, Héctor. 2001. "Medio Ambiente y Acción Publica," in *Medio Ambiente, Cuidad y Orden Jurídico,* eds. Bassols, Mario and Mele, Patrice. Mexico City: Miguel Angel Porrua Grupo Editoral and Universidad Autónoma Metropolitana.

Pan American Health Organization. October 1999. Structures and Mechanisms for Technical Cooperation on Health in the U.S.–Mexico Border Meeting, Final Report. El Paso: PAHO.

PASE (Programa de Asistencia Estudiantil para Mexicanos). Office of International Programs University of Texas at El Paso n.d.

Peña, Devon. 1997. *The Terror of the Machine Technology, Work, Gender, and Ecology on the U.S.–Mexico Border* (Austin, TX: Center for Mexican–American Studies, University of Texas)

Pérez López, D. 2001. "Flor y Fauna de la Antigua Cuenca del Bravo: Lo que el tiempo se llevo," *El Diario de Juárez,* July 8, 2001:B3.

Polk, Wendy White. March 5–11, 2000. "Ann Schaechner (Interview): Nonprofit Professionalism, *El Paso, Inc.*

"Presidents Call for BECC-NADB Reform." 2001. *Borderlines,* 9, 10, November.

Prieto, Antonio. 1999. "Coalition for Justice in the *Maquiladoras:* An Interview with Martha Ojeda. www.igc.org/isla/mex2

Putman, Robert. 2000. *Bowling Alone: The Collapse and Rival of American Community.* Cambridge: Harvard University Press.

Reagan, Leslie J. 2000. "Crossing the Border for Abortion: California Activists, Mexican Clinics and the Creation of a Feminist Health Agency in the 1960s," *Feminist Studies,* 26, 2, Summer, 323–48.

Red Casa del Migrante (www.migrante.com.mx/cuidadjuarez.html)

Regelbrugge, Laurie. 1999. *Promoting Corporate Citizenship: Opportunities for Business and Civil Society Engagement.* Washington, D.C.: CIVICUS.

Reich, Robert. 1992. *The Work of Nations.* NY: Vintage.

Resultados Definitivos, Tabulados Básicos: Chihuahua Censo 2000. Instituto Nacional de Estadística e Informática, 2001.

Reyes, Rosario. 2001. "Trafican con micas en los puentes." *El Diario de Juárez,* June 19: 2A.

Reyes, Silvestre. 2001a. Reports of the 16th Congressional District, El Paso, Texas.

Reyes, Silvestre. 2001b. News Releases, 16th Congressional District (various).

Reza, Ernesto et al., 1996. "Observations on the Implementation of the North American Agreement on Labor Cooperation: Emerging Issues and Initial Impacts if United State–Mexico Labor Relations," *Journal of Borderland Studies* 11, 1: 59–72.

Rio Grande-Río Bravo Basin Coalition. (October 21, 2000). Join us in cele-brating el Día del Rio 2000, Information pamphlet.

Rio Grande-Río Bravo Basin Coalition. 10 million people, 335,00 square miles: 1 fragile resource, Information pamphlet.

Rippberger, Susan and Kathleen Staudt. 2002. *Pledging Allegiance: Learning Nationalism in School at the U.S.–Mexico Border.* NY: Routledge/Falmer.

Rodríguez, R. (July 7, 2001). "Mexico Applauds Desert Initiative," *Star-Telegram,* web.star-telegram.com/content/fortworth/2001/07/29/state/fw010402-0729-XB001-mexico.htm.

Rodríguez, Victoria. 1997. *Decentralization in Mexico.* Boulder, CO.: Westview Press.

Rodríguez, Victoria and Peter Ward. Eds. 1995. *Opposition Government in Mexico.* Albuquerque: University of New Mexico Press.

Rodríguez, Victoria and Peter Ward. 1999. *Reaching Across the Border: Intergovernmental Relations between Texas and Mexico.* Austin: LBJ School of Public Affairs, University of Texas.

Saguaro Seminar. 2001. *Better Together: Civic Engagement in America.* www.saguaro.org.

Saint-Germain, Michelle. 1998. "Re-Presenting the Public Interest on the U.S.–Mexico Border," in *The U.S.–Mexico Border: Transcending Divisions, Contesting Identities.* Boulder: Lynne Rienner Press, 59–82.

Salant, Tanis J. et al., 2001. *Illegal Immigrants in U.S.–Mexico Border Counties: Costs of Law Enforcement, Criminal Justice and Emergency Medical Services.* Commissioned by the U.S./Mexico Border Counties Coalition. Tucson: University of Arizona Institute for Local Government.

Salzinger, Leslie. 2001. "Making Fantasies Real: Producing Women and Men on the *Maquila* Shop Floor." *NACLA Report on the Americas* 34, 5, 13–19.

San Diego Dialogue. www.sddialogue.org.

Scherrer, Paul and Kate Randall. 2000. "Texas Executes Mexican National," www.wsws.org/articles/2000/nov2000/exec-n11.html

Schmidt, Steffen et al., eds. 1977. *Friends, Followers, and Factions: A Reader in Political Clientelism.* Berkeley: University of California Press.

Scott, James. 1990. *Domination and the Arts of Resistance.* New Haven, CT: Yale University Press.

Shapleigh, Eliot. n.d. "Texas Borderlands: Frontier of the Americas," Senate District 29, www.elpaso.net/~borderlands/TBOverview.htm

Sharp, John. 1998. *Bordering the Future: Challenge and Opportunity in the Texas Border Region.* Austin, TX: Texas Comptroller of Public Accounts.

Shirley, Dennis. 1997. *Community Organizing and Urban School Reform.* Austin: University of Texas Press.

Sloan, John W. and Jonathan P. West. 1977. "The Role of Informal Policy-Making in U.S.–Mexico Border Cities," *Social Science Quarterly* 58, 2, 277–82.

Smith, C. E. 2000. *Inevitable Partnership: Understanding Mexico–U.S. Relations.* Boulder, CO: Lynne Rienner Publishers.

Smith, Peter. 1970. *Labyrinths of Power: Political Recruitment in Twentieth-Century Mexico.* Princeton: Princeton University Press.

Spener, David and Bryan Roberts. 1998. "Small Business, Social Capital, and Economic Integration on the U.S.–Mexico Border," in Spener and Staudt, co-eds. 83–104.

Spener, David and Kathleen Staudt, co-eds. 1998. *The U.S.–Mexico Border: Transcending Divisions, Contesting Identities.* Boulder, CO: Lynne Rienner Press.

Status Report on the Water-Wastewater Infrastructure Program for the U.S.–Mexico Borderlands, 2001. Office of Water, United States Environmental Protection Agency.

Staudt, Kathleen. 1998. *Free Trade? Informal Economies at the U.S.–Mexico Border.* Philadelphia: Temple University Press.

Staudt, Kathleen. 1985. *Women, Foreign Assistance and Advocacy Administration.* NY: Praeger.

Staudt, Kathleen and Randy Capps. 1998. "Con la Ayuda de Dios? El Pasoans Manage the 1996 Welfare and Immigration Reforms." Prepared for the University of Houston Center for Immigration Research. Condensed and forthcoming in *Living in the Interim: Immigrant Communities and Welfare "Reform" in North America,* eds. Ana Aparicio, Phil Kretsedemas, and Kalyani Rhai. NY: Greenwood-Praeger.

Staudt, Kathleen, Shirin Rai, and Jane Parpart. 2001. "Protesting World Trade Rules: Can We Talk about Empowerment?" *Signs: Journal of Women in Culture and Society* 26, 4, 1251–8.

Staudt, Kathleen and David Spener. 1998. "The View from the Frontier: Theoretical Perspectives Undisciplined." In *The U.S.–Mexico Border: Transcending Divisions, Contesting Identities,* Spener and Staudt, co-eds. Boulder, CO: Lynne Rienner Publishers, 3–33.

Stoddard, Ellwyn. 1978. "Patterns of Poverty Along the U.S.–Mexico Border." El Paso: Center for InterAmerican and Border Studies, University of Texas at El Paso.

Stone, Deborah. 1997. *Policy Paradox: The Art of Political Decision-Making.* NY: W. W. Norton.

Story, Dale. 1986. *Industry, the State, and Public Policy in Mexico.* Austin: University of Texas Press.

Stowers, Carlton. 2001. "The Angel of Juarez," *Dallas Observer,* January 4.

Tannen, Debora. 1996. *Gender and Discourse.* NY: Oxford University Press.

Tarrow, Sidney. 1998. *Power in Movement: Social Movements and Contentious Politics.* NY: Cambridge University Press.

Texas Immigration and Refugee Coalition. 1996+ Newsletters.

Texas–Mexico Border Health Coordination Office. www.panam.edu/dept.tmbhco/publication.htm.

Texas, State of, www.texas.gov.

Tiano, Susan. 1994. *Patriarchy on the Line: Labor, Gender and Ideology in the Mexican Maquila Industry.* Philadelphia: Temple University Press.

Torney-Purta, Judith et al., 1999. *Civic Education Across Countries: Twenty-Four National Case Studies from the IEA Civic Education Project.* Amsterdam: International Association for the Evaluation of Educational Achievement.

Uchitelle, Louis. 1993. "America's Newest Industrial Belt," *New York Times,* March 21. Business.

Ugalde, Antonio. 1970. *Power and Conflict in a Mexican Neigborhood.* Albuquerque: University of New Mexico Press.

UNICEF-DIF. 2000. "Boy and Girl Victims of Sexual Exploitation in Mexico." www.ssw.upenn.edu/restes/Mexico_Final_Report_001015.pdf.

United States Commission on Civil Rights. 1971–4. *Mexican–American Education Study.* Washington, D.C.

United States Department of State. 1983. Environmental Cooperation: Agreement between the United States of America and Mexico. August 14. TIAS no. 10827. United States and treaties and other international agreements. Washington, D.C.: GPO.

United States Department of State, Dispatch 623, September 14, 1993.

United States Department of State, Travel Advisory. www.travel.state.gov/mexico.html.

United States Environmental Protection Agency (EPA). 1999. Border XXI. Program Overview, Spring Fact Sheet.

Untied States Environmental Protection Agency (EPA). Office of Cooperative Environmental Management. Good Neighbor Environmental Board. www.epa.gov/ocem/gneb/htm.

United States Environmental Protection Agency (EPA). Region 6, Office of Environmental Justice. www.epa.gov/oeca.main/ej/nejac.

United States Environmental Protection Agency (EPA). Region 6, Dallas (U.S.–Mexico), monthly newsletters. www.epa.gov/region6/border.htm.

United States Environmental Protection Agency (EPA). Washington, D.C., 2000. Fourth Report of the Good Neighbor Environmental Board.

United States Environmental Protection Agency (EPA). Washington, D.C., Good Neighbor Environmental Board, n.d., pamphlet.

U.S. Mexico Business and Trade Community. n.d. *The Seven Principles of Environmental Stewardship for the 21st Century.* Washington, D.C.: U.S. EPA.

U.S.–Mexico Border Health Association website. www.usmbha.org.

U.S.–Mexico Border Program, San Diego. American Friends Service Committee information pamphlet. n.d.

U.S.–Mexico Border XXI Program, Framework Document. 1996. United States Environmental Protection Agency, Washington, D.C.

University of Texas at El Paso, (UTEP). 2000. *NAFTA Impact on the Border: Problems and Solutions.* Conference Proceedings. October. (Summary in Borderlines. December 2000 by Frank López and Kathleen Staudt.)

UTEP, Center for Civic Engagement. 2001. *Community Links.* Directory of Organizations.

Van Schoik, Rick D. Presentation to the Good Neighbor Environmental Board, July 25, 2001, San Diego, California.

Vélez-Ibañez, Carlos. 1996 *Border Visions.* Tucson: University of Arizona Press.

Walshok, Mary. 2000. "A Research University Perspective," *Civic Responsibility and Higher Education,* ed. Thomas Ehrlich. Phoenix: American Council on Education/Oryx Press, 295–305.

Ward, Peter. 1999. *Colonias and Public Policy in Texas and Mexico.* Austin: University of Texas Press.

Ward, Peter and Victoria Rodríguez, co-eds. 1995. *Opposition Government in Mexico.* Albuquerque: University of New Mexico Press.

Warner, David C. 1999. "The Medical Care System in Mexico and the United States: Convergence or Deterioration? The View from the Border." *Life, Death and In-Between on the U.S.–Mexico Border,* Martha Loustaunau and Mary Sánchez-Banes, eds. Westport, CT: Bergin and Garvey, 177–90.

Washington Valdez, Diana. 2001a. "Bodies Everywhere, *El Paso Times,* June 25: B1.

Washington Valdez, Diana. 2001b. "Border Conference to Discuss Pollution Prevention," *El Paso Times,* June 25: B1.

Washington Valdez, Diana. 2001c. "Phone Taps in Mexico Uncovered," *El Paso Times,* July 9: B1.

Washington Valdez, Diana. 2001d. "Some say Laws Hurt Women" *El Paso Times,* August 27: B1.

Washington Valdez, Diana. 2001e. "Some Rights Advocates Feel Ignored by Reyes" *El Paso Times* August 13: B1.

"Water Quality in the U.S.–Mexico Border Region." 1998. *Borderlines,* vol. 6, no. 3, April.

Weiner, Myron. 1993, *International Migration and Security.* Boulder, CO: Westview Press.

Weintraub, Sidney et al., 1998, *Migration between Mexico and the United States Binational Study* Mexico City, Mexican Ministry of Foreign Affairs, Washington, D.C.: U.S. Commission on Immigration Reform.

Weiss, Larry. 1999. "Coalition for Justice in the *Maquiladoras:* 10 Years of Cross-Border Organizing. www.americas.org.News/Features.

Westerhoff, Paul. Ed. 2000. *The United States Mexican Border Environment: Water Issues along the U.S.Mexican border.* San Diego, CA: Southwest Center for Environmental Research and Policy, San Diego University Press.

Williams, Heather L. 1999. "Mobile Capital and Transborder Labor Rights Mobilization," *Politics and Society* 27, 1, March 139–66.

Wilson, James Q. 1993. *Political Organizations.* NY: Basic Books 2nd edition.

Winer, Michael and Karen Ray. 2000. *Collaboration Handbook: Creating, Sustaining, and Enjoying the Journey.* St. Paul, MN: Amherst H. Wilder Foundation.

World Bank. 1999. *World Development Report: Knowledge for Development.* Washington, D.C./NY: World Bank/Oxford University Press.

Yin, Robert K. 1994. *Case Study Research: Design and Methods.* Newbury Park, CA: Sage Applied Social Research Methods Series, Volume 5.

Zúñiga, Cynthia. 2001. "Organizaciones no Gubernamentales en Perspectiva Comparativa Ciudad Juárez/El Paso," unpublished research paper.

Index